Micro-Politics

Micro-Politics

Agency in a Postfeminist Era

Patricia S. Mann

University of Minnesota Press
Minneapolis
London

Published by the University of Minnesota Press
2037 University Avenue Southeast, Minneapolis, MN 55455–3092
Printed in the United States of America on acid-free paper

Library of Congress Cataloging-in-Publication Data

Mann, Patricia S.
    Micro-politics : agency in a postfeminist era / Patricia S. Mann.
        p.   cm.
    Includes bibliographical references and index.
    ISBN 0-8166-2048-2 (alk. paper). — ISBN 0-8166-2049-0 (pbk. : alk. paper)
        1. Feminist theory.   2. Social sciences—Philosophy.   3. Gender identity—
    Philosophy.   4. Postmodernism—Social aspects.   I. Title.
    HQ1190.M35   1994
    305.42′01—dc20   93-28965
                                                                                        CIP

The University of Minnesota is an
equal-opportunity educator and employer.

To the family and friends who have been there for me in so many ways.

Contents

Acknowledgments

I would like to thank many people for dialogue and encouragement over the years during which I was writing this book. Without the following friends and colleagues my ideas would surely not have evolved into their present form: Jane Roland Martin, Tom Rockmore, Elayne Rapping, Alan Olson, Leonard Harris, Chris Costan, Margaret Walker, Lee Quinby, Mary Katherine Wainwright, Carole Cole, Milton Fisk, Sohnya Sayres, Stanley Aronowitz, David Weissman, Barrie Karp, Betsy Shevey, Rosamond Rhodes, Ruth Spitz, Ann Snitow, Terry Cochran, Biodun Iginla, Ann Klefstad, Jane Marcus, and my CUNY Women's Studies graduate students.

I would also like to extend thanks to the following groups for providing me with the intellectual give and take without which I might never have figured out my proximate place in the academy: the New York Institute of Humanities Seminar, "Sex, Gender, and Consumer Culture"; the Legal Theory Workshop of Columbia University; the CUNY Women's Studies Colloquium; the NYU Colloquium for the Study of Law, Philosophy, and Social Theory; the Society for Philosophy and Public Affairs of NYC; the Philosophy Colloquium of the Graduate Center of CUNY; the Social Text Collective; the Baruch Colloquium for Philosophy, Politics, and the Social Sciences; the New York Institute of Humanities Seminar on Psychoanalysis and Sexual Difference; and the Karl Jaspers Society of North America.

I am also grateful on a daily basis for the complexly woven micropolitical fabric of NYC; I cherish its streets and its schools, its uncountable public and private nooks, spaces, and moments for engaging with strangers and friends. It is my beloved terrain of social analysis, and my home.

Introductory Reflections

i. Origins of This Postmodern, Postfeminist Project

Like it or not, ours is an era that will be remembered for dramatic changes in basic social relationships, within families, workplaces, schools, and other public spheres of interaction. We negotiate these changes in the course of our day-to-day lives, usually without thinking about them in any systematic way. Indeed, it is difficult to achieve any sort of perspective on the dynamic societal picture of which we are part. In this book, I develop a theoretical framework intended to provide insight into our complicated nexus of social relationships. I formulated this theory of individual agency in response to gendered social transformations that I believe provide the basic foundation for all other social transformations today, and I call it a "gendered micro-politics." However, this schema of micro-political analysis is applicable as well to other contemporary sites of conflictual social and political interaction. I will begin to broach the implications of a micro-political theory of agency for multicultural sites of social transformation in the last chapter of this work. A fuller analysis of the micro-politics of the academy and civil society is an undertaking for my next book.[1]

This is a work of postmodern philosophy/social theory. The slash is important; I cannot conceive of doing philosophy except as a social theory, and I cannot conceive of doing social theory without the categories and concerns of philosophy. I am a postmodern philosopher in a quite literal sense. I believe that the social and political frameworks of modernism are exhausted and incapable of making sense of the most important contemporary problems. Unlike the insightfully pessimistic Anglo-American philosophers Bernard Williams and Alasdair MacIntyre, I do not believe that ethical philosophy will end with the collapse of the modernist frameworks they so devastatingly criticize.[2] The modern period has been a particularly difficult one for ethical theory, given the dominance of the economic-man paradigm of social identity and the non-ethical conceptions of rational agency associated with it. I am relieved to think that in this postmodern moment we may take up the analysis of individual and social behavior from a fresh starting point. Unlike the poststructuralist philosophers Jacques Derrida and Michel Foucault, I do not believe that current criticisms of previous metaphysical traditions demonstrate any sort of ultimate crisis of philosophical rationality. In fact, I think it is possible to show the roots of a postmodern philosophy within modernism, and in this book I attempt to trace a path of philosophical development leading us beyond modernist paradigms.

This is also a book of postfeminist theory by a feminist who believes that changing gender relations are the most significant social phenomenon of our time. The modern philosophical frameworks of liberal individualism, as well as Marx's critiques of them, were grounded in the reorganization of Western society that occurred after feudalism, corresponding with developing capitalist economic and scientific relations. Today, it is the reorganization of society associated with changing kinship structures and gender relationships that requires and enables us to move beyond the intellectual paradigms of modernism. Feminism, like Marxism, was a powerful reactive social and intellectual movement within modernism. For women who grew up in the 1940s, 1950s, or 1960s, the "second wave" of feminism that began in the late 1960s and continued through the 1970s was an intense, transformative period of changing consciousness and social relationships. Looking back, there was some indefinable moment during that decade when the previous normative identification of humanity as an exclusively male enterprise came to an end, partly as a result of the feminist movement and partly as a consequence of other important social and political factors associated with the decline of modernism. Postfeminism, the postmodern offspring of feminism, begins with the historic end of the amazingly enduring normative identification of humanity with men and masculinity.[3]

I am grateful, as an individual and as a philosopher, to have been born in the midst of these great changes, and to have experienced only very briefly the plight of women in a society in which humanity was ideally manly. The second wave of feminism was just hitting its stride as I graduated from college in 1973. There was no such thing as a women's studies program yet at Bates College, but I read Simone de Beauvoir's *The Second Sex* and Kate Millet's *Sexual Politics*, rose many mornings at dawn in order to integrate racquetball courts still reserved for men during normal playing times, and belonged to "the women's group" on campus, as well as to a consciousness-raising group in the local town of Lewiston, Maine. I felt thankful for not having been born in an earlier generation of women.

"Woman as Other" was still a very real phenomenon, but we were confident witnesses to its becoming a phenomenon of the past.

My generation of women experienced that Past as children and teenagers; it was often the stories of our mothers that made it most real to us as women. World War II had provided social opportunity and independence for my mother's generation of women during the 1940s in the name of patriotism; but with men returning from the war, the patriarchal family was reinstated in the 1950s with a cartoonish intensity. My mother proudly worked her way through the University of Michigan, only to put away her Phi Beta Kappa key and a bit of her pride to stay home and care for me and my younger sisters and brother. My father, loyal to values learned as a child during the Depression, suppressed his desires to become a writer and followed his father into the automobile industry, working twelve-hour days, six days a week as an industrial engineer in the River Rouge Ford plant.

I spent adolescence as an alienated tomboy, refusing to participate in the extracurricular social rituals, from jump-rope to after-school dances and cheerleading, through which girls acquired appropriate feminine attitudes and social skills. I knew I did not want any part of these, but alternative modes of participation were considered psychologically deviant. Rebellious tactics of the sort recently hailed by Judith Butler as "parodic practices" were indeed considered "disruptive and troubling" in the mid-1960s, but were barely recognized as acts of political resistance, even by those committing them. I will not forget the inchoate fury of a little girl who cut her hair very short and wore inappropriate shoes with her dresses to debating contests and orchestra performances, and who was repeatedly reprimanded for her antisocial behavior.[4] Even though I had never seen the inside of a courtroom, I was set upon becoming a "lean and arrogant" trial lawyer. Vaguely angry at a great many things, I thought the courtroom seemed an ideal platform of verbal resistance. Yet I was metaphysically troubled by the fact that women had not been trial lawyers in the Past, and I could not explain what made it a possibility now, if only for a few "exceptional" women. Moreover, even a professional career did not promise complete escape from the normalizing regimes of kinship that seemed so oppressive to both of my parents.

As I went off to college, however, middle America began to come unglued. First the civil rights movement, then the new left and antiwar movements, and finally gay pride and feminism began to challenge the gamut of traditional presuppositions that had constituted the grim horizon of social behavior for previous generations. At the height of these movements, major social changes seemed not only possible but imminent.

Simone de Beauvoir's existentialist challenge to women acquired political bite: "If woman seems to be the inessential which never becomes the essential, it is because she herself fails to bring about this change," she asserted.[5] I, for one, was ready to do whatever was required to bring about this change. We all were, pedaling home from our consciousness-raising groups filled with a sense of historical destiny. Whatever it took, we of the second wave of feminism felt that the emancipation of women, and men as well, from the oppressive and repressive structures of patriarchal capitalism was our allotted task. It may be impossible to convey the intense, shocked sense of relief we experienced in those years, as the patriarchal link between masculinity and normative humanity was finally severed. For the first time in history, it was really and fully OK to be a woman. In fact, as the new revolutionary subjects, we often felt it was great to be a woman.

Needless to say, progress has not come as readily as we anticipated. It has taken almost twenty years simply to gain a realistic sense of the processes of social change we committed ourselves to so long ago. At this point, I think, we require new conceptual machinery for assessing where we have come and where we may go as feminists, and as postmodern persons headed into a new century. Notice that I use verbs, signifiers of action rather than terms of identity or subjectivity. In periods of social change, identities become unstable and multiple, crumbling and growing all at the same time. Individual consciousness becomes volatile and unpredictable, ahead of the action or lagging behind, sometimes somewhere else entirely. Everyday actions are liable to lead onto uncharted personal turf, jarring us out of the calm sense of who we were yesterday. We act as we feel we must, or as we wish, or simply out of indifference, and subsequently we find that we see ourselves and our relationships to others somewhat differently.[6]

I believe that insofar as social identities are presently unstable we should stop focusing so intently upon these fragile notions of selfhood. Instead, I suggest that we think more about the quality of our actions, or in the terminology of social theory, upon our *agency*. In seeking to better understand our actions we will be confronting the moral and political issues of everyday life in the best way possible during a time of social confusion. We should think of ourselves as conflicted actors rather than as fragmented selves.

The perplexing quality of contemporary life has several sources. It is in part due to the fact that transformations in the gendered structures of family and workplace call upon people to live in new ways. For example, while previous generations of working-class and black women worked outside the home, they aspired along with more privileged women to the middle-class feminine ideal of becoming housewives and mothers, economically supported by men. By contrast, women of all classes and races today aspire to good careers unavailable to women in the past, and they believe they should be able to combine the responsibilities of motherhood with those of a career. Men are increasingly expected to share housework and child care with women who sometimes take their professional careers more seriously than their male spouses do theirs. The organization of family life is changing quite radically, and the organization of the workplace is being affected as well.

During times of social turmoil it is not only people's behavior that changes, however, but also the social meaning of their behavior. We can make sense of controversial issues such as abortion or sexual harassment only by adopting a conceptual framework that thematizes alterations in the social understanding of individual actions. For hundreds of years the Catholic church considered abortions in the first months of pregnancy (prior to "quickening") to be legitimate. No longer. Many of the patriarchal meanings of motherhood that were a basic component of religious teachings are losing their social grounding, and the Catholic church and many fundamentalist Protestant churches have chosen abortion as a symbolic site upon which to do battle against the gendered tides of change. Accordingly, abortion rights have come to signify for many feminists a watershed of women's emancipation from patriarchal kinship relationships.

Sexual harassment is another example of a historically embedded form of social behavior that has only recently become explicitly identified and defined as a morally and legally wrongful action. In this case, feminists have caused a furor by pointing out that traditional male sexual attitudes toward women conflict with liberal norms of personal autonomy and respect within the workplace.[7] We are struggling fiercely over the social valuation of different practices on a variety of fronts. The old social game board is still visible beneath our feet, yet there are new players, new moves, and new rules to be negotiated. It is an old game and a new one at once.

ii. Why a Theory of Agency?

When I first came to think seriously about gender issues in 1982, they were a highly seductive site of intellectual inquiry because they raised so many important philosophic questions in radically new ways. Yet feminist theory was also a frightening field to immerse oneself in as a philosopher, insofar as its links with traditional forms of inquiry were so undeveloped and tenuous. Moreover, the more one investigated gendered problems, the more evident it became that previous philosophic traditions, whether of liberalism, Marxism, psychoanalysis, or phenomenology, were all conceptually incapable of representing current issues associated with changing gender relationships. For me, there were years of confusion as I very gradually figured out how to conceptually ground my theoretical analysis. In the early chapters of this book, I show some of the issues that had to be worked through in order to arrive at what, I hope, is a philosophical framework that does justice to the social problems we are now faced with.

Modernist ethical and political theories tend to emphasize notions of identity, whether personal identity in the liberal tradition or social group identity in the Marxist tradition. Yet one of the most interesting aspects of our contemporary situation involves the erosion of gendered as well as other forms of personal and social identity. Women and men today, for example, quite typically pursue activities and relationships that lie outside traditional boundaries of male and female identities. As a consequence of this phenomenon, neither our personal nor our social identities have the sort of defining hold on us that they had on previous generations. Many if not most individuals operate quite effectively outside the parameters of traditional gendered, ethnic, class, professional, or kinship identities, relying instead upon highly fluid, ad hoc, tentative working identities.

The decline in previously gendered identities explains some of the difficulties feminists have encountered in attempting to reform a modern institution such as the family. On the one hand, liberal norms of justice seem to make it obvious that once women are working to support the family economically in the public sphere alongside men, men should begin putting in a fair share of time alongside women in the home. On the other hand, it has proven anything but simple to actually redistribute the labor within the family, to many women's surprise and disappointment. In chapter 1, I consider the difficulty of applying various liberal notions of individual rights, as well as Marxist conceptions of social justice, within contemporary families. Aristotle's subtle analysis of the relationships within a Greek household allows me to show why liberal and Marxist political conceptions of equality and justice fail to apply to a woman so long as her identity remains that of what I term a "subsumed nurturer" within a family headed by a "patriarchal benefactor."

Indeed, within our liberal democracy, the recent entry of large numbers of women into the public sphere, a process I term the "social enfranchisement" of women, has caused these intrinsically hierarchical male and female family identities to be fundamentally undermined.[8] Women and men are trying out various new public and private roles today. Insofar as clear-cut familial identities have waned, however, it remains difficult to apply abstract notions of individual rights or fair behavior within specific domestic situations. According to Aristotle's formal principle of proportional justice, "those who are equal in relevant respects should be treated alike, and those who are unequal in relevant respects should be treated differently in proportion to their difference."[9] Within families today, women and men have a multitude of different positions in relation to each other, and formal notions of justice are quite inadequate to adjudicate these situations. Liberal categories of individual rights and justice provide an important basis for feminist critiques of the patriarchal family, but they hardly offer a sufficient conceptual basis for reconstructing domestic relationships.

In the second place, and even more problematically, with the decline of patriarchal family identities, the experience of familial agency is undermined, sometimes to a small degree and sometimes to a very large degree. Women and men become uncertain of their basic desires and responsibilities in relation to family life. The analytic philosopher Donald Davidson has attempted to analyze situations in which individuals operate without a strong sense of individual agency. The problem, according to Davidson, is that individuals experience their actions as surd, or meaningless, whenever they fail to follow the dictates of their own best conception of rational action. He believes that the problem of meaningless action typically arises when we allow some form of habitual behavior to win out over our own rational conception of what it is in our best interests to do. The solution, according to Davidson, involves cultivating the virtue of acting rationally, much as Aristotle directs us to cultivate courage and other virtuous modes of action.[10]

Davidson is quite right in recognizing that a deficient sense of rational agency is currently a problem for individuals; it is a major concern for women and men alike in professional as well as familial contexts. What Davidson does not realize is that our present standards of rationality contribute to these problems of agency, through dictating hierarchies of desire and self-interest, as well as relationships between self-interest and obligations toward others that no longer make sense of women's or men's private and public lives. The problem of surd behavior arises insofar as neither traditional notions of gendered behavior nor the abstract welfare-maximizing rationalities of the public world can indicate the appropriate actions for a man or a woman in any of a multitude of public and private situations today.

We have rationally criticized patriarchal male and female kinship roles,

crude confusion between what people do and value, and fundamental categories

* Why think they ever could, except for blind, selfish or self deluded people?

yet we fall back upon traditional familial roles for lack of alternative ways of fulfilling our desires and responsibilities. As Davidson warns, there may be a gnawing sense that such habitual actions have lost their meaning when real maternal and paternal interests conflict with standard welfare-maximizing principles of public-sphere economic rationality. It is not hard to see that actions and attitudes that were appropriate for a full-time housewife are not necessarily rational for a woman who is both a mother and a professional woman. Yet public-sphere notions of rational self-interest can tell women little about how to balance their public and private lives today. Likewise, men who are fathers and spouses can no longer confidently apportion responsibilities between their families and high-salaried jobs that preclude spending time with their families. Notions of meaningful and rational action are still associated with incommensurable, gendered conceptions of social identity. There is no formal notion of rationality, no pregiven mode of calculating appropriate individual behavior in many contemporary situations.

Because individual and social group identities remain highly unstable in class, ethnic, and sexual as well as gendered contexts, we can hardly hope to base our decisions about how to act upon notions of rationality or meaningfulness associated with such identities in the past. These identities come to us only in the fragmented, disaggregated narratives of previous generations. We need to rethink the significance of many of our actions in more basic ways than are encouraged by currently available notions of rational action, whether defined in terms of economic self-interest, utilitarian or deontological morality, or various traditional social roles and identities. The question is how we can accomplish this.

In fact, we have experiential access to more basic data of meaningful actions. We may be uncertain of who we are. Yet we usually have some sense of what we want in a particular situation, as well as a sometimes competing sense of what our obligations are. Of course, when we attempt to force these desires or responsibilities into the patterns of previous generations we are likely to be plagued with feelings of inadequacy and meaninglessness. It is as counterproductive for us to evaluate our lives according to previous standards of happiness or welfare-maximizing behavior as it is to yearn for now-unavailable gendered notions of personal and social identity. Instead, individuals need to recognize that their own experiences of desire and obligation provide the specific grounds for reconstituting notions of meaningful action.

Chapter 1 ends on this speculative note: personal identity problems are quite real, but not resolvable in the immediate future, given the continuing flux of social relationships. It is problems of agency, uncertainties about what to do in many situations, and questions about the significance and meaning of the actions available to us which are more immediately troubling, in any case. But these agency problems are also more open to solution. With the critique of former notions of social identity, women and men alike are placed in positions in which they can and must decide how best to accommodate their particular desires and responsibilities according to their own particular social circumstances. Immediately below the roiled surface of identity problems and rationality anxieties lie relatively clear variables of individual agency. I think that a theory of individual and social agency can be constructed that will help individuals comprehend and reorganize this data. Such a theory will also constitute an appropriate framework for analyzing contemporary gendered and multicultural issues, quite generally.[11]

iii. Toward a Definition of Agency

It is necessary to rethink agency, or the significance of our actions, in the context of recently destabilized gender relationships. We will need to investigate not only the kinship structures which have determined the everyday interactions of men and women, but also the patriarchal structures of sexuality which have operated to enforce kinship relationships, while also providing a vehicle for transgressing them. As women began to enter the public sphere in large numbers in the 1970s, they inevitably challenged patriarchal definitions of sexual identity and agency. It is unsurprising that the arrival of women was greeted with deepseated forms of male resistance and hostility. It has taken twenty years, however, for women to begin to articulate these problems as legal issues around which women can build viable cases of rights infringement.

Women had long been aware of a male "sexual gaze" which lurked, always ready to eroticize their presence and deny their non-sexual interests and achievements. As women ventured into formerly male workplaces, however, they experienced the oppressiveness of this ubiquitous male gaze with a new intensity as they sought to be taken seriously on a daily basis in various public forums. Pornography was an obvious objective correlative of this otherwise intangible sexual gaze, and a feminist anti-pornography movement gained unexpected momentum as an important outlet for the anger of women who felt diminished by the sexual gaze. Chapter 2, accordingly, begins with a discussion of the pornography debates that dominated feminism for several years during the late 1970s and early 1980s. Radical feminists such as Andrea Dworkin and Catharine MacKinnon argued that pornography was oppressive to women and _no such thing as non patriarchial pornography?_

should therefore be subject to statutory regulation, while feminists who gave priority to civil libertarian concerns and the freedom of speech opposed all forms of regulation, arguing that pornography was merely a symptom of "real" economic and political forms of patriarchal power. From a contemporary political perspective, educated by Foucault to think of our actions as inscribed within various hegemonic discourses, it is possible to go beyond the opposing stances within the pornography debates. We can comprehend pornography as a symptom of patriarchal signifying assumptions within institutional discourses today, and also as a material embodiment of these assumptions. The "sexual gaze" continues to be a quite real constraint upon women's agency.[12]

When we analyze how patriarchal sexual identities have helped produce gendered forms of social agency, we notice several interesting features of agency. In the first place, we become aware of the relational construction of sexual agency, and of the complementary distribution of several different dimensions of agency between men and women. Sexual desire was identified as a particularly masculine feature of sexual agency and women were presumed to lack this desiring dimension of agency, quite generally. Women are considered sexually passive insofar as they are not presumed to direct a sexual gaze at men, or to otherwise exhibit active desire for others. Yet a different quality of sexual agency in women is apparent if we consider the significance of women's responsibility for recognizing male sexual desire and its implications for them. Women traditionally fulfilled their sexual responsibility by either encouraging male desire or avoiding it. Patriarchal social relationships were built upon a foundation of generous female recognition of potential male sexual and social agency.

Indeed, another feature of agency that emerges as we analyze patriarchal sexual and social relationships is the significance of "recognition" as a dimension of individual agency. Within sexual contexts, the knowing female gaze anticipated the physical power of men over female bodies, and corresponded with a broader female obligation for anticipating and encouraging male actions in the world. Patriarchal discourses articulate male-identified forms of sexual and social agency almost exclusively, creating the discursive reality of male performances. These discourses encourage the recognition of male agency by men and women alike, and make it exceedingly difficult to properly recognize and reward the actions of women. Women have entered the public sphere under the rubric of liberal political discourses that incautiously defined social agency in universal terms of desire and responsibility, which women now rely upon for their inclusion. Yet women have discovered that their new economic and professional desires and responsibilities are not an adequate basis upon which to ground successful social agency. If the desires, obligations, and achievements of women are not properly recognized and rewarded by others, their very existence is diminished. Women today find that their social agency is frequently undercut by inappropriate forms of sexual recognition which displace the specific forms of social recognition and reward their actions deserved and would have received if they had been performed by men.

According to Jacques Lacan's psychoanalytic theory, individual desire for the recognition of others provides the originary basis for all human activity. Individuals seek the recognition of others within the languages and other signifying systems of their society. Lacan is quite aware that women remain fundamentally unrecognized within the patriarchal signifying systems of our society; indeed, that is made quite explicit by his theory of "the primacy of the phallic signifier."[13] Lacan does not realize the significance, however, of the fact that women today are coming to be partially defined as social agents in terms of patriarchal signifying systems which still presume the social invisibility of women. I maintain that women are constituted as radically critical social agents insofar as they find their desires and responsibilities increasingly defined in terms of patriarchal discourses which yet deny them the social recognition that would be conferred upon men for similar actions.

The consideration of sexuality in chapter 2 has thus brought me to an explicitly social analysis of the category of agency. In the first place, it has become clear that many individual actions are socially and psychically partial and can only be understood in relation to the complementary actions of others. This becomes evident in chapter 2 with the analysis of patriarchal sexual situations, where female agency only becomes visible in its relation to dominant forms of male agency. In the second place, it becomes apparent in considering sexual forms of agency that the particular distribution of the dimensions of agency between women and men corresponds with the prevailing power relationships between men and women. As privileged social agents within patriarchy, men are presumed to have sexual as well as social forms of desire, and are recognized and rewarded for the actions they perform in private sexual and public social contexts. As subordinate social agents, women were not recognized as autonomous agents of any sort, but were held responsible for recognizing male agency and acting appropriately in relation to it. Even now, when women perform as men do, their actions are frequently overlooked. Social recognition and reward are a fundamental and relatively autonomous dimension of individual agency which is typically denied to less powerful members of society.

Insofar as our actions have had a fundamentally gendered quality under patriarchy, our very desires determined according to whether we were socially identified as a man or as a woman, any analysis of agency that does not attend to its social construction will overlook basic variables of meaningful action. Furthermore, this gendered analysis of agency leads us to recognize other social dimensions of action. Once we notice that agency has been determined by gendered binaries, it becomes apparent that other hierarchical social divisions have helped produce our notions of agency as well. In our society, race, ethnicity, class, and sexual preference have all provided the grounds for differential notions of individual and group agency. Within these power-laden social relationships the dimensions of agency are distributed in characteristically unjust ways which we can now evaluate and critique. Racism, for example, is articulated in terms of a particular distribution of the forms and dimensions of agency, as are heterosexism, ageism, and class biases. The women's movement may be understood as demanding a substantive redistribution of the various forms and dimensions of social agency, and so may other oppositional political movements. As social relationships change and are renegotiated, we all have reason to become concerned with altering various definitions of agency and redistributing dimensions of agency. And we may expect dramatic transformations in modes of social interaction as a consequence.

This social theory of agency contrasts markedly with the psychological model of individual agency presumed by Anglo-American philosophy today. Whether they are doing ethical theory, political theory, or action theory, analytic philosophers take the individual as the necessary and sufficient unit of agency. For those, like Donald Davidson, who do "action theory," discussions of agency continue to be framed in terms of metaphysical issues first raised by Descartes in the seventeenth century. Descartes theorized a metaphysical separation between mind and body which gave rise to concerns about whether individual actions had a mental/spiritual or a merely physical origin. Philosophers still seek to identify the psychological features of intentionality that distinguish a person exercising free will (mind) from one whose actions are determined by external (bodily) causes. While Hegel interpreted the mental component of agency in a social way, and Marx explained the material basis for agency in a social way, Anglo-American philosophers typically ignore these nineteenth-century Continental theorists. Their latter-day Cartesianism is, at this point, thoroughly embedded within a scientific/mechanistic perspective upon individual agency. Action theorists focus on specific, isolated physical actions of persons raising their arms or turning a light switch on and off, the better to evaluate the metaphysical quality of intention that person manifests.[14] Ethical theorists speculate upon supposedly intrinsic psychological features of ethical intentionality, or its lack today.[15] Even political economists who are concerned with the social variables affecting individual economic transactions assume a theory of rational welfare-maximizing behavior in which alternative desires are the only significant individual variable.

As a philosopher concerned with contemporary gendered social issues, I have two choices. On the one hand, I may accept the institutional authority of analytic philosophy, and conclude that my analysis of gendered forms of social agency does not fall within the bounds of philosophy. On the other hand, I may decide that the inability of analytic philosophy to recognize the philosophical significance of the social issues raised by changing gender relations is indicative of serious limitations in the way that Anglo-American philosophy has developed over the last two centuries. Indeed, while I appreciate and respect many aspects of analytic philosophy, I feel a moral and political responsibility to insist upon the philosophical significance of gendered as well as other social relationships.

The work of the poststructuralist philosopher Michel Foucault provides an immediate and critical source of support for this endeavor, insofar as he supplies a theoretical framework for debunking the foundationalist and universalist metaphysical claims of modern philosophy. For Foucault, modern philosophy is but one of a number of humanist discourses supporting a succession of regimes of power/knowledge operating in a liberal democratic mode. Yet my gendered postmodern vision assumes the possibility of reconstructing contemporary discourses as part of an ongoing micro-politics, a project that finds no more support from Foucault and other "first-generation" male postmodern thinkers than it does among Anglo-American philosophers. It is the moral and political philosophy of Aristotle, with his complex analysis of the social fabric within which individual actions take place and his broad interest in the various private and public domains of action, that is one of the most important foundations for my project. My gendered postmodern individual would be quite foreign to Aristotle, but he and she might speak together sympathetically about the problems of doing social philosophy.

iv. Putting a Theory of Gendered Agency to Work

Feminists and other social theorists tend to use the notion of "agency" very freely today, its relevance all too apparent, its meaning, however, still quite elusive. We want to signal those moments when individuals finally "take action" in a great many different circumstances, yet the very idea of what it means to act has become difficult to pin down. This book chronicles my efforts to arrive at a conception of "agency" that would allow me to evaluate those actions, both historical and contemporary, that appear significant from a gendered perspective. The resulting theory of agency has become the conceptual pivot around which I attempt to generate a postmodern and postfeminist analysis of contemporary social issues. I define "agency" in the following way: *"Agency" refers to those individual or group actions deemed significant within a particular social or institutional setting. While we are accustomed to thinking in terms of distinct forms of agency, as in economic, ethical, or sexual agency, I emphasize that there are also three distinct "dimensions" of agency operative either together or apart within the context of individual actions. Individual agency is always associated with one or more of the following dimensions: motivation, responsibility, and expectations of recognition or reward. I also emphasize that individual agency is typically interactive, necessarily understood in terms of relations between two or more individuals.*

There are two basic premises underlying the theory of agency I propose in this work: (1) We require a more complicated social analysis of agency to ground an adequate historical appreciation for the actions of women and the relationships of women and men under patriarchy. (2) A more complex and politicized theory of agency is necessary for us to analyze conflicted social relationships today, as well as for reconfiguring these relationships in an evolving postmodern society. Feminism has always addressed issues of agency implicitly. Our society, like most others, has quite blatantly preferred male actors and activities to female ones. Patriarchy systematically devalues the social significance of actions characteristic of women. And it excludes women from participating in those activities that have been deemed significant and full of agency. Insofar as historical and even contemporary accounts of significant social events are populated almost exclusively by men, it tends to look like women are not the sort of beings capable of significant social actions.

It is a founding principle of feminism that women deserve to be recognized as significant social agents, and feminists have challenged the patriarchal preference for male-identified forms of social agency on two distinct fronts. In the first place, feminist thinkers from Mary Wollstonecraft to Simone de Beauvoir have asserted the (equal) ability of women to perform those acts that men deem socially significant under patriarchy. Second, feminist theorists from Catharine Beecher to Sara Ruddick have demanded that domestic and maternal activities primarily identified with women under patriarchy deserve to be recognized as (different) sites of social agency alongside the public activities of men.[16] The arguments of "equality" and "difference" feminists, as these two variants of feminism have been labeled, have been important. Both rely, however, upon relatively static, binary, and gendered notions of social identities and forms of social agency. As I attempt to show in chapters 1 and 2, gendered notions of both identity and agency are undergoing significant mutations as the roles of women and men overlap, merge, sometimes reverse themselves, and finally develop in quite unexpected new directions.

Reproductive issues are one of the most compelling sites of such contemporary changes, putting a postfeminist resolve to move beyond the gendered frameworks of modernism to a stringent test. Chapter 3 takes up the issue of abortion, arguing that there have been serious feminist difficulties in providing an adequate ethical analysis of abortion, and suggesting that the problem results from an enduring feminist inclination to celebrate an organic vision of motherhood. So long as we assume a naturalistic conception of maternal agency, pregnancy appears to organically implicate women in the moral responsibilities of motherhood. A nonnaturalistic vision of procreative agency can be found in Donna Haraway's cyborg myth: she suggests that the boundaries of the natural and the artificial have become blurred in many situations to such an extent that we may imagine a hybridization of human being and machine which she calls a cyborg. I recommend a notion of cyborgean maternal agency as a metaphoric vehicle for radically altering the way we think about human reproductive processes.

Cyborg imagery immediately calls to mind robotic figures, but the force of Haraway's cyborg concept is to emphasize the merging of organic, natural forms of agency and the inorganic, artificial devices we use to enhance human agency within social life today. Artificial knees and hips empower us to go on being physically active social agents; the mechanical capacities of computers meld quite seamlessly with the organic intellectual resources that enable us to write articles and books. For heterosexual women today, various artificial, inorganic substances and devices enable us to be sexually active human beings without becoming pregnant. Our organic reproductive capacities are no longer determinative of our reproductive lives once we rely upon contraception. Insofar as organic facts no longer determine our reproductive lives as women, and we rely throughout our adult years upon various chemicals and devices to keep us from becoming pregnant, our relationship to motherhood ceases to be organic and becomes cyborgean. Organic phenomena no longer determine our relationship to reproduction, and no longer determine the ethical quality of our agency as adult women, in general. Insofar as this is so in a general

What is this
saying?

way, it would seem that a particular organic fact, like that of pregnancy, must also be insufficient to determine the morality of a particular woman's path of action. For cyborgean reproductive agents, the morality of a decision to produce a child is no longer determined by, and indeed may no longer be reduced to, an organic factor such as pregnancy.

Note that this conclusion does not require us to adopt an antireligious position, any more than did Newtonian mechanics, Galileo's telescope, or any of the other theories associated with the Copernican Revolution.[17] It is only if we associate God exclusively with the organic component of human reproduction that we need fear offending him/her with abortions. If we more generally associate God with the efforts of human beings to act morally in the context of their particular social world, there would presumably be many situations today in which abortion would be a morally justifiable act in the eyes of God.

This notion of cyborgean procreative agency may serve as a defining feature of a postfeminist theory, distinguishing it from prior feminist positions as well as from postmodern positions developed without the advantage of a gendered perspective. Second-wave feminism, as I have explained it, was a movement operating from within a modern patriarchal society in which there remained a normative identification of humanity with masculinity. In this context, it is understandable that feminists such as Adrienne Rich and Sara Ruddick would respond to an essentialist patriarchal social metaphysic with an attempt to celebrate that which seemed most essentially different about women's lives and capabilities. If men were deemed naturally superior because of being born with a penis, then women could respond in kind by competitively asserting the natural value of women's wombs.

I have explained postfeminism as beginning at that moment when the normative identification of humanity with men and masculinity became open to question. No matter how formal and superficial the normative critique of patriarchy remains today, it corresponds with changes in social relationships that can only deepen the critique over time (as I explain in chapter 4). Postfeminists no longer need to assume a reactive essentialist feminism in relation to essentialist patriarchal values. We may value very highly our bodily maternal capacities as individual social agents, but the celebration of women's organic female constitution ceases to be a component of postfeminism. Just as we have ceased to respect claims about the organic capacity of penises to endow men with social meaning and authority, we may no longer plausibly insist that there be particular social meanings associated with the "natural" bodily capacity of women to become pregnant and produce children.[18]

This analysis of postfeminist reproductive agency also provides a basis for beginning to distinguish poststructuralist political theories which articulate radical politics in terms of a notion of resistance, à la Michel Foucault, from the more constructive notions of political agency available to a postfeminist theory. Michel Foucault focuses upon the institutional discourses within which our subjective identities, as well as our experiences of desire and rationality, are produced. According to Foucault, hegemonic social discourses constitute individual subjects who participate in society from various positions of domination, subordination, or resistance. All individual actions are inscribed within particular discursive power/knowledge relationships, and resistance is simply one mode of political interaction.

While this approach generates important insights about the power-laden quality of daily social interactions, it is not capable of explaining or even recognizing the dynamic aspects of our contemporary milieu. Foucault explains how hegemonic discourses work, not how they break down. His analysis can explain all possible individual actions within a well-defined sociopolitical moment, to the extent that such moments exist. But when serious conflicts develop between social discourses, or when hegemonic institutional relationships erode and become unstable, a number of different discourses may become competitively and/or chaotically relevant to understanding individual actions. While power relationships will always circumscribe individual actions, and while subordination or resistance will always be a possible set of alternatives in relation to these power relationships, it is necessary to expand the vocabulary of political actions in order to make sense of individual agency in moments of discursive uncertainty and political change.[19]

The procreative activities of women and men today, for example, are chaotically "inscribed" within waning patriarchal kinship and religious discourses, ascendant technological discourses, and unstable economic and political discourses of late liberal capitalism, as well as within various tentative progressive discourses. To explain such individual actions as discursively determined has little analytical force. Considering the chaotic state of both reproductive technologies and their juridical status, it is politically myopic to evaluate the procreative decisions of individuals primarily in terms of their relationship to hegemonic structures of power. Women must, of course, remain vigilant in resisting patriarchal forces and figures, ever lurking and ready to seduce them into dark corners or reduce them to lesser lives. Yet the most serious and difficult issues facing individuals undertaking procreative relationships today have to do with constructing viable postmodern family and community relationships.

Neither liberal concepts of participation nor radical political concepts of
resistance will comprehend individual reproductive decisions despite the
fact that these decisions are likely to have serious political consequences.
My postfeminist account attempts to explain alternative trajectories of
procreative agency, linking them with other forms of possible micro-
political action.

v.   Historicizing this Theory of Individual Agency

Many analytic and continental philosophers believe that Western society
is experiencing some form of social or theoretical crisis, but there is little
agreement about what it involves. Jacques Derrida, from a poststructuralist perspective, and Richard Rorty, from a postpragmatist one, both
pronounce upon the purely textual residua of once-grand Western metaphysical theories, but neither manifests much concern for the extratextual
political signs of fragmentation and decline. Jürgen Habermas, on the
other hand, maintains that we are in the midst of a crisis in political leadership and institutions that he calls a "legitimation crisis," but he is confident
that consensual political solutions may be "communicatively achieved"
through political mechanisms available within modernism. Jean-François
Lyotard identifies a crisis in the Western master-narratives of emancipatory progress and totalizing truth, and specifically repudiates Habermas's
belief in a consensual political solution, but he suggests that sophisticated
modernists can learn to get along without these narrative comforts. Mean-
while, Gilles Deleuze and Felix Guattari dramatically debunk psychoanalytic understandings of "Oedipal" desire, but show little interest in the implications of their "nomadic" account of "desiring-production" for
gendered social structures such as the family. In an Anglo-American context, philosophers are concerned about a decline in moral agency. We have
become "first personal" individuals, according to Bernard Williams, and
"ghostly individuals," according to Alasdair MacIntyre, and each philosopher believes we have lost our capability of making reasoned ethical and
political decisions; yet neither holds out serious hope that new grounds
for ethical reasoning might be possible. [20] These philosophers all continue
to assume important aspects of modernism as given, even as they critique
other aspects, and each therefore remains unable or unwilling to conceive
of solutions that would require them to venture very far beyond its
paradigms.

     My experience of the crisis, on the contrary, is too encompassing to ad-
mit of a partial critique. I see problems of rationality and action, of desire
and responsibility, of social and political identity, all rendered equivocal

or faint by processes of transformation reaching across the social spectrum. The philosophical challenge, as I see it, is to propose a framework for explaining how such diverse forms of change may be understood in relation to each other. Chapter 4 begins to articulate such a framework.

Without suggesting that our weary liberal tradition is a candidate for radical theoretical surpassing, Alasdair MacIntyre offers three useful criteria for any theory that seeks to resolve the theoretical crises brought on by the decline of a social tradition.[21] First, the theory must be capable of providing answers to problems associated with the decline of a tradition, enabling people to deal with social and political difficulties in ways that only become conceivable in light of its new theoretical perspective. By interpreting our present social woes as originating in a crisis of individual agency, I hope to provide a categorical pivot for turning away from modern oppositions of self and other, of economic and moral rationality, of personal and impersonal motivations. It is reasonable to hope that by rethinking their agency in some of the ways I suggest, engaged postmodern individuals will confront current theoretical and social dilemmas more productively.

Secondly, MacIntyre argues, a new theory must explain why the current tradition has become incoherent. My answer, in brief, is that a specific gendered organization of society has precipitously declined, with several immediate consequences. On the one hand, forms of identity and agency that were meaningful within patriarchal kinship structures have eroded, leaving individuals uncertain about who they are or how they should act in many situations. On the other hand, a whole spectrum of needs formerly satisfied within patriarchal kinship relationships have come unmoored from them. Insofar as these needs presently evoke individuated, experimental responses by men and women within public as well as private contexts, we are experiencing the inevitable intellectual confusions attendant upon a moment when diverse new modes of behavior are chaotically filling the gaps left by the decline of long-prescribed gender- and kinship-based relationships.

Thirdly, MacIntyre avers, such a theory must explain the ways in which a newly evolving tradition will be continuous with the previous tradition. My response is that the current social conjuncture provides us with a basis for reconceptualizing the historical development of notions of agency and individualism. Marx went along with the classical political economists in emphasizing the relationship between the development of capitalism and that of individualism. However, I maintain that transformations within gendered kinship relationships currently provide the basis for a further developmental stage of individualism. I propose that we are now entering upon a second major stage of individualism, involving new modes of individual agency and identity that are gradually transforming the forms of social behavior with which we are familiar. As the social structures and discourses of a liberal, patriarchal individualism wane, they will be replaced by those of a postmodern society organized around transactions between persons I will refer to as "engaged individuals."

The modern period of liberal individualism is generally understood as beginning with the end of feudalism in sixteenth- and seventeenth-century Europe. I explain this first stage of individualism as resulting from the physical unmooring of individuals from stable feudal communities within which their social and material needs had been satisfied in communally prescribed ways. As serfs were evicted from the agricultural lands of their ancestors, their survival came to depend upon individuated responses to material forms of neediness. The material-based notions of individual agency characteristic of liberal individualism began to develop at this point. They continued to develop for several hundreds of years, providing a dynamic infrastructure for the complex society we live in today. Liberal notions of personal identity, with all their psychological, social, and political subtleties, have been constructed upon a foundational notion of agency understood in terms of individuated responses to material forms of neediness. From the seventeenth to the twentieth centuries, not just economic theory but political, ethical, and psychological theories and all the human sciences assumed that rational social behavior could be traced back to fundamental individual motivations, responsibilities, and rewards of a material nature. Theories of democracy and totalitarianism, justice and injustice, moral development and deviant psychological development, all took individuated material motivations, responsibilities, and forms of recognition and reward, or what we commonly refer to as "economic agency," as the background against which other modern forms of rational and irrational behavior had to be understood.

While liberal individualism was not overtly articulated as a gendered form of agency, the various social structures and political norms of modern society enforced the fact that men were liberal individuals and women were not. Women were instead ensconced as key figures within the patriarchal kinship structures characteristic of liberalism which I refer to as "incorporated male family selves." This incorporated family structure provided men with the personal and psychological mooring that enabled them to perform as "autonomous" individuals in the public sphere of an industrial society. The agency of liberal individuals can only be fully understood in the context of their ties of desire, responsibility, and reward to this private family self.

The agency as well as the oppression of women can be understood in the context of this family self. Women's desires, responsibilities, and rewards were defined wholly in terms of their role within the family self. While women were understood to exercise important forms of social agency within the family, their identities were subsumed within the families of their fathers and husbands. They were not allowed individual desires exceeding the bounds of their familial existence, and they could expect no individual recognition for their achievements. Within liberal society, economic independence was a necessary precondition for full personhood, yet women remained materially dependent upon men, their needs and indeed their lives submerged within the incorporated family selves of liberal men.

The second stage of engaged individualism, and the end of modernism, begins with the economic unmooring of women from the incorporated male family. The initial phase of this process is deceptive, in that it appears as if women are simply becoming liberal individuals within the public sphere alongside men. It only becomes apparent that something more complicated is going on when this process of "socially enfranchising" women fails to proceed as smoothly as might be expected. Women today experience anger and frustration over a host of problems that seem to have been exacerbated by the process of social enfranchisement. In part, the anger is a result of the rising expectations of women, and is occasioned simply by the fact that the equalization of women with men in various public and private venues does not occur faster. In part, the anger may be explained as a response to what Susan Faludi has identified as a "backlash against women" who have "made waves," on the part of men and patriarchal cultural institutions such as the media.[22] But a large component of the anger and frustration of women, and of men as well, has to do with the fact that the social enfranchisement of women has triggered more fundamental social changes which are difficult even to conceptualize, much less deal with, in terms of the structures and norms of liberal individualism.

We can understand the current situation if we have the hubris to insist upon the social and historical significance of the gendered transformations now occurring in daily life. In the first place, it is evident that as large numbers of women began to leave the home each day to participate in the public sphere, the incorporated family began to decline. When men became economic individuals they also became incorporated family selves, with all the responsibilities and rewards of being the head of a patriarchal family. Contrarily, as women become economic individuals their economic independence promotes the breakup of incorporated family selves.

People still live within family units, of course. But there is no more life-time incorporation under a male head of household. Families are now limited partnerships. The end of modernism is assured when the familial moorings of men, women, and children basic to modern liberal society cease to be either practically or normatively secured, and the social struc-tures of kinship, and of workplace as well, cease to function in predictable ways.[23]

The problems associated with the social enfranchisement of women can only be understood once we properly identify the full extent of the current process of *familial unmooring* and analyze its implications. In many ways the results of this familial unmooring are analogous to those that occurred with the unmooring of the serfs from the feudal manors. In addition to the material needs of women and children that are loosed from the patriar-chal family of liberalism, however, a great many personal and psychic forms of neediness of men, women, and children have also become un-moored. I will refer to these as *psychic relational forms of neediness*: they com-prise a broad set of basic psychic requirements, from childhood needs for nurture to adult needs for various forms of personal and psychological connectedness.[24] It is initially difficult to recognize the significance of this spectrum of psychological needs insofar as they were formerly attended to silently and "naturally" by women within the incorporated patriarchal family. These needs cease to be attended to silently or naturally by women, or by anyone, with the breakdown of this family structure. As children leave the home each morning along with their parents, and as adults experiment with the degrees of autonomy possible in a society that no longer demands familial connections, various psychic forms of needi-ness are frequently neglected. As developmental problems in children and assorted forms of psychic stress in adults emerge, it appears that our sur-vival now depends upon developing individuated responses to this newly visible multitude of psychic relational forms of neediness.

Loosed from their moorings in patriarchal kinship relationships, our personal and psychic forms of neediness must be satisfied in individuated and contingent ways. Accordingly, what I term "interpersonal" forms of individual agency have become a newly important component of in-dividual lives. *I define "interpersonal agency" as "those actions in which we seek to create and maintain affirmative psychic connections to others."* While these forms of agency always existed, they were not a significant basis for in-dividuated forms of action in a society within which the maintenance of basic psychic connections was considered the natural responsibility of mothers and wives within incorporated male families.[25]

As we begin to evaluate sites of nascent and potential interpersonal agency it is already apparent that these forms of agency will often be associated with very different sorts of motivations, responsibilities, and expectations of recognition and reward than forms of agency grounded in material needs. For one thing, psychic needs and the interpersonal agency we exercise in responding to them generate more direct forms of relationship between individuals, contrasting with the relatively indirect contractual relationships that arise in the context of satisfying material needs. It required several hundred years for liberal economic and political structures to develop, however, and our notions of agency remain deeply embedded in their practices, despite their increasing ineffectiveness. A theory of interpersonal agency suggests strategies for rearticulating individual agency within particular institutional frameworks. It also allows us to speculate upon how forms of interpersonal agency may augment or even come to displace materially based forms of agency.

vi. On the Ultra-Social Status of Postfeminist Theory

What is the status of this account? As a postmodernist, I am thoroughly critical of the metaphysical presumptions of prior philosophy. But as a postfeminist philosopher my reasons for denying the metaphysical truth claims of philosophy are very much connected with a desire to assert a socially bounded truth potential for philosophy. As a gendered postmodernist, I lost any predispositions for metaphysical truth at a very young age, as a reaction to being repeatedly confounded by patriarchal theories that clashed not only with my emerging sense of self, but with my socially developing expectations for a nonpatriarchal world. I remember, for example, deciding to read Plato's *Republic* at the suggestion of a teacher who said Plato argued for the equality of women. Yet in making a preliminary examination of the dialogue, I noticed a repeated Platonic refrain of "women, and children, and slaves." Disgusted, I put the book down for years. To my quite partisan eye, Plato was writing a brazenly patriarchal Greek text which offended me, whatever arguments he made for training women alongside men to rule as Guardians of his utopian Republic. (Indeed, Plato refers to the relationship between male and female dogs as a means of explaining the relationship between male and female Guardians, leading one to suspect his concerns are primarily ones of breeding.) Out of an emerging gendered sense of selfhood, I was forced to evaluate the *Republic* as a social and historical text, rather than as even potentially an expression of metaphysical truth.

It was evident that had I lived in the eras of Plato, Descartes, Kant, Marx, or even John Rawls, they would not have recognized me as both a woman and as a potentially significant philosopher, and this fact made it personally necessary for me to disqualify their claims of metaphysical truth. Insofar as I could not have existed for them as a philosopher, I could not be fully inducted into their worldview. I could not be seduced to fully participate in a philosophic gaze that was incapable of adequately recognizing me. I claim no metaphysical basis for denying their patriarchal worldviews, or for proclaiming the truth of my own efforts to construct a postpatriarchal worldview. It is simply a fact that my own philosophic actions could not be constituted in the terms of these prior philosophic discourses insofar as they denied my female theoretical agency, more or less explicitly. My gender in this late-patriarchal, emergent postpatriarchal age required and enabled me to distance myself from the cultural power of prior philosophic visions in a quite special way. To a certain extent, my gendered stance has been socially and theoretically disabling, for all the psychological and political reasons feminist thinkers have explained. However, it has kept me from succumbing to the metaphysical faith effects of dominant philosophical discourses that thinkers such as Derrida, Foucault, and Rorty so vehemently deplore, while yet bearing traces of these within their own critical stances.

There is for me a very clear distinction between the metaphysical and the social status of philosophic claims. As a woman and a philosopher in this chaotic postmodern, potentially postpatriarchal age, I perceive a lot of work to be done in reconfiguring dominant discourses and institutions. I feel an opportunity and a responsibility to engage in rethinking the dominant social and political discourses. I believe in the social significance of such efforts insofar as I am committed to bringing about a postpatriarchal age. Richard Rorty is correct, in a sense, when he argues that philosophers never do more than offer new vocabularies which either prove socially useful or do not. Yet the Ur-Cartesian assumptions that still color his vision lead him to believe that if a theorist cannot presume to give an objective account of what is "out there," then he can do no more than subjectively respond to internal psychological urges that lack any necessary social connection.[26] Of course, Continental thinkers, from Hegel to Foucault, have explained that subjectivity, or the theoretical and psychological performances I experience as subjectivity, are socially conditioned or constituted. I take it for granted that my psychological and theoretical urges are part of a social relationship to the world around me.

If my psychological urges and theoretical products gain potential significance as part of a relationship to the world around me, however, then so do those of Plato, Aristotle, or Descartes. It is clear that I must respect the philosophical relationships of such previous thinkers to their societies if I am to believe in the seriousness of my own philosophical relationship to my society. I consider it an act of futile metaphysical wishfulness to become overly indignant at the prior exclusion of women from philosophy, and to attempt to explain it as the product of particular failures in a masculine theoretical project.[27] The philosophic deck is stacked against efforts to prove the metaphysical deficiency of patriarchal worldviews and the superiority of feminist worldviews. And if we succumb to the urge to deny the works of Plato or Descartes legitimacy as socially and historically bounded theories, we undermine the legitimacy of our own theoretical efforts to replace them. If, instead, I simply assume that the most basic philosophic account is a socially and politically bounded one, I can calmly accept previous philosophies as powerful articulations of worlds I cannot quite imagine living within. I can gratefully appropriate particular aspects of these theories as discursive gifts, transmitted across astonishing historical and social distances. I can remain tenaciously focused on a thoroughly contemporary project of postmodern theorizing. I would therefore insist upon *the ultra-social status* of postfeminist theories.

vii.   Renegotiating Agency: Seizing the Micro-Political Moment

A postmodern, postfeminist era has begun. While liberal discourses remain dominant, they are conflict-ridden and unstable as a consequence of the social enfranchisement of women, and the unmooring of women, men, and children from patriarchal kinship relationships. The identification of humanity and masculinity is no longer normatively or structurally secured by the ailing institutions of late liberalism. And so, the actions of women and men, as well, have a peculiarly radical/constructive potential. Yet it will remain difficult to appreciate or to act upon that potential so long as we continue to assume modernist visions of change and political agency.

Chapter 5 identifies particular examples of micro-political agency and attempts to explain some of the complicated ways in which such forms of agency now operate. Although they may eventually have societywide consequences, micro-political forms of agency typically occur and must be evaluated within particular institutional contexts. Micro-political struggles involve issues of race, class, and sexual preference as well as gender, requiring a new sophistication with respect to what Kimberlé Crenshaw has termed the "intersectional" quality of many situations. One of the most important features of a micro-politics is its analysis of how these various forms of domination interact with each other in particular situations, and its strategic concern for opposing multiple forms of domination.[28] An apparent defeat in one institutional moment of micro-political struggle may become the basis for success in later struggles that carry forward themes raised by the earlier one.

I utilize the 1991 Senate Hearings in which Anita Hill made her charges of sexual harassment against Supreme Court nominee Clarence Thomas to illustrate each of these points. Anita Hill's appearance before the Senate Judiciary Committee was an inadvertent result of the racial politics surrounding President Bush's attempt to appoint an ideologically conservative black man to Thurgood Marshall's seat on the Supreme Court, and her dramatic charges of sexual harassment failed to derail this project. Yet a year after Hill's humiliating treatment by the twelve white male members of the Judiciary Committee, voters galvanized by this sexist media spectacle elected record numbers of women to Congress, among them a black woman, Carol Mosely Braun, and a white woman, Diane Feinstein, who have been appointed to that same Senate Judiciary Committee.

More important, the intense and extended public discussion of sexual harassment occasioned by the Senate hearings has had an electrifying impact on perceptions of the workplace. Women of all ages and social positions have begun to reevaluate their own experiences in light of the legal category of sexual harassment, discovering that it is readily applicable to their everyday professional relationships with men. A year after Hill's testimony, sexual harassment has come to be seen as a pervasive problem within military, academic, political, and economic institutions, and various strategies have been developing for dealing with it. In one frequent scenario, numerous women testify to their sexual harassment by a single well-known man, providing evidence of a history of oppressive sexual behavior toward female employees, often by a man formerly held in high regard for his public attitudes toward women. The hope is not only to force this man to change his behavior but to make him an example by which other men will relearn the boundaries of appropriate behavior. The problem with this approach is that we tend to focus on the pathological psyche of the famous man, taking a stereotypical quality of sexist behavior for granted. Men who are not particularly powerful and who have not engaged in stereotypical forms of harassment are not required to think critically about their own behavior.[29]

In a more recent micro-political tactic, Earline Hill, a New York state assemblywoman, issued a public statement explaining three diverse acts of harassment she had recently experienced. She said she was not interested in punishing the men who committed the acts but rather in publicizing the problem and focusing attention on the highly varied forms harassment may take. She encouraged people to analyze each action for its unique quotient of hostility / triviality / social hurtfulness. There was much debate over the precise quality of the creatively sexist acts she described, and whether they were "truly" acts of harassment. In fact, within a few days colleagues came forward to apologize profusely and publicly for committing the two least serious of the acts.[30] Earline Hill's approach was valuable in downplaying both her own victimization as well as the malign intentions of her harassers. The goal of a sexual harassment micropolitics is to alter the fabric of public relationships between men and women, rather than to celebrate or condemn particular political subjects. The immediate micro-political goal is that of reconfiguring specific relationships to require appropriate degrees of respect between men and women within a particular institutional setting. As large numbers of women engage in specific critiques of institutionally embedded patterns of sexualized power, they may cumulatively alter the standards for male behavior toward women more generally. As this process goes forward, the public agency of all women will be enhanced.

A gendered micro-politics may also concern itself with transforming relationships that have been exempt from political judgment within liberalism by virtue of their personal and private character. I have analyzed patriarchal sexuality as presuming a complementary and quite unfair division of the dimensions of sexual agency between men and women. Men have been accorded the right to act upon their sexual desires, and been given positive recognition for all their sexual activities, while women have been held responsible for physically securing their persons against male sexual desire not sanctioned by marriage, and punished for extramarital sexual incidents, regardless of whether they sought them out.[31] A sexual micro-politics seeks a redistribution of the dimensions of sexual agency such that women will have as much right to feel, express, and act upon their sexual desires as men have. Men will be obliged to be as concerned with women's sexual desires, positive or negative, as women are with the desires of men. The patriarchal asymmetries that now define heterosexual relationships will be replaced by more symmetrical forms of sexual agency.

A sexual micro-politics will take place primarily within the diversely personalized and privatized settings of individual sexual relationships. Yet insofar as patriarchal sexual relationships are thoroughly embedded in a diverse set of public discourses, ranging from the Bible and the legal system to Freudian psychology and contemporary film conventions, any successful challenge to patriarchal sexual practices must have a large public discursive component as well. Chapter 5 analyzes the trials resulting from Patricia Bowman's and Desiree Washington's accusations of date rape against William Kennedy Smith and Mike Tyson as media events providing an occasion for a popular discussion of the sexist biases of legal and psychological discourses. Serious criticisms of patriarchal patterns of sexual agency were discussed publicly in response to these trials, and the gendered distribution of sexual desire and responsibility was highlighted quite well. Yet they were disappointing events from the perspective of a sexual micro-politics. While issues of race and class intersected with the sexual politics in distracting and troubling ways, the largest difficulties arose from the script of date rape trials themselves. As a hybrid form of traditional rape trials, the legal script for a date rape trial is a fundamentally patriarchal one, a woman needing to prove that she was an unwilling victim of a criminal act of sexual assault. Whether a woman wins or loses in such a legal context, the trial results say very little about the need for changing normal forms of sexual interaction between men and women who would define themselves as neither criminals nor victims. Yet it is normal forms of sexual relationships that a sexual micro-politics seeks to alter.

While Patricia Bowman lost her case and Desiree Washington won hers, a year later it appears that Washington may have been the bigger loser. She has publicly stated that the outcome of the trial has ruined her life, and that "for as long as Mike Tyson is in prison, I will also be in prison," as a consequence of the harsh public reaction to her as a black woman who caused a famous black man to be convicted of date rape.[32] The racist history of lynchings of black men accused of rape in the South has made it all too easy for public opinion to avert its eyes from the sexual violence Tyson inflicted upon Washington. Had Tyson been a white athlete, his conviction would have been attended by more critical reflection upon the sexual perquisites commonly accorded to male athletes, movie stars, and political figures, among others. The rape paradigm is sufficiently harsh, however, to make such convictions unlikely.

I recommend in chapter 5 that instead of resorting to date rape trials women bring civil suits against men who have acted in sexually coercive or assaultive ways. In demanding monetary damages for the psychic and physical injuries men have inflicted upon them, women will be speaking to men as angry sexual agents of a new sexual order rather than as traditional female victims of male lust. Of course, the idea of women suing men for monetary damages in response to sexual misconduct profanes deeply held assumptions about the intangible quality of heterosexual encounters. This is all to the good, I think, insofar as various romantic mystifications of sexuality presently impede the progress of micro-political renegotiations in bedrooms across the land. By challenging patriarchal notions of male sexual dominance within civil suits, women will provide a legal forum for theoretically dissecting the forms and degrees of male coerciveness common within patriarchal sexual relationships. Women and men today need such public discursive support insofar as they wish to transform their individual sexual relationships. Civil suits will provide valuable legal and symbolic encouragement for a contemporary sexual micro-politics.

I also analyze recent gendered micro-political struggles within the military in chapter 5, discussing the ways in which women soldiers challenged the ultra-masculine quality of military identity in the context of their participation in the 1991 Persian Gulf War.[33] Since the Gulf War, the military has experienced an embarrassing rash of micro-political problems. In 1992, revelations about egregious and collective acts of sexual harassment at the annual Tailhook convention of naval aviators again brought the institutionalized masculinity of the armed services under severe scrutiny.[34] Most recently, with the election of President Clinton, the micro-political issues have shifted somewhat, as the new President has sought to honor his campaign pledge to lift the ban on gays and lesbians in the military. Bill Clinton has begun to sound postmodern on this issue, arguing that a fair military policy requires that we judge an individual solely on the basis of conduct or military performance rather than his or her gender status or sexual identity.

Actually, it is neither the conduct nor the identity of the homosexual individual that is presently generating the most severe military anxiety, but instead the avowed sexual agency of homosexual men. As members of a patriarchal culture that continues to assume that predatory male heterosexual desires for women are natural and even desirable, military men are obviously vulnerable to fears that homosexual male desires for other men will take an equally predatory form once they are recognized as legitimate. While women are challenging the macho ethos of uncontrollable and potentially violent male sexual desire in the context of domestic abuse, for example, the high level of sexual violence against women within the armed services is evidence of its continuing strength.[35]

So long as a predatory conception of sexuality remains a feature of the ultra-masculine military identity, gay male sexuality may evoke unspeakable dread from otherwise fearless soldiers. Of course, once the ban on gays and lesbians is finally rescinded, and it becomes obvious that gay men do not find it natural or necessary to prey upon available straight male bodies, the whole notion of uncontrollable male sexuality will be undermined. The intersectional quality of postmodern politics is ultimately an advantage in this case. As women in the armed services increasingly prosecute men for sexual harassment and other forms of sexual assault, and as gay men provide positive evidence for the ability of men to exercise control over their sexual desires, naturalistic claims about the predatory quality of male sexuality will appear less and less persuasive, even as a component of an ultra-masculine military identity.[36]

One of the ironies of the current confrontation between the military and President Clinton is the fact that a major opponent of an executive order ending a ban on gays and lesbians is Colin Powell, the chairman of the Joint Chiefs of Staff. As a black man, Powell owes his military position to an executive order issued by President Truman in 1948, which brought racial integration to the armed services for the first time. The idea of racial integration aroused as much opposition and fear within the military in 1948 as Clinton's proposal does today. Yet Powell's military identity is wholly defined in terms of the current institution, and he sees no similarity between its former (unjust) exclusion of blacks, and its current (just) exclusion of homosexuals. He maintains that the dangerous sexuality of gay men is a threat to military discipline and morale, and that because homosexuals pose a real *sexual* danger there can be no parallels between the military policy of excluding homosexuals and its unfounded discrimination against black men. Yet Powell conveniently forgets that exclusionary racial practices were frequently justified in terms of white perceptions of the dangerous sexuality of black men. Powell's confident distinction between the discrimination against blacks and that against homosexuals is historically inaccurate. Insofar as fears based upon stereotypes of black male sexuality were features of racial oppression, there are clear parallels between current arguments against lifting the ban on homosexuals in the military and arguments against integrating it in 1948.

Powell's military identity is neither historically nor racially nuanced. His agency is rigidly defined in terms of perpetuating the military institution, which just happens to be patriarchal and homophobic, within which his actions have been (rewardingly) inscribed during his thirty-five-year career.[37] The military is one of the last remaining communities within which such a narrow, unconflicted sense of identity can still be cultivated within our society, and current micro-political struggles within the armed services indicate that it will not remain possible much longer even here. While Colin Powell's exclusionary attitudes are presumably shared by much of the current military leadership, opposition to women and homosexuals is hardly universal. For example, in recent hearings on the question of allowing women into combat, several top generals firmly supported women's equal right to assume combat roles, arguing along with feminists that military positions, like all others in society, should be assigned solely on the basis of a person's ability to perform the duties of the position.

Brigadier General Thomas V. Draude explained that he had been led to question the military's exclusion of women from combat due to his own daughter's decision to train for a career as a Navy pilot.[38] His parental pride in the capabilities of his daughter, and his desire that she be allowed to achieve her highest ambitions in an age when women have been socially enfranchised within most other social institutions, were contradicted by the imperious patriarchal stance of the military institution of which he remains a part. His sense of parental interest and responsibility finally overrode the military parameters of his public agency. He became willing to criticize the institutional discourses that had defined his professional career in order to advocate the rights of women like his daughter to fly combat missions.

I take General Draude's experiences struggling with conflicting kinship and military loyalties as a good example of how even the most entrenched institutional identities are subject to disaggregation today as diverse professional and familial discourses come into conflict with one another. One wonders what would happen if Colin Powell had a gay or lesbian child who wanted a military career. The disaggregation of fixed identities is a process that has reached an advanced stage in many individuals today. As multiply-engaged individuals, we create our daily lives out of a bricolage of competing and conflicting forms of agency. We are micro-political agents insofar as we manage to operate within various institutional discourses without ever being fully inscribed within any of the familial, military, economic, or other corporate frames of reference that engage us.

viii.   Summary Thoughts

A micro-political analysis has several purposes. In the first place, it demonstrates that there are serious political implications in many of the everyday decisions individuals make with respect to how they will act in a given circumstance, even when these decisions are not accompanied by traditional forms of political consciousness. Second, it offers a framework for acting as intersectional agents within various institutional settings. By encouraging individuals to evaluate what sort of actions are likely to contribute to the perpetuation or, alternatively, to the erosion of complex, intersectional relations of domination within a particular situation, a micro-political analysis provides grounds for creative and unconventional forms of political organizing and struggle.

The chapters in this book chronicle my efforts to formulate a social perspective appropriate to an emergent postmodern age as we head toward the twenty-first century. I analyze contemporary social conflicts in terms of the individuated struggles through which we are jointly negotiating changes in social relations of power and authority, and articulating new forms of agency and individualism. In a society dominated by economic relationships, we have associated shifts in social power primarily with shifts in the distribution of economic power. But as interpersonal forms of agency and the need for individuated responses to the various forms of psychic neediness gain in social significance, shifts in social power will have to be articulated in more complicated terms.

While economic power remains very much a condition of freedom and justice in our society, in these globally recessionary times a disjuncture between the mandates of economic agency and existing ideals of individual achievement and freedom is increasingly evident. Our substantive political ideals will be transformed as they come to reflect the new qualities and distributions of agency that are increasingly necessary to explain the actions of postmodern individuals. Engaged individuals are experimenting with multiple and changing forms of individual agency, struggling to maintain a shifting and always contingent sense of psychological and social integrity. As micro-political agents, we are often conflicted actors but not fragmented selves. We are institutionally engaged selves who can only function insofar as we become capable of individually integrating diverse desires and obligations on a daily basis through creatively reconfiguring our practices and relationships.

1

Love and Injustice in Families

Women have made it to center stage in the historical drama. The problems of contemporary women in relation to work and family are society's problems. From the feminization of poverty, to abortion and surrogacy, to sexual harassment, the new choices and responsibilities of women have created the need for major realignments at every level of our social institutions.[1] These problems are typically treated as practical political issues, however, and are rarely recognized as expressions of philosophically interesting changes in the human condition. There is even a tendency to believe that in stretching our categories and conceptual frameworks to deal with such problems we are becoming unphilosophical. Perhaps we are, but only insofar as we are placing demands upon our philosophical resources to which they are not yet capable of responding.[2]

In this first chapter, I begin with a problem of contemporary family structure with which a majority of adults will grapple at some point in their lives. The familial division of labor is frequently unjust today. While individual men are struggling alongside women with the burdens of single and working parenthood, it is not unreasonable to generalize and assert that new patterns of family responsibility have shifted the burdens unduly onto the shoulders of women. The origins of the problem lie in the recent movement of American women into the sphere of public employment. As women first began leaving the home in large numbers to participate in the public sphere of wage labor, it seemed reasonable to suppose that male spouses and living partners would take on previously female duties within the home in some roughly commensurate degree. As a simple adjustment in the division of labor, as a matter of basic reciprocity, men would assume substantial domestic roles as women took on major economic obligations for the family. Surprisingly, this balancing out of economic and personal responsibilities between men and women has not, for the most part, occurred. Moreover, although men "help women out around the house" more today, no fundamental balancing seems to be even on the horizon.[3]

i. Toward a Dynamic Conception of the Private Sphere

How can we explain this new phenomenon of gendered injustice? We have a name for it already; it is referred to as the "double day" of working women. But how can we explain the willingness of women to take on the economic burdens of their fathers while continuing to perform the traditional domestic duties of their mothers? How can we explain the readiness of men to accept the economic contributions of female partners while continuing to expect an array of personal services from them?

It is a situation of transparent injustice with an apparently straightforward solution, an issue readily raised and discussed on the first day of a women's studies course. It is unjust that men enjoy the advantages of sharing their traditional economic responsibilities with women without taking on a goodly portion of the domestic duties. Women are truly oppressed by their new double burden; the men who share their lives are capable of relieving this burden and are morally culpable for not doing so. It is all quite obvious, yet the problem persists. Men rarely take on an equitable share of internal family-sustaining activities when their female partners work outside the home. Women frequently accept their new double burden, in some cases even discouraging major changes in the division of domestic responsibilities. The intractability of the problem suggests that we do not yet fully understand what is at stake.

I will argue that this current riddle of gender-skewed family responsibility resists solution in terms of the moral and political concepts we typically bring to bear on it because it rests upon a substratum of issues about personal identity and rational agency that remain unexplored. I think that in contemporary gender relations we are asking anew what sorts of persons men and women can now become (the identity question), and also asking what sorts of activities can be rationally chosen by such persons (the agency issue). Domestic duties are presently defined in such a way that they fail to become the rationally chosen activities of many men, even when these men are sympathetic to the career aspirations of women. For women, on the other hand, domestic activities are bound up with traditional forms of identity to which many women continue to feel drawn, even when they have rationally chosen to pursue a public career that conflicts with their familial obligations.

Four sets of assumptions provide the background of this investigation.

1.   I assume the value and the significance of a private sphere of personal relations and activities. Such a "familial community" involves relations of daily intimacy, love, and domesticity between two or more adults and, in many cases, children. This "family" is not necessarily heterosexual,

and not necessarily limited to two adults. It may or may not include children.

2. Historically, there were reasons why the family, as the social institution organizing the private sphere of our lives, did not generate philosophical interest. Family units, until very recently, were lived as natural, necessary spheres of male and female activity. Individuals were born into gendered family roles that structured their beliefs, intentions, and values, as well as their behavior.[4]

3. Despite recent turmoil and what appear to be changes in its basic structure, the contemporary family and the private sphere generally have continued to be treated by most philosophers as sites of natural and necessary affective bonds. David Heyd, for example, is representative of many contemporary philosophers in maintaining that a mother's sacrifice for her child belongs "to the sphere of natural relationships and instinctive feelings (which lie outside morality)."[5] Such a philosophical position has, perhaps unintentionally, conservative implications today. Family relationships seen in these naturalistic terms remain invulnerable to moral and political critiques. Even liberal philosopher John Rawls overlooks the family as a site of injustice in contemporary society in his *Theory of Justice*, a work celebrated as providing the most comprehensive political vision of his generation.[6] Only by reclassifying the family as a socially contingent set of relationships can we effectively critique patterns of domestic injustice in terms of categories of individual rights and social justice.

4. The family sphere of personal relationships has become a philosophically interesting site today, as a consequence of the increasing economic and sexual autonomy of women from men. It is no longer plausible to think of the family as a site of natural and necessary roles and relationships of men and women. Kinship relationships now involve each individual in a broad spectrum of daily choices. These individual choices are clearly subject to normative social evaluations, as we scramble to articulate our preferred conceptions of "family values." And conflict-ridden relationships between women and men within the family now invite evaluation in terms of categories such as justice and injustice.

I believe that any adequate analysis of family relationships must begin with a description of the recent changes in the social status of women. Accordingly, I suggest a notion of *the social enfranchisement of women* to designate various material and symbolic aspects of women's expanding participation in liberal society. Consciously echoing the category of political enfranchisement, I intend the concept of social enfranchisement to refer to the breadth of economic and political rights, responsibilities, and rewards associated with full participation in liberal society. In addition, I assume that social enfranchisement involves participation in culturally specific forms of public identity and rational agency that articulate the possible beliefs and goals of reasonable citizens.

A concept of the social enfranchisement of women is warranted by the fact that over the last thirty years we have come to assume, and our laws have come to give force to the presumption, that women have the right and the capacity to participate in the public sphere, bearing the full social responsibilities of such participation, on a basis of at least formal equality with men. With the social enfranchisement of women, the family ceases to function as a traditional moral practice, with roles and relationships determined by standards internal to the practice.[7] Activities and obligations within the family cease to be seen as wholly natural and necessary choices and become discretionary acts for both women and men.

This means, however, that public values of individual freedom, equality, and autonomy suddenly loom within family life as confusing and threatening new considerations. Traditional familial identities of men and women have lost some degree of legitimacy insofar as they involved hierarchies of gender and were hardly imbued with the voluntariness of fully discretionary choices. Seemingly fundamental features of family life such as mutual dependency between adult family members have now become problematic in circumstances where the values of individual freedom and autonomy seem relevant to one or more family members. "The family begins to dissolve," Hegel warned quite presciently, "when the naturally enduring lifetime commitments which bind family members come to be seen primarily as contractual or legal agreements."[8]

With the new status of the family as a sphere of discretionary activities, family-sustaining activities are subject, for the first time, to potentially unlimited competition from public-sphere activities associated with individual achievement and economic success. These family-sustaining activities were previously performed by women in the home silently and without social recognition, philosophers never having conceived of the home as a site of individual achievement. Yet professional activities are now a constant alternative choice to family-sustaining activities. Men and women both are called upon to choose between responsibilities to an employer and to a sick (or healthy) child or spouse.[9]

Unless the family is reconceived as an alternative site of rational individual purposes, this new choice will be weighted toward public sphere activities, since the public sphere is still identified as the primary site of freely chosen individual achievements. Unless our basic assumptions about the constituent features of rational agency and personhood expand, the commitment of men to the sorts of activities that sustain families cannot be expected to increase greatly. And the commitment of women to the family may be expected to diminish, insofar as it must now be justified in competition with other projects more identified with public norms of achievement. This problem — the balancing-out of economic and personal responsibilities between women and men within families — is a tangible embodiment of new problems of personal identity and agency consequent upon the new status of women (and as I will show, the new status of men as well) in the contemporary family.

This contemporary situation is anything but static, however. It is unfortunate that the two political models we most often apply to gendered family relations, liberalism and Marxism, both conceptualize the situation in terms of traditional political issues of equality and domination. I will analyze the strengths and the shortcomings of these models in their treatment of gendered conflicts in families today. Then I will utilize two further models, Orlando Patterson's slavery analysis and Aristotle's theory of unequal friendship, to better assess patriarchal relations in terms of the personal forms of domination and support existing between women and men within families. I conclude by considering the problems men and women have in reconfiguring gendered identities within family relationships.

Roberto Unger has written that "modern social thought was born proclaiming that society is made and imagined, that it is a human artifact rather than the expression of an underlying natural order."[10] Modern social thinkers from Thomas Hobbes to Roberto Unger himself, however, tend to accept personal and gendered relationships as an unchanging substrate upon which important social relationships are constructed.[11] I intend to demonstrate that with the recent social enfranchisement of women, the private sphere becomes another site of social relations that must be imagined anew, in accordance with new needs and purposes of women and men.

ii. Equality and Rights within Liberal Families?

I take classical liberalism, as promulgated by modern political thinkers such as Thomas Hobbes and John Locke and founding fathers of the American Constitution such as Thomas Jefferson and James Madison, as the dominant source for contemporary political values of equality, personal achievement, freedom, and autonomy. As the gaze of contemporary liberalism has finally come to rest, at least now and again, upon the situation of women and men in the family, its ideals of equality and mutual respect are potentially offended by quite basic aspects of the patriarchal family.[12]

There are a variety of possible defenses as well as criticisms of contemporary family structures from within liberalism.[13] Jean Bethke Elshtain voices a relatively conservative critique, asserting that the role of women in the family should be valued equally with the role of men in the public sphere, in a way that it now is not. A more thoroughgoing application of liberal principles to evidence of domestic inequities between women and men is to argue, as A. I. Melden does, that equal respect between men and women in the family implies that a husband and wife each has the right to the support of his or her individually chosen goals by the other person. Each of these approaches fails finally, I think, to engage fully with the predicaments women and men actually face today, but their failures are instructive with respect to the specific shortcomings of liberal ideals in this context.

Proposing a solution she labels "social feminism," Elshtain attempts to reconcile traditional gender roles with a liberal commitment to equality. Arguing for "a feminist perspective that enables contemporary women to see themselves as the daughters of Antigone," she opposes the belief that feminist goals are to be achieved by women taking on the public activities of men.[14] For Elshtain, the need for a feminist solution is grounded in the fact that women have been subordinate in their relationships to men, and in many cases subject to male coercion or tyranny. But if we believe the traditional role of women had social importance, we should not abandon it; we should instead demand that the private-sphere activities of women be valued as much as the public activities of men.

I think that one can agree with Elshtain that the traditional family activities of women should be valued much more highly, without thinking that the traditional gender division of public and private roles could or should continue. Elshtain focuses on an opposition between the public values represented by Creon, king of Thebes, and the private, family values of Antigone. At issue, however, are not merely values but particular activities associated with traditional roles. In the case of women's traditional social role, we are talking of personal services of care and nurture, performed by women on behalf of men and children. If we come to value women as highly as men, is it not reasonable to assume women deserve to receive such services of personal care and support from men? And if we come to appreciate the social significance of these private activities of women is it not reasonable to assume men would desire the privilege of practicing them as well? That is, if we truly come to value the family commitments of Antigone, we would expect Antigone's tradition to be carried on by her sons as well as by her daughters.

Moreover, "social feminism" ignores the fact that Elshtain and most of her female readers along with a majority of American women have already "gone public," devoting a large part of our efforts toward projects outside the home. Socioeconomic projections indicate that this trend of women's increasing public participation will continue. Even if we think that women may have a greater biological propensity than men for the various family-sustaining activities, women's energies are now divided, and they have less of themselves to give to the family sphere. Unless men take up the slack, the private sphere "social feminism" celebrates would seem destined to have a smaller, less important part in all of our lives.

A. I. Melden's approach seems more plausible, initially. He sees the family as a moral community created by an agreement between a man and a woman who love and respect each other. The most basic feature of moral respect for another person in this context as in others, according to Melden, is respect for "the right of persons to pursue their interests."[15] Thus each person who agrees to join his or her life to others in a family has, Melden argues, the right to expect the support of his or her individual agency by the other family members. That a traditional wife could be expected to wholly subordinate her interests to those of her family Melden deems morally offensive, and indicative of a failure to recognize the full moral personhood of women. He asserts the right of women today "to pursue those interests which go beyond those social roles to which they have been restricted by custom and tradition." In addition, he claims for each married woman that "her husband owes her as a matter of her right, the kind of treatment that will enable her to develop interests of her own."[16]

These are strong statements. Yet Melden is too quick in his assessment of the immorality of traditional family relations; his prescriptions for the present situation take on an obviousness and clarity that is only superficial. Insofar as agency was a gendered category, marriage was an agreement by a man to support the natural and necessary female purposes of childbearing and homemaking, in return for a woman's support for his male public forms of agency. There has been a radical but indeterminate expansion in our notion of the potential scope of female agency in the last fifty years. Melden rightly criticizes the continued derivation of moral rights and obligations between men and women from patriarchal family relationships. But he also acknowledges that the obligation to support someone can become questionable when one perceives an "unreasonable design" in this person's conduct.[17] Radically different assessments of *which* particular interests of a man or a woman are reasonable or unreasonable are still very common today, and they continue to provide grounds for gendered asymmetries in familial support relations, often between persons who would claim total respect for each other.

Even more problematic may be an inherent vagueness in the understanding of what constitutes "support" for another's agency. Male support of women was traditionally economic, while female support of men took the form of personal services. Women today have assumed economic responsibility for their own lives as well as for those of men and children in many cases. They may now require a different *quality* of support from men—various forms of personal care and nurture, rather than financial support. Men may only be willing to offer the traditional economic forms of support for which they have been trained, and may deem it unfair or unreasonable of women to demand a different quality of support. Moreover, men may feel hurt when women unilaterally decide to alter the quality of their support for men, deemphasizing the personal services to which men were accustomed. Melden does not confront the problems arising from the changing qualities of support that women and men may need from each other within relationships in which both persons pursue their own individual interests. Nor does he consider the specific nature of male resistance to offering types of support traditionally associated with women.

This problem illustrates the tenuousness with which Melden's moral doctrine of rights and obligations rests atop an underlying economic model of exchange relations. Melden very clearly distinguishes his theory of the moral agreements incurred by promises between people who respect each other from any mere theory of contract. A contract only commits each person to explicitly stated actions, while moral promising creates more wide-ranging responsibilities, presuming "a moral background of understanding" between persons.[18] But during a time of changing social relationships between men and women, a moral background of understanding between persons is precisely what cannot be taken for granted. Hierarchical relationships were the moral background of understanding within the patriarchal family, and insofar as Melden criticizes these he cannot base a notion of rights and obligations within the family upon any prior moral background of understanding therein. This moral background must be renegotiated before it can serve as the basis for a new notion of familial rights and obligations.

One of the strengths of the liberal theory of exchange relations is that a procedure for the negotiation and renegotiation of any economic relationship is fundamental to its structure: Each party to an economic contract has the right to receive only what another person chooses to offer, and only for so long as they choose to offer it. This determinate specification of the voluntariness that must permeate any transaction between contractual equals suggests the quality of problems that may arise in attempting to render the right of a contemporary woman to reasonable support of her interests compatible with a contemporary man's right to refuse to engage in particular activities, for whatever reason. Some such "refusal right" will be part of any relationship between equals. Regardless of my respect for the seriousness of your interests, there may be certain sorts of activities I am simply not willing to engage in in support of these interests. If I consider certain sorts of activities demeaning, or simply not appropriate acts for someone such as me, my support for you may fall short of what you would wish from me, or even what you would offer to me. To commit myself to more than this, to agree to do *anything* in support of the legitimate interests of a loved one, would constitute some degree of sacrifice of my personhood, even enslavement to a loved one. Unfortunately, many traditional female forms of support have long been considered demeaning or inappropriate to male personhood. Insofar as this affects men's willingness to engage in certain activities in support of women and children they love, it must be addressed.

John Hardwig, along with many feminists, has criticized any appeal to rights in the context of family relations as introducing public-sphere values of individual self-interest and competition into a situation where these are inappropriate.[19] In fact, issues of economic rights will enter the family sphere as soon as both women and men define themselves, to whatever degree, in terms of their economic agency. I think Melden is correct to argue that claims of rights can be much more broadly grounded in notions of the respect owed to persons, and indeed, concern with the quality of respect owed to one's spouse is an appropriate response to recent conflict within the family.

The problem is that while we have a standard notion of the rights accruing to economic agency, and of the rights and obligations associated with traditional gender roles, the content of a new right to personal support within an egalitarian family situation is underdetermined by previous practices, and to some extent even contradicted by them. The framework of rights may not be inherently suspect, as many feminists and theorists in the Marxist tradition claim; but it is a formal framework that must acquire its social content from a pool of shared values and practices. It is rendered helpless in the face of fundamental disagreements of the sort emerging today in the family, about the activities that constitute the basis of personhood.[20]

iii.   Marxism and Material Relations of Power in the Family

Marx's theory of the social relations of production was offered as an anti-
dote to the formalism of the liberal theory of individual rights. It is misleading to speak of political equality and individual rights, Marx argued,
so long as one class of people controlled the means of production and
thereby had the power and the motivation to exploit the labor power of
all those who must work for them. It was Engels who first applied this
model of economic power to the relationship between men and women,
asserting that men oppressed women within the family in the same way
that capitalists oppressed workers in a factory.[21] While Engels located the
source of male as well as capitalist power in the control over private property, feminists soon pointed out that patriarchal power relationships existed long before any system of private property. Patriarchy currently
structures the relationships between men and women in every social class
and in noncapitalist cultures as well. The socialist feminist revision of Engels is clearly put by Heidi Hartmann when she states that "the material
base upon which patriarchy rests lies most fundamentally in men's control
over women's labor power."[22] Private property is *only one of many* sources
of male power over women.

   With this qualification, however, socialist theory has seemed quite relevant to the feminist problematic. Male power in our society is expressed
in economic terms even if it does not originate in property relations;
women's activities in the home have been undervalued at the same time
as their labor has been controlled by men. Moreover, socialism proposes
a tangible political project. If women's traditional domestic labors were
seen as having productive value, and if women gained control over their
labor power, the material grounds for patriarchy within the home would
diminish. To this end, many feminists have argued that women's activities
within the family must be conceptualized in terms of their productive
value. Ann Ferguson, for example, emphasizes the need to expand our
theoretical understanding of what sorts of activities might count as
productive labor, suggesting that the traditional labor of women be
thought of as "sex/affective production." Margaret Benston, as part of a
"wages-for-housework" movement, argued that the work of women
within the home must become paid labor within the public economy.[23]

   Although a "wages-for-housework" movement was unsuccessful, the
economic revaluation of women's traditional labor has recently begun to
take place on wholly practical grounds. Women have realized they can
wrest control over their labor power from individual husbands, indirectly, through employment for wages outside the home. As women

enter the sphere of wage labor, their former child-rearing and homemaking activities must often be shifted to someone else who does them for a wage. The extremely low wages of domestic and child-care workers reflect a continuing low valuation of traditional female activities, of course.

One of the most direct means for women to gain control over their labor power within the family is by utilizing contraception and other means of reproductive control. Indeed, Mary O'Brien has argued that we are experiencing a revolution in "the relations of reproduction" (the classical Marxist way of referring to production in the home), brought about by women's access to the means of contraception. She maintains that this revolution in the social relations of reproduction is as significant as the revolution that Marx hoped for a century ago in the relations of production.[24]

There is a sense in which O'Brien is right; dramatic social realignments are in the making, and their generative source seems to lie in the breakdown of gendered family roles and relations. Yet to identify the traditional family activities of women as activities of production, or even reproduction, seems a reductive formalist exercise. To interpret family relationships in these terms is to settle for a partial view that ultimately distorts our understanding of relations within the family. We might even say that a Marxist account of the family is analogous to a liberal narrative of the nineteenth-century industrial workplace. The relationships of capitalist production cannot be portrayed fully by means of liberal exchange theory, and patriarchal family relationships cannot be adequately understood in terms of either Marxist theories of domination or the various liberal categories of equality and individual interests.

Contemporary nontraditional variations on patriarchy within the family highlight the inability of Marxist concepts to capture more than a portion of the conflicts affecting women and men within gendered family structures today. It is generally assumed, as it was not a generation ago, that there are many circumstances under which a woman can and even should exercise her social autonomy and leave a spouse who mistreats her. Individual men do not possess the absolute control over the labor power of women that they once did, nor even the degree of power that capitalist employers wield over a worker in many circumstances.[25] Yet many, if not most, publicly employed married women choose to remain in situations where they bear an unfair burden of domestic, family-maintaining activities.

In Marx's terms, it is as if an exploited factory worker went out and found a way to support himself as an entrepreneur, and then came back to the factory to work the night shift because he missed the assembly line and the camaraderie with the boss. Of course, a women's choice to come home at night after a hard day of work and serve her husband dinner has to be seen in more complicated terms. We must assume that women today have a variety of possible reasons for deciding to ignore the unfairness of their responsibilities as employed and married women. From within the Marxist theoretical framework, however, only the continued economic dependence of women upon men can explain behavior that is quite certainly a function of a more complex set of motivations.

Notice that the refusal of husbands to take on a fair share of domestic activities may be understood quite well by referring to the Marxist model. What would be the likely response of the capitalist boss to the naive worker who came back to the factory for sentimental reasons, while also suggesting that out of fairness the boss should take his turn on the assembly line? From the viewpoint of the satisfied husband/capitalist, the return of the devoted wife/worker means that family/production relations can go on as before. No alternative set of relations is conceivable so long as his patriarchal-kinship/capitalist-producer identity remains intact.

Such an understanding of male reasoning illustrates a further problem with the Marxist paradigm. For Marx, the ineradicable selfishness of the capitalist was presumed, as was the need to destroy the class of capitalists in order to achieve socialism. If the desire of women to continue to associate with men is to be trusted, then we must be as concerned with understanding why men would *choose* to participate more fully in the family as with why women would wish them to do so.

iv.   "Women and Children and Slaves," said Plato

In comparing traditional gender relations to master/slave relationships, I hope to reveal some characteristic features of traditional familial relationships, as well as of female and male social identities, which are not addressed by liberalism or Marxism. Theorists in both of these traditions, conceiving of their emancipatory project in terms of an idealized set of public relationships between men, only recognized those features of private or family relationships that could be plucked out of the family context and used to illustrate liberal theories of reciprocal exchange or Marxist theories of production. Hegel's Master/Slave dialogue in the *Phenomenology* became renowned as an explanation of the instability of human relationships in which there was domination and lack of liberal forms of reciprocity. Marx responded by diagnosing production relationships within capitalism as wage slavery, exemplifying precisely the coercion and lack of mutual respect Hegel thought liberalism had put behind itself. Marx also believed, however, that such relations of domination, wherein one's labor was appropriated by another, were fundamentally unstable and would see their end in the near future with the proletarian revolution.

Orlando Patterson has proffered a subtle analysis of slavery with notably more ambiguous social implications. He focuses on the coercion and control exercised by a master over every aspect of a slave's life, contrasting this image of enslavement with a very common eighteenth-century notion of freedom defined as an absence of external human impediments upon an individual's action. Patterson views this quite formal and negative conception of individual freedom as gaining its social meaning through a constant if implicit contrast between the personal liberties of the male citizen and the harsh constraints upon the activities of the slave. He concludes *Slavery and Social Death* with the tantalizing assertion that our notion of freedom only came into existence as a function of slavery, and thereby exists in a parasitic relationship with a notion of enslavement. He provocatively queries, "Are we to esteem slavery for what it has wrought, or must we challenge our conception of freedom and the value we place on it?" Patterson clearly implies that our conceptions of freedom deserve to be criticized as being implicated in the denial of the slave's personhood basic to the institution of slavery.[26]

A woman's status in the family was in some ways much better, and certainly very different from that of a slave. Yet I will suggest that patriarchy involves a denial of women's personhood similar to the denial of personhood Patterson analyzes as constitutive of slavery. And I think that liberal norms of autonomy and individual achievement are similarly implicated in the denials of women's personhood basic to the institutions of patriarchy. Ideals of male autonomy, or freedom from dependency upon others, rested upon a denial of women's personhood such that it was possible to dismiss the social significance of male dependency upon women within the family. Ideals of male achievement under capitalism, of answering only to oneself and one's own interests, and of devoting oneself singlemindedly to the pursuit of material forms of wealth, presupposed wives whose services and interests could be *wholly subsumed* within those of the liberal man.

In many ways, the similarities in the life conditions of a woman and a slave are startling, including not only the expectation of unlimited, unpaid service to a household but also the denial of any individual public existence unmediated by the husband or master. When a woman married she entered a man's house, and from that time forward had no separate space of her own, no time of her own, no wage that would give her consumption rights of her own. She had no social existence separate from that of her husband. Her life was lived, as much as twenty-four hours a day, in the service of her family. Moreover, she gave up her name when she married and took that of her husband, just as a slave was forced to take the name of his master. Patterson cites this ritual of renaming as a primary step in the process of enslaving someone.[27]

The great difference between the position of a slave and that of a wife lies in the social meaning attributed to their lives of service. Aristotle attempted to make a case for the natural inferiority of both women and slaves. A slave was merely "an instrument of action" insofar as he possessed "no deliberative faculty at all," while a woman was a "permanently unequal subject," having a deliberative faculty "without authority" insofar as it was her natural role to obey her husband.[28] Despite Aristotle's sincere efforts to explain the institution of slavery naturalistically, he had to admit the typically violent *social* process by which a free man is made into a slave after being captured or defeated in war. In Patterson's dramatic phrase, the process of enslavement entails "the social death" of a man, the negation of his personhood such that he could no longer pursue his own purposes or even have individual purposes, but must become a mere instrument of the needs of his master.

By contrast, women's subordinate status continued to appear both natural and necessary until quite recently. The patriarchal subordination of a woman could not be condemned as a social death, insofar as there was no conception of a female person's purposes to be denied within patriarchal families. It was at the originary moment of her birth as a girl-child that she was denied the full personhood associated with having individual human ends. Marriage and procreation were from that point onward deemed to be her natural purposes; she was destined to seek the completion and fulfillment of her female self in serving a husband and children. It was taken for granted that she would submerge herself in the lives of her husband and children and participate in the larger world through them. I will refer to this belief that a woman was destined to find meaning and fulfillment within a patriarchal family as the "subsumed nurturer" model of female identity.

Thus the meaning of life was very different from the perspective of a slave and a woman. But notice that, from the perspective of the husband and the master, in both cases he was being served by someone he did not need to acknowledge as a full person. Patterson gives numerous examples of situations in which slaves attained positions of great power and influence—in military and administrative roles in Rome, as chamberlains of Byzantine emperors, even as rulers in Islam. Yet, whether in public positions in Rome or Islam, or in positions of menial intimacy as the body servants of emperors, a slave's tremendous influence only existed in the context of the fact that his personhood could never be acknowledged.[29]

A traditional wife was in a similar position, potentially wielding great influence over her husband's life, but always in the context of her status as a mere woman, her wifely identity subsumed within the public identity of her husband. Notice, however, that a husband who did not have to acknowledge the significance of a wife's role in his life could also ignore the significance of the needs—his personal and psychological needs—to which the wife ministered. The ideal of male political autonomy rested upon a solid foundation of unacknowledged private neediness and dependency. The hypocrisy of this liberal ideal of autonomy only began to become apparent with the social enfranchisement of women. On the one hand, women began to demand acknowledgment of the personal services rendered unto men in the privacy of the home. On the other hand, when women chose to leave family responsibilities behind men could experience, often with surprise, the character of a more fully autonomous life.

Closely related to the liberal ideal of autonomy is the celebration of a self-interested basis for individual achievements. Our political tradition, at least since Hobbes, has presumed that material scarcity along with an egalitarian distribution of human desires guarantees a fundamental opposition between the self-interested purposes of oneself and others. John Locke's image of "mixing one's labor with nature" in order to satisfy material needs through the creation of private property, further embeds the assumption of self-interestedness into that of individual achievement. Kant's association of moral and political freedom with self-given laws consolidates this reflexive ideal of personhood. Orlando Patterson, accepting this aspect of the liberal political tradition, identifies the degradation of slavery with slaves having to act wholly "for others," in contrast to acting "for themselves" as any normal free man would wish to do.[30] Free men do not serve others voluntarily, or without hidden ambitions of consolidating personal power or interests.

When we look at the traditional role of women, however, it seems clear that there is a complexity to the caring or serving activities of women in the family that we are at risk of losing sight of if we interpret them in terms of such notions of individual achievement and autonomy. If we look closely at the case of women, it is clear that this particular conceptual dichotomy between "actions for oneself" and "actions for another" does not capture the meaning of women's agency in the family. One of the ways in which the traditional role of a wife was distinguished from that

of a slave was through the presumption that a woman's nature was so constituted that in acting for the others of her family, she was acting *at the
same time* to fulfill herself. When feminists first identified women as oppressed within patriarchal relations, there was a tendency to dismiss this
identification between her interests and those of others as a mere illusion
imposed upon women. By contrast, as feminism began to consciously celebrate the traditional values of women, there was a growing presumption
that, at least to some degree, this identification between a woman's interests and those of others she loves and cares for is both possible and
desirable. One can act in one's own name and yet also act very consciously
on behalf of others, according to what is often presented as a "maternal"
model.[31]

Someone might perhaps question the basis upon which we morally
condemn patriarchy if the traditional woman's role of acting on behalf of
others is not to be considered inherently degrading. In fact, it is quite simple to identify a further aspect of the relationship that makes us think a
traditional woman's humanity was denied, even if her purposes truly
coincided with those of her family. Women were traditionally excluded
from the sphere of public activities and public recognition. Like a slave,
a woman took the name of the man she married, and thereafter could act
upon the world only through exerting influence on her husband and children. The position of the slave, as well as that of a woman, can be criticized in terms of the inhumanity of denying a person the possibility of action on the world in his or her own name. While it is not necessarily the
case that in acting on behalf of another one's own interests are denied, it
is necessarily the case that in acting *in the name* of another, one's own purposes, one's own selfhood, cannot be recognized.[32]

In light of this analysis, it is troubling to see that the practice of women
taking men's names upon marrying remains quite healthy today, even
among women who act in other ways as independent individuals. Some
women are surely intending to make their new name a conscious expression of their own independent identity, as well as of their union with a
particular man. Yet the gendered asymmetry of the act is all too meaningful. In at least a symbolic sense it is a residual denial of female personhood.

Unfortunately, the continued acquiescence of women in this ritual
denial of female personhood makes all too much sense in terms of the current dynamics between women and men within families. The social enfranchisement of women creates personal dilemmas for modern men insofar as it implies the full personhood of women. In light of the foregoing
analysis of the liberal ideals of autonomy and individual achievement, we
can understand the sorts of domestic tensions created by the new social

status of women. Women have public identities of their own, even when they take a man's name in marriage. Yet women still perform many of the traditional wifely services for their husbands, despite the fact that men can no longer think of their wives as having lives subsumed in their own. A man who accepts the personal services of a wife must acknowledge a certain degree of voluntary dependency upon this woman whom he now recognizes as a full person. But a modern man also entertains anxieties about the underlying motives of a wife who continues to voluntarily perform personal services for him. Because she is now formally an equal, and because of liberal assumptions about the self-serving parameters of rational individual motivation, a modern husband may wonder whether a wife, in caring for him, is really attempting to dominate him.[33] In taking the name of the man she marries, a woman performs a formal act of traditional subservience which may serve as something of a foil to the changing power relationships within the family.

Women who are seeking to gain social control and authority in relationships with men are better advised to get a high-paying job than to rely upon the influence they wield through activities of care and nurture, in any case. While it is easy to demonstrate that those who serve others are often engaged in honorable and important activities, abstractly considered, it is a fact that in this society, activities involving a large component of personal service are devalued to such an extent that any person who chooses to devote a life to such activities is typically not considered worthy of very much respect. Those who are paid to perform activities associated closely with a traditional woman's role, such as domestic workers, prostitutes, and teachers of small children, are accorded the lowest possible professional status in our society.[34]

Faced with increasingly stark evidence of various forms of community breakdown, and troubled by the rising incidence of what Alasdair MacIntyre has termed "ghostly individualism," we are slowly beginning to admit personal and psychological needs into our public notions of personhood. Freud broke down a great many barriers, insofar as he made sexual desire the underlying basis for even worldly economic motivations.[35] But Freud was as invested in reigning patriarchal notions of identity as anyone; male forms of psychic neediness were sublimated in the public activities of healthy adult men, and were heterosexually expressed in relation to subordinate female objects of desire. Personal forms of neediness and activities that minister to forms of psychic neediness are not yet appreciated as the basis for socially significant interactions. Even when such relationships occur within the public sphere and within institutions employing a proportionately large number of men — within the upper levels of education, for example—when one person's activities must be understood primarily in terms of their effects upon another, as in teaching, these activities are accorded a low level of social respect, and those who engage in them are poorly paid, in relative terms.[36]

Philosophers and social thinkers have grown increasingly willing to criticize purely self-interested notions of human motivation, but do not recognize the strong ties between the attribution of motivations and available forms of social recognition and identity.[37] David Gauthier, for example, proposes to replace an ideal of selfhood narrowly bound up with economic rationality with a broader, more humanistic conception of "the liberal individual."[38] According to his model of human motivations, we would continue to explain all rational activities as originating in individual preferences, but we would deny any presumptions that individuals are "hardwired" for self-interested activities. We would now take care to emphasize that many "tuistic," or other-directed activities, could also be chosen as a matter of personal preferences.[39] If women freely choose to devote themselves to the happiness of their husbands and children, this, like any other freely undertaken course of action, must be understood as simply a matter of personal preference.

But if we ask a doctor to diagnose our difficulties in sleeping and he responds that we apparently prefer not to sleep regularly, we will question his medical abilities. Gauthier's alternative-preferences model of human behavior begs the question of why women continue to prefer to perform personal services for men, and why men prefer not to perform such services for women. Gauthier sidesteps the pressing question of why a whole set of human preferences, those particularly associated with the traditional role of women, retain such a low social status, even when performed for wages in the public sphere. Not only does a preference model fail to provide any deep insights into gendered, asymmetrical domestic preferences, but in combination with dominant cultural ideals about personal achievement and autonomy, it leaves us with the predisposition to believe that persons who choose lives of personal service are either somewhat masochistic, or perhaps lazy, or motivated by the desire to control others. We are increasingly aware that some persons must remain motivated by caretaking preferences, but we are not yet capable of according very much respect to these motivations or to the persons who possess them.

Contrast this with the unthinking respect we offer to those we perceive as engaging in competitive economic behavior. Much of this behavior—the willingness to be very bored by a high-paying job, to live where one does not otherwise wish to live in order to receive a large salary, or the obsessive concern with rising through the ranks of a company—could surely be understood in terms of deviant psychological tendencies toward masochism or the desire to control others. But only when a person's job, living situation, or competitiveness results in overt personal problems do we think to question the appropriateness of such typical priorities. For the most part, we simply assume the overriding logic of economic self-interest. Persons motivated by economic self-interest have placed themselves upon a trajectory of social achievement that is so dominant that most people identify with it without recognizing either the quality of their motivations or the possibility for acting according to different priorities.

Even in the public sphere, wage-earning behavior engaged in for the sake of noneconomic goals is often suspect or simply not comprehended, as artists, musicians, and writers will attest. In the private sphere the lack of economic motivations to explain acts of personal service in the family renders them doubly suspect. We know that until very recently women and servants performed these activities in conjunction with a subordinate position in society. While we are prepared now to recognize such behavior as formally equivalent to other forms of chosen activities, we are not prepared to explain why a person might rationally prefer to engage in activities of personal service, choosing such modes of social engagement over more typical and socially recognized modes of rational agency and social achievement.

The typical female decision to continue to engage in many traditional nurturing activities on behalf of others in the family is a purposive choice we need to make sense of constructively. Although we have concluded that the influence she exerts on others through these activities cannot be properly understood in the traditional terms of self-abnegating service, none of the models surveyed so far indicates a satisfying way of comprehending such activities. There are obvious positive grounds for individuals to choose to nurture and care for others, and similar reasons for persons to choose to teach or to write books. It is quite straightforwardly true that in directly influencing others one can have an effect on the world, and thereby gain a sense of the significance of one's own existence. It is easy to link acts of personal agency in the family to humanly significant ends. Were we to assume an overarching category of rationally purposive behavior defined in terms of humanly significant acts, we might have the basis for making direct comparisons and alternative choices between economic activities, other sorts of public achievement, and various acts of personal agency. At present, however, we do not look to any such overarching category of human significance when we evaluate individual choices. We tend to confine our attributions of rational purposiveness to, acts that take place in the public sphere, and give preference to acts with materially tangible, economically valued results.

The slavery paradigm allows us to analyze more precisely what has and has not changed with the social enfranchisement of women. Women have ceased to be subsumed nurturers and are now social agents insofar as they can act in their own names. But the sorts of personal and interpersonal agency particularly identified with women are not yet comprehended as the sorts of acts that anyone would want to do in one's own name. We can still appreciate that women want to do these activities, in some non-theoretically articulable way; but we can also understand why women might no longer choose to perform them. And we can explain all too clearly why men would not choose to engage in them.

v.   Aristotle and Patriarchal Benefactors

Aristotle is one philosopher who did consider personal service on behalf of others to be a rationally purposive form of action. His theory hardly provides a blueprint for contemporary gender relationships because, for Aristotle, male and female practices within the family were a consequence of the natural hierarchy existing between husband and wife. But because of this conscious presumption of a natural gendered hierarchy within the family, Aristotle's theory provides insights into traditional male and female motivations and features of gendered personal identity other theoretical rubrics have avoided discussing.

The husband/wife relationship was a form of unequal friendship, according to Aristotle. While ideal friendships could only exist between equals, the ubiquity of social hierarchy in classical Greece meant that one also needed to be able to understand the basis for congenial, stable relationships between persons of very different social status. Aristotle distinguished friendships, equal and unequal, from exchange relationships by virtue of the different motives of the participants. While each person enters an exchange relationship in order to receive something, people become friends, Aristotle argued, in order to act in a virtuous and loving fashion.[40] In an unequal friendship, each person has different forms of love to offer. The lesser person, be it the younger or poorer man, or indeed a child or a wife, offers forms of care and personal service as his or her acts of love. The greater person, be it an older or richer man, a father, or a husband, offers the benefits of his social position, status, and monetary support.[41]

While Aristotle denies that either party in an unequal friendship is motivated primarily by the desire to receive something, he never really attempts to show any sort of intrinsic meaning or purpose in the acts of care and service provided by the lesser person. Consequently, it appears as if the wife or any lesser friend is motivated either by encompassing structures of social authority that leave them no other options but a life of personal service, or by the social benefits she or he will receive. Thus Aristotle's model does not offer any direct support for a revaluation of female acts of personal service as acts of rational personal agency outside a context of social hierarchy or dependency.

It is Aristotle's explanation of the meaning of the loving actions of the husband, father, or any dominant friend that is psychologically interesting. This person, Aristotle explains, functions as a benefactor of the lesser person, and tends to see the person who benefits from his gifts as his creation, his "handiwork." "We exist by virtue of activity, and the handiwork *is* in a sense the producer in activity; he loves his handiwork therefore, because he loves existence." [42] As a poet loves his poem, as a painter his painting, thus does a man love his wife and children. It is a relationship of both creation and possession; a man sees his family as a projection of himself. I will refer to this as the "patriarchal benefactor" model of male kinship identity.

Notice how well Aristotle's benefactor analysis can continue to function as an explanation of the male role in the family after other such relationships had been repudiated by the modern philosophy of individualism. Insofar as the male head of a family identified himself with his wife and children, even the most narrowly focused theory of Hobbesian self-interest could accommodate the assumption of a man's generosity toward his family. Since a man saw his family as a mere extension of himself, the selfish individual had every reason to act on behalf of his family, and consider such actions as self-enhancing deeds. The most egoistic individual had a de facto social purposiveness in his familial relationships.

With the social enfranchisement of women, the male benefactor role is severely undermined, however. Men have no right to claim authorship of a wife/woman, no matter what benefits they have bestowed upon her. As a full person, a woman is presumed to create herself, and efforts to unduly control that process are no longer socially acceptable. Even if a man settles for feeling pride insofar as he has helped a wife to realize herself, he cannot possessively assume rights over her future self. Even if she is grateful for the help he has given her, she may at any time decide to leave him, and seek to realize herself elsewhere. The male benefactor relationship to his children may appear unchanged by the new status of women. And yet, male access to children is typically through the mother. In losing rights of possession over women, men's hold upon their children also becomes more tenuous.

Furthermore, when a man ceases to identify with his family as a creative projection of himself, the services he has traditionally been expected to perform for the family take on a new set of meanings. If the family can no longer be seen as an extension of the male self, then in acting on behalf of his family a man is acting on behalf of distinct others. If he accepts the liberal dichotomy between freely "acting for oneself," and only "acting for others" in the face of some sort of coercion, a man may begin to feel enslaved by family obligations, coerced by society or his wife into sacrificing his own interests on behalf of these others.[43] On the other hand, as a man's wife begins to act in her own name, her domestic services may signal female authorship of the family scenario.

A man's sense of his own personhood may seem to be called into question by remaining in the family under these circumstances. The traditional role of a male benefactor has become uninhabitable, in typical circumstances. Yet if the male family identity of patriarchal benefactor is no longer available to men, then on what basis can a man understand his own presence in a family today? What needs, desires, purposes does it serve? We have, I think, arrived at further evidence of the need to rethink gendered family identities, and the relationships of personal care and support upon which they are founded.

vi.   Surd Behavior and Problems of Familial Identity

I began this chapter with the statement of a contemporary social problem: the startling new patterns of inequity in the still highly gendered distribution of family responsibilities. I then analyzed theoretical responses to this problem according to accepted moral and political frameworks. According to A. I. Melden's account of the moral rights of persons in families, it would seem that men who dwell in family situations, putting in a single day alongside women who put in a double day, are acting in an unprincipled fashion and are morally culpable. At best, such men are presumed not to see the actual situation for what it is, and their actions are judged to originate in a biased patriarchal worldview. The liberal moralist can maintain that men *ought* to educate themselves to overcome this bias, but as with other normative conclusions, there is little sense of what might bring this about. According to feminist political accounts emphasizing the material grounds of male power, patriarchal forms of consciousness will persist and domestic relationships between men and women will tend to remain oppressive for so long as men are dominant within the economic and political structures of our society.[44]

I criticized such responses for not adequately representing the specificity of current domestic situations, and for consequently failing to recognize the quality of the issues women and men are struggling with in kinship relationships. Utilizing Orlando Patterson's model of slavery to uncover changes in women's sense of personal identity resulting from their social enfranchisement, I explained the recent transformation of women from subsumed nurturers into individuals capable of acting in their own names. Now that women's needs, desires, and purposes are no longer limited to the familial sphere, however, the question is how to revalue the status of activities within the family so as to make them commensurable with the activities that provide the basis for women's new identities in the public sphere.

Appealing to Aristotle's theory of unequal friendship, I suggested that the traditional familial identity of men could best be understood in terms of their status as benefactors of women and children. As a patriarchal benefactor, a man could think of his wife and children as his personal handiwork. With the social enfranchisement of women, however, a man's economic support of his family no longer affords him the control or status of the patriarchal benefactor. The question is how to reconfigure a male family identity so that it is not predicated on men's previous sense of possessive authority over women, and how to comprehend men's actions of familial support and care as commensurable with individual forms of behavior performed in the public sphere.

At the beginning of this chapter I alluded to the fact that analytic philosophers typically dismiss issues of gender as failing to raise philosophically interesting questions. As presently formulated, however, the predicament of women and men within families allows us a critical perspective on current philosophical discussions of agency and personal identity. I will conclude this chapter by considering the work of two analytic philosophers whose ideas are quite pertinent to the situation of women and men today in the context of changing gender identities.

Donald Davidson has been concerned with problems in the theory of action, and one of the classical problems he analyzes is that which has been referred to as "weakness of the will." According to Davidson, "An agent's will is weak if he acts, and acts intentionally, counter to his own best judgment."[45] Previous philosophical thinkers, from Aristotle to Dante to R. M. Hare, have assumed that weakness of the will is essentially a moral problem, best illustrated by cases in which we experience our moral principles as being overcome by momentary passions or desires. Davidson takes issue with a moral understanding of the problem, insisting that there are numerous cases where acting against our better judgment has nothing to do with succumbing to temptations to do something bad or sinfully pleasurable. Davidson offers the example of a late-night toothbrusher who has gone to bed, and upon remembering that he did not brush his teeth decides that, all things considered, he should *not* get up to do so. Nevertheless, he does get up to brush his teeth, responding to the urge of habit or hygiene in a way that Davidson characterizes as "incontinent," insofar as it prompts an action contrary to his own best reasoning about how he should act.[46]

Such incontinence has psychologically disorienting personal consequences, according to Davidson, who concludes that "what is special in incontinence is that the actor cannot understand himself: he recognizes, in his own intentional behavior, something essentially surd." Davidson treats this failure to act according to one's own best reasons as a problem of self-discipline. Acknowledging that it may be difficult to always know and do what is best, he yet suggests that the cure for incontinence is simply a greater commitment to performing the action one has judged to be best, comparing the effort to practice rational continence to efforts to practice other virtues such as chastity and bravery.[47] Our motivation for continent behavior is supplied by Davidson's rather stark judgment that "to the extent that we fail to discover a coherent and plausible pattern in the attitudes and actions of others [and presumably ourselves as well] we simply forego the chance of treating them as persons."[48]

Davidson's analysis of the problem of incontinence is surely relevant to the predicament of women and men today in the context of changing gender identities. Contemporary women and men in families may frequently find themselves in positions analogous to that of Davidson's late-night toothbrusher. We have all been conditioned from childhood to accept a number of gender-specific familial roles, and the practices that correspond with them. Finding ourselves in specific circumstances where our own better judgment tells us that we should not act in accordance with these roles, we may yet find ourselves acting as the role dictates. Davidson's arguments against treating incontinent actions as moral problems are quite consistent with my own arguments for understanding inequities in the current distribution of familial obligations as the consequence of confused individual notions of familial duties due to changing conceptions of gendered agency and personal identity.

Davidson's belief that these sorts of problems of action and identity can be overcome by practicing a "virtue of continence"—seeking to consistently perform those actions indicated by the best available reasons—is not supported by an analysis of the situation of women and men in the context of changing gendered identities, however. Obviously, there are cases where women and men should attempt to follow the dictates of their best reasoning, and refuse to follow any longer the intuitive motivations of their previous conditioning. A young mother, for example, tempted to quit a job she is very happy with, and pull her child out of a very good day-care center so that she can fulfill her sense of traditional motherhood, would be advised to stick to her better judgments and resist her conditioning to reenact a patriarchal ideal of maternal identity.

Given the current undervaluing of a broad range of activities traditionally associated with women, however, we should often be suspect of the social rationality that defines the best actions of ambitious men and women alike in terms of liberal public-sphere priorities. The young father who would like very much to take time off from his boring, high-paying job to be with his new child, but who cannot provide good reasons for doing so to his boss or to himself, might be advised "to cast reasons aside" for the moment. After the fact, he may well have developed an experiential basis enabling him to explain the valuable features of this activity so that he could rationalize such a choice in the future. But in cases like that of the young father, it may be best to give priority to activities and commitments for which we do not yet have substantive articulable reasons, at least at the time when we make the decision to act. In other cases where public and private commitments pull us in two directions, we may have reasons for both decisions and yet lack any method for deciding which among our conflicting but incommensurable good reasons is best, all things considered. In neither case will a virtue of continence direct us toward the appropriate actions.

In taking the problem of incontinence out of the moral realm and locating it firmly in the theory of action, Davidson provides an analytic basis for comprehending what would seem to be a common current sensation of personal confusion, resulting from fundamental conflicts in our decisions about how to divide our actions between demanding but incommensurable spheres of responsibility. In my analysis of changing gender identities I have attempted to provide a systemic social analysis for this contemporary experience. When we look closely at examples of the sorts of surd behavior Davidson's analysis highlights, we may question, however, whether we should continue to label such behavior incontinent, insofar as much of this behavior makes sense in social terms. It is not at all clear that we would want to encourage continent behavior, even if we knew how to do so. Men who are no longer patriarchal benefactors, for example, may find themselves immobilized within newly egalitarian family contexts if they assiduously cultivate the virtue of continence while lacking the creativity or confidence to articulate reasons for new modes of familial participation. Better that they should just act.

The surdity of the devoted young father's decision to take a leave of absence from his job may indeed test his own sense of personhood, as well as his identity in the eyes of others. Such behavior challenges modern ideals of male identity and rational behavior, which assume that a well-adjusted man has a patriarchal vision of how his professional and personal responsibilities and goals can be rationally organized into a life plan. And yet in a time of social change such as ours, personal honor and integrity would seem to demand the willingness to make risk-laden decisions like those of the devoted young father. The well-adjusted individual today does not cling to anachronistic familial identities, but instead attempts to act in ways warranted by a particular situation, renegotiating, when necessary, the terms of personal identity to make room for such choices.[49]

Davidson's idealized criteria for rational personhood reflect the dominant viewpoint of modern philosophy and psychology, whose behavioral models still assume a unitary sense of personal identity extending over the duration of an individual's life. Those who are committed to such models judge the present moment harshly, threatened by the fragmentation of traditional gender identities, and not wanting to confront the dynamic quality of the personal confusion and risk within conflicted family relationships. Derek Parfit is the rare contemporary philosopher who has attempted to formulate a notion of selfhood capable of tolerating the high degree of personal confusion, as well as the potential for radical transformation, affecting individuals' lives today. He argues that prior notions of personal identity, exemplified by the separately existing mental or spiritual substance of the Cartesian Pure Ego, are not defensible. And he asserts that a more determinate notion of psychological unity, specifically a notion of "psychological connectedness and/or continuity," which he terms the "R relation," is all that really matters when talking about persons.[50]

Considering possible objections to this theory, Parfit imagines the hypothetical medical possibility in which three siblings are in an accident: while my brain is not injured, my body is destroyed; the bodies of my two sisters remain whole, while their brains are destroyed. Making the best of things, surgeons successfully divide my brain in two and place half of it in each of the bodies of my two siblings. The question is whether I survive. Parfit claims that I do, even though neither of the two resulting persons are me, exactly. If we are committed to a Cartesian notion of personal identity, I have not survived; but if we believe that the R relation is what counts, then I have survived, even though my R relation has taken "a branching form." The division of my brain has resulted in my "double survival."[51]

Contemporary philosophers invariably deploy physicalist images, but if we transpose Parfit's discussion of the problem of branching and double survival into the social realm, an interesting perspective on the experiences of women and men with changing gender identities emerges. We may think of the social enfranchisement of women as involving the *social* branching of the R relation of a subsumed nurturer, and her double survival in a new public self and also a new private self. The subsumed nurturer has become two new selves, neither one having a psychological make-up identical with that of the woman who was a subsumed nurturer. But both of these new selves reside in the body of the former subsumed nurturer. In the case of social branching, a Cartesian sense of personal identity tends to make us blind to the seriousness of the problems experienced by the socially enfranchised woman insofar as she appears to be identical in some indeterminate spiritual sense with her former self. Parfit's rather frightening image of the double survival of my divided brain in two different bodies may actually be a good metaphor for the divisiveness of the social claims upon the contemporary woman, however. For she must now somehow choreograph the R relations of public and private selves whose psychological make-ups have previously been distributed between individuals of different genders and roles. The contemporary woman has not so much a double day as a double life.

The problems of the contemporary man can be imagined in terms of another of the hypothetical situations Parfit uses to call into question traditional notions of personal identity. In science fiction, he relates, there are machines that can "teletransport" a person to far-off planets instantaneously by making a blueprint of relevant personal data, and then replicating the person on whatever distant planet the person has as their destination. Parfit argues that while the replica of the person is not identical with the original person, it possesses the requisite psychological continuity and connections that would make it reasonable for a person to think of teletransportation as a mode of travel rather than as a death sentence.[52] I think we may usefully apply this metaphor of teletransportation to comprehend the experience of the married man who loses at least a portion of his identity as a patriarchal benefactor when his wife begins to work outside the home. He returns from work one evening to find himself upon a new domestic planet which no longer rotates around *his* work schedule, where meals no longer appear magically on the table, and dust collects oddly on furniture. It is a strange, uncomfortable familial environment, at first. He knows he will survive the changes, but probably not as the same identical person. Perhaps we may depict the disorientation we all experience within personal relationships no longer organized in terms of traditional gender roles and expectations through Parfit's image of teletransportation to a strange planet.

We must take issue with Parfit's belief that issues of personal identity have ceased to be an interesting site of philosophical problems, however. If we focus upon the R relations of contemporary women and men in almost any social context, we immediately notice problems that seem to concern personal identity. Parfit is correct that the important issues of personhood today have little to do with the Cartesian metaphysics of mind and body, and they will not be resolved by positing some indeterminately existing mental or spiritual substance labeled "personal identity." But if Parfit is right in thinking that the significant issues of personhood today can be understood in terms of the R relations of psychological continuity and/or connection, we are beset with a whole new cluster of identity problems. The nature of these problems is dramatically indicated by contemplating the social scenarios suggested by Parfit's science fictional metaphors of "branching and double survival," and "teletransportation and replication on a distant planet." Contemporary women tend to be faced with the need to reconstitute the R relations of psychological continuity and connection between radically different and conflicting spheres of their new lives. And contemporary men are frequently confronted with the need to adapt the R relations that were serviceable within patriarchal situations to the quite different social environments on this new planet of egalitarianism, where women expect to be treated as equals within public and personal relationships.

How could Parfit have overlooked these quite obvious social grounds for problems of personal identity in terms of R relations? And how could he have believed, ironically enough, that individuals who learned to understand themselves in terms of their R relations would have less trouble in feeling connected with others?[53] In fact, the analytic philosopher's frame of reference is a highly individualistic one which encourages the belief that basic psychological features of individuals can be understood apart from any particular social context. Thus once Parfit has shown that even extreme physical operations like the dividing of my brain, or the teletransporting of my body and brain to another planet, do not sever my R relations of psychological connectedness, he is content with having shown that R relations of psychological connectedness and/or continuity will analytically secure my personal and social existence. This notion of R relations becomes the intellectual machinery that allows Parfit to reassert a confident notion of personhood, replacing the spiritual conception of personal identity which founded the Cartesian notion of personhood with a version more serviceable in an age of computers and cyborgs.

There are social grounds for predicting a widespread experience of psychological disconnectedness and discontinuity as a result of drastically altered gender roles. In fact, Donald Davidson's argument for a nonmoral understanding of the problem of incontinence provides indirect support for such a social analysis. And Parfit's emphasis upon the importance of R relations has the effect of pinpointing the social location of new problems of personal identity, as well as the gendered reasons for feeling disconnected from others, rather than explaining away these contemporary concerns.

vii.   Acting beyond Unjust Identities

What seemed initially to be a rather simple moral problem of unfair male domestic behavior no longer seems simple at all. A generalized mooting of traditional gender identities is one of the consequences of the social enfranchisement of women. Women and men have become unsure about their respective roles within the family, and about the value of whatever domestic activities they choose to perform or to forego. It seems reasonable to think that the vast majority of women and men will experience personal confusion and uncertainty within whatever familial relationships they undertake today. Psychologists tend to link a muddled sense of personal identity or rational agency with individual pathology, while analytic philosophers seek to uncover theoretical pathologies. Both overlook the social origins of individual disorientation in changing gender relationships. Feminists, along with social critics of both radical and conservative orientations, tend to interpret contemporary conflicts within the family in ideological terms which neglect the significance of individual efforts to construct solutions appropriate to specific situations.

We need to appreciate the pathos and the volatility of relationships between women and men within families, recognizing the present turmoil as a necessary stage within a process of social transformation. We need to respect the individual struggles of women and men alike within domestic relationships, as challenging current parameters of gendered social identities, and as demonstrating the need for acting beyond their boundaries.

2

Glancing at Pornography: Recognizing Men

Pornography, like housework, may appear at first sight to warrant a quite straightforward feminist analysis. What woman has not suddenly felt herself the object of a humiliating, leering male gaze? When a radical-feminist antipornography movement developed in the late 1970s, anger in the face of this everyday modern female experience galvanized scores of women who had never before identified with feminist causes to join an emotion-charged crusade against the pornography industry's sexual exploitation and degradation of women. At the height of the movement in 1983, two feminist theorists, Catharine MacKinnon and Andrea Dworkin, drafted a human rights ordinance which declared pornography to be a practice of sex discrimination and a violation of women's civil rights. Under this ordinance, it became a civil offense to "traffic" in pornography or to coerce participation in its making or use. First proposed and debated in Minneapolis, the ordinance was adopted in Indianapolis on May 1, 1984.[1] Within a year, however, a federal appeals court had struck down the ordinance as unconstitutional, and in 1986 the Supreme Court affirmed this decision.[2] The antipornography ordinance had run afoul of First Amendment concerns with protecting the freedom of expression, and with its immediate hopes of political victory dashed, the antipornography movement faded.

As a political issue pornography turned out to be more complicated than anyone might have imagined; it proved highly divisive even within feminism. While opinion polls taken during the height of the controversy showed a majority of Americans believing that pornography is degrading and harmful to women and supporting legal restrictions on its production and distribution, large numbers of feminists were vehemently opposed to legal sanctions against pornography.[3] I will begin this chapter by briefly analyzing the different feminist perspectives occasioned by the pornography controversy. In hindsight, this bitter debate forecast a disconcerting broadening of feminist concerns and heralded the politically transgressive quality of the multiple voices of women.

Sexuality is such a ubiquitous and yet intangible medium of gendered communication and exchange that the apparent concreteness of "pornography" renders it as seductive for social analysis as for politics. In the remaining sections of this chapter, I will attempt to articulate the issues of sexual agency and identity that began to emerge in the course of the pornography debates. As in each chapter of this book, my primary concern lies in probing and evaluating current processes of gendered conflict and change as they develop in diverse social locations. The pornography debates provide a good framework for investigating a gendered dimension of agency involving both active and passive forms of sexual and social recognition. Typically overlooked as a dimension of agency even now, patriarchal regimes of sexual recognition are finally, a decade after the pornography controversy, being challenged on a variety of legal and political fronts. But the processes of social renegotiation in sexual harassment and date rape cases, to name two contemporary examples, will succeed only if we appreciate the dynamic underlying structure of recognition relations, which I investigate in this chapter.

i. The Feminist Debate over Pornography

Antipornography feminists emphasize the relationship between pornography and the institutionalization of male supremacy in our society. Insofar as pornography objectifies women's bodies, sexualizes their human presence, and eroticizes the male subordination of women, the very existence of pornography does violence to the desires of women for equality and relations of mutual respect with men, according to antipornography theorists Andrea Dworkin and Catharine MacKinnon.[4] They argue that male violence against women is endemic to all aspects of pornography: (1) in the production of pornography, where women and children are sometimes coerced into participating;[5] (2) in the images of pornography, whether in "snuff films" in which women are murdered, or in representations of female sexual degradation by means of boots, whips, or just physical force;[6] (3) in the social reception of pornography by men as well as by women. The political psychology here is that the identities of men and women in our society are heavily influenced by the eroticization of male domination of women within pornography—to such an extent that, in MacKinnon's opinion, "Women will never have that dignity, security, compensation that is the promise of equality so long as pornography exists as it does now."[7]

Of course, the portrayal of women as sexual playthings and servants is hardly confined to pornography. One need only turn on the television or scan one of innumerable mass-market magazines while in line at the supermarket to gain a quite definite sense of gendered social hierarchies, and whether it is one's masculine lot in life to actively express sexual desire or instead to accept one's feminine responsibility for satisfying the desires of a man. No law regulating pornography could possibly begin to eradicate all the graphic sexual representations of patriarchy that bombard us in our daily lives. While this might seem a conclusory argument against legal sanctions, MacKinnon justifies her antipornography ordinance in terms that sidestep this criticism. For her, the goal of a civil rights ordinance against pornography does not lie in eradicating it, but in revealing the pervasive eroticization of male power in the visual media, and enabling women to speak out against it in such a way that they can be heard. Representations of women as sexual objects undermine women's social authority so effectively that they make it difficult for women to protest its effects. "To the extent pornography succeeds in constructing social reality," MacKinnon argues, "it becomes invisible as harm. . . . So the issue is . . . how the harm of pornography is to become visible." By enacting into law the antipornography ordinance, MacKinnon believes that women "would have this recognition and institutional support for our equality [and] . . . there could come a day when she would speak in her own voice and you would hear her."[8] Pornography silences women. The antipornography ordinance intends to restore to women their voice.

The antipornography movement's goals, at least as articulated by its most sophisticated theorists, were those of a symbolic politics. There was no question of eliminating all images demeaning to women, and not even the hope of putting an end to the production and distribution of pornography per se. The aim was rather to make people aware of the ideological power of such images, and to empower women to give voice to their anger at being so portrayed. Indeed, the antipornography movement served as an important focal point for the outrage of a great many women who were just beginning to be conscious of how men "looked at" them in a variety of situations. Women were beginning to become wary of possible links between a boss's casual reading of *Hustler* on his lunch break, his embarrassing sexual innuendos in the hallways, and his refusal to pay them the same salary as male co-workers. The antipornography movement was fueled by a growing fury on the part of women newly confronting the fact that the male world looks most readily at women with a sexual gaze, disdaining to recognize women's accomplishments, even disregarding their presence in nonsexual contexts.[9]

Those feminists opposed to the regulation of pornography do not so much dispute the anger of the antipornography feminists as question its efficacy. They offer two related critiques of the antipornography movement. In the first place, they insist that no matter how reprehensible the images and ideas it communicates, pornography is merely a form of speech or expression; they contrast the repellent images of pornography with actual physical forms of abuse suffered by women at the hands of men. Never denying the psychological forms of male tyranny and domination experienced by women within sexual relationships, these feminists question the significance of pornographic representations in creating the conditions for such forms of domination. Second-wave feminists coming out of a Marxist tradition of material social analysis are skeptical of claims that pornography is any more than a cultural reflection of more basic forms of patriarchal power. As Varda Burstyn confidently asserts, "Sexist pornography is a product of the economic and social conditions of our society — not vice versa. . . . It follows that these are the conditions we must change if we want sexist pornography to disappear."[10]

In the second place, "pro-sex" feminists, as they often identify themselves, celebrate the goal of sexual freedom and the new possibilities for liberatory and egalitarian sexual relationships created by the social enfranchisement of women. Rejecting the tendency of the antipornography movement to focus on the sexual victimization of women by pornography, they emphasize that pornography is a transgressive form of sexual expression in a culture with a long tradition of sexual repression. Insofar as women today are casting off oppressive patriarchal notions of sexuality, they need to see themselves (and are surely seen by others) as engaging in sexually transgressive forms of speech and behavior.[11] For feminists to align themselves with the religious fundamentalists and social conservatives who most typically call for laws regulating pornography on the grounds of its sinfulness is both foolish and dangerous, argue these theorists. Such allies are quite likely to turn around and demand the suppression of what they perceive to be radical feminist depictions of deviant and immoral sexuality. Ironically, feminist-inspired antipornography laws will provide "a useful tool in antifeminist moral crusades," and small feminist journals challenging the boundaries of conventional sexuality will be more vulnerable to censorship than financially successful mass-market publishers of pornography.[12]

There were persuasive feminist arguments on either side of the pornography controversy. At the time, it seemed as if discussion of the issue was short-circuited by the legal framework of American liberalism. Any proposal for regulating individual behavior in our legal system must qualify according to the standards of the Harms Principle, first articulated by J. S. Mill in the mid-nineteenth century. Alarmed by the regulatory enthusiasm of Utilitarian social reformers Jeremy Bentham and James Mill, his father, J. S. Mill famously argued in *On Liberty* that governmental restraints upon individual behavior must be justified by the goal of preventing a harm from occurring. And in addition, he maintained, governmental action is warranted to prevent a harm only if the goal can be achieved without creating greater harms as a result of the regulatory procedures themselves.[13] In the United States, a hallowed tradition of First Amendment law has created a strong presumption that there are very great harms in regulating forms of speech or expression, and it has generally been accepted that restrictions should be placed upon speech only if there is shown to be a compelling state interest requiring such restrictions.

In ruling that the Indianapolis antipornography ordinance was unconstitutional, Judge Frank Easterbrook said, "We accept the premises of this legislation. Depictions of subordination tend to perpetuate subordination. The subordinate status of women in turn leads to affront and lower pay at work, insult and injury at home, battery and rape on the streets." That is, he did not deny claims that pornography is a harm to women. On the other hand, he did not find the state's interest in sex-based equality, according to the Fourteenth Amendment, sufficiently compelling to justify what he deemed the even greater harm of infringing upon First Amendment guarantees of free expression.[14] Constitutional norms seemed to weigh in heavily on behalf of the anticensorship, pro-sex feminist position.

In recent years, however, a surprising variety of theoretically compelling arguments have been made that suggest the legal issue might deserve to be reopened. According to Rae Langton, pornography places the state's interest in promoting the equality of women under the equal protection clause of the Fourteenth Amendment in direct conflict with its commitment to an individual freedom of speech. She suggests that if we apply currently accepted forms of legal reasoning to the pornography issue, the equality interest will be seen as "trumping" the state's concern for free expression.[15] Taking another legal tack, Yale law professor Owen Fiss argues for a broader reading of the state's obligation to protect the freedom of speech. He maintains that the state's interest in the freedom of speech should be interpreted not simply as a commitment to protecting individual speech acts, but as a responsibility for promoting a democratic process of discussion. Insofar as pornography serves to silence women to any significant degree, restrictions upon pornography may well enhance a democratic process of free and uninhibited discussion.[16] David Dyzenhaus contends that J. S. Mill himself might have supported restrictions upon pornography, out of his strong concern for opposing male tyranny over women and encouraging the autonomy of women.[17]

Despite the availability of plausible legal arguments for reopening the pornography issue, there seems little political impetus for doing so. The reason, I think, is that many of the issues first raised in the context of pornography are now being joined more effectively in a number of other legal venues. In later chapters, I will trace the legal and political legacy of the pornography debates in struggles over abortion rights, sexual harassment, and date rape. In the rest of the present chapter, however, I will attempt to unravel the confusing strands of fraying sexual agency and identity that continue to make the theme of pornography a rich fabric for social analysis.

ii. An Interactive Model of Sexual Agency

Pornography has a deceptive simplicity about it, representing quite viscerally the reality of female sexual objectification and passivity under the eye of a patriarchal sexual gaze. Lying unself-consciously and nakedly on a table before us, the pornographic object also seems quite vulnerable to either feminist wrath or defanging. On the one hand, we can imagine reaching out with both fists to crumple it and toss it with little further ado into a wastebasket. Perhaps if enough women crumpled enough pieces of paper we could finally be free of the demeaning images of women in our society. On the other hand, we can imagine this pornographic magazine or video undergoing a sex change. In the place of female bodies it would be filled with male bodies passively displayed for female sexual approval. Artfully posed to emphasize unusually large or perfectly formed sexual parts in states of erotic tumescence, the complete sexual objectification of these men would prove the existence of a female sexual gaze to rival that of the male sexual gaze. The sexual gaze would no longer be associated with patriarchal oppression insofar as it had either been destroyed or become symmetrical.

But pornography is not immediately vulnerable to either the wrathful destruction or the liberatory mimicry of feminist responses. For pornography is not so much a literal record of obnoxious male psychological patterns as it is a sign system constructed atop a set of late patriarchal social asymmetries which cannot be destroyed or reversed so readily.[18] We need to investigate the asymmetries in patriarchal relationships, and particularly the asymmetries within patriarchal systems of recognition, in order to understand the social context for current responses to pornography.

Without succumbing to biological essentialisms of sexual difference we may begin by emphasizing the quite radical asymmetry in biologically based male and female forms of sexual agency.[19] Historically, the male ability to rape and impregnate a woman provided an important ground for patriarchal sexual and social power relationships. Consider the immediate asymmetries indicated by male spermatic agency. A man, qua man, was physically capable of getting a woman, any woman, with child, and leaving her with child. Because of his relative size and strength he was generally able to do this with or without her consent. He was thus able to leave an indelible mark of his momentary pleasure or release upon a woman, imposing upon her a nine-month labor of physical reproduction as well as a future life of motherhood. Any man could thus act upon any woman in a way she could neither refuse, nor reciprocate, nor forget (given pregnancy as a consequence). While such a man might not disavow his physiological paternity, the social anonymity of his sperm after conception made it possible for him to do so. The rather amazing temporal asymmetry of immediate male spermatic potency and long-term female connection and obligation thus provided a material and social basis for more general forms of male domination over women.[20]

In chapter 1, I analyzed patriarchal notions of agency as constructed in relation to the characteristically different location and status of activities socially assigned to women and men. Male activities were typically identified with the public sphere and respected as embodying forms of social rationality, while the activities of women within the domestic sphere were not presumed to require rationality or any other uniquely human qualities insofar as they were "natural" forms of human behavior. Women's struggle for identity and social empowerment in this context has involved proving they can take on male-identified public forms of economic and political agency, and also requires a revaluing of familial activities as important forms of social agency in which men as well as women will participate.

Patriarchal hierarchies are established very differently with respect to sexual agency, insofar as male and female forms of sexual activity and power are defined interactively. Male sexual domination of women is not based upon notions of male sexual rationality or upon the exclusion of women from the site of male sexual activities. Men celebrate the irrationality of their sexual passions, and ardently solicit the participation of women in their sexual scenarios. Male sexual superiority seems to have been a contingent historical function of a man's physical ability to unilaterally act upon a woman in a socially significant way. This ability to act unilaterally upon women anchors the social discourses that represent men as active and women as passive, men as having desire and the sexual gaze and women as lacking sexual desire and being the object of the sexual gaze.

When we seek to make the social mechanisms of male sexual domination explicit, its interactive quality becomes evident. We need to understand complementary forms of male and female sexual agency involving the shared recognition of the social significance of the male ability to act upon a woman. We may say that patriarchal forms of sexual agency are defined dialectically in terms of such recognition relations. A man's ability to rape or impregnate a woman only gains its social significance insofar as this ability is recognized by women as having particular social implications; a woman's recognition of male abilities to rape and/or impregnate her will correspond with particular female strategies to control the conditions under which this may occur. Thus forms of social recognition become both actively and passively a component of gendered agency and identity within patriarchy.

We may even consider this sociosexual interaction in terms of a ritualized male-female dialogue of asymmetrical forms of recognition. Given the shared social knowledge that a man had the capacity at any moment to act sexually upon a woman, a mere look of sexual interest was enough to convey this possibility to a woman, and to constitute an act of sexual intimidation. A woman was required to recognize herself as the object of this male's sexual desire, and the potential repository of his seed, along with the extensive physical and social obligations this seed carried with it. Thus threatened, a woman was forced to accept her generic sexual vulnerability, and was rendered subject to male demands for lesser acts of service or obedience. In other words, through a word or a mere glance communicating his sexual interest a man could assert his sexual power to act in some future moment upon a particular woman. And he could use this sexual communication as grounds for exerting social control and subordination over a woman, exacting various acts of service from any woman wishing to forestall his sexual threats.[21]

Seen in this light, patriarchal marriage, as an institutionalized structure of kinship placing social boundaries on the physical vulnerability of women, offered obvious advantages for a woman. By accepting the sexual and social demands of one man, by agreeing to provide him with heirs and to serve him, a woman could secure his protection from the sexual threats of other men. Such protection would operate most effectively, of course, insofar as a woman was willing to remain in private familial spaces except when accompanied by her male protector. To be present in the public spaces of social recognition and acclaim meant for a lone woman to be vulnerable to multiple glances of male sexual recognition, reduction, and intimidation. We may well associate women's recognition of the asymmetries of gendered sexual agency with women's "willingness" to accept the confines of a familial sphere, thereby articulating the drastic male exclusion of women from public spaces of social interaction with a strategic female withdrawal. Insofar as the asymmetry of sexual agency imposed kinship boundaries upon women's social participation, we may directly link male spermatic potency with exclusionary male social agency.

Within the normal orderings of social metaphysics we are accustomed to thinking that events occur, or people perform actions, and then recognition follows eventually in response. Recognition is a secondary, cognitive phenomenon, and is even a bit capricious, sometimes failing to occur altogether, at other times exaggerated or distorted in its relationship to the prior performance or occurrence. But whatever its degree of reliability, social recognition exists within the order of social perception or knowledge, and follows or presumes to follow consequentially upon some prior social phenomenon. I am proposing, however, that the asymmetries of sexual agency were such as to reverse the ordering of social metaphysics and epistemology, and most dramatically so in the lives of women.

The social logic ordering women's existence began with their recognition of what men could potentially do to them, and their own sense of agency could only be predicated upon their strategies for dealing with this possibility. Women's position within patriarchy must be understood in the context of asymmetrical relations of sexual recognition, and specifically in terms of women's *anticipatory recognition* of male sexual and social potency. In women's anticipatory recognition of what men could do to them sexually lay the grounds for seeking out marriage so as to avoid becoming prey to random, unexpected acts of male sexual assertion, and for accepting the obligations of a subsumed nurturer within patriarchal kinship relationships.

In women's anticipatory recognition of what men could do to them sexually we can also discover the seed of a further form of characteristically female anticipatory recognition. The male gaze of sexual interest gained its power as a phallic promissory note, and the responding female gaze not only acknowledged male sexual potential but also elaborated on it. Having accepted her exclusion from direct participation in the public sphere, it made sense for a woman to invest her male partner with all the powers of social activity she could now only imagine and plan. Renouncing the possibility of accomplishing worldly projects herself, female self-realization could vicariously root itself in the nurturance and support of male social potential. Insofar as she could identify with the prospective agency of a particular man, a woman could experience herself as participating in worldly events.[22]

Female fear and acquiescence in anticipatory recognition of male sexual power was transformed by patriarchal institutions of kinship into a generous, supportive, potentially manipulative faith of wives (and mothers) in the capacity of their husbands (and sons) to accomplish worldly goals which women might initiate or help to formulate in the protected space of the home. This anticipatory female recognition and encouragement of prospective male deeds served an important role in empowering the individual economic and political activities of men within liberalism. Romantic modes of mutual recognition whereby men and women sought completion in marital union can be understood as resting upon such a dynamic of gendered anticipation. We can only appreciate the scope of women's social agency by acknowledging the importance of these anticipatory forms of recognition.

Notice that anticipatory forms of social recognition not only preceded performance but were quite capable of existing independently of it. It was not the male act of rape or impregnation so much as the communication of his capacity to do so that socially signified. It was the chain of recognitions ensuing upon a male sexual gaze and the female reception of this gaze; it was the mutual accord as to the meaning of the male gaze that made sense of gendered subjectivities under patriarchy. *Patriarchal power was a power that existed at its very source in the subjunctive form, in the communication of possibility.* Unlike the whip of the slave master, the violent, coercive meaning of which could not be denied, male sexual potency was long ago accepted, domesticated, and submerged within elaborate rituals of patriarchal love and kinship, providing a foundation for male forms of social agency and identity extending far beyond the private sphere.[23]

The interactive and subjunctive qualities of gendered recognition relations provide insight into some peculiar, and from the perspective of feminism quite disappointing, features of the present social moment. Technologies of contraception have given women the power to contravene male sexual potency, and to become "determinate in the last instance" with respect to reproduction.[24] And social enfranchisement has given women rights and responsibilities to participate directly in political and economic forms of agency. Women's lives can no longer be understood in terms of strategies dictated by the anticipatory recognition of male agency and power. Mary O'Brien has gone so far as to herald a Contraceptive Revolution, proclaiming that the social transformations resulting from women's new procreative control within relations of human reproduction will be as dramatic as the changes Marx predicted from a Communist revolution.[25]

Yet the subjunctive quality of the dialogue of sexual recognition has provided men with a certain cushion against acknowledging their loss of an important material component of patriarchal sexual agency. Male sexual performance could always be deferred in the past, a veiled phallic power source that men and women anticipated and finally took for granted. It seems today that the patriarchal sexual gaze and the ritualized forms of recognition between men and women that it mandated have attained a degree of social autonomy. Many women's current sense of being victimized by pornography, despite having achieved positions of social power and authority countervailing pornography's message of subordination and silencing in their own lives, bears witness to a disheartening autonomy of the patriarchal sexual gaze. It would not be logically impossible for the "memory" of patriarchal sexual and social forms of power to persist indefinitely in this perverse, two-dimensional form.

Yet recognition relations comprise a practical dimension of social agency; we cannot afford to dismiss patriarchal modes of recognition as merely the stuff of bad memories. Neither pornography nor the persistently low wages of women, to mention another currency of social recognition, are merely cognitive artifacts of a senile patriarchal culture. If men still fail to "get it" with respect to women's capacities for worldly achievements, then it must be that they do not want to "get it." Insofar as we are dealing with male resistance to changing relationships between men and women, a failure of recognition can often be interpreted as a refusal of recognition.

In fact, such refusals of recognition are on a continuum with more overtly negative reactions to women's changing status. We may link the impassive denial/recognition of women's changing sexual and social status in the gaze of pornography, for example, with more active forms of denial/recognition within personal relationships. Recent reports indicate that domestic forms of abuse against women increase as women assert greater social independence, and women incur the greatest levels of violence, even death, at the hands of sexual partners they have decided to leave.[26] Confident patriarchal power could once assert itself with a mere glance—no longer. Women may still cower psychologically and feel victimized by the patriarchal gaze of pornography. But increasingly women stand up for themselves within patriarchal institutions of power, saying "No" in the face of coercive sexual and nonsexual demands. Male violence in response to women who leave them and male responsiveness to pornographic images of women who cannot say "No" are surely both acts of patriarchal resistance. In a sense, they constitute an anticipatory male recognition of the radical implications of women's changing status.

We saw that recognition relations were a constitutive part of gendered forms of agency and power in the past. It should hardly surprise us that they continue to play a primary, practical role in the struggle to transform, and to resist the transformation, of gendered relationships. We need to develop better strategies for critically engaging with defensive patriarchal recognition relations, however—which brings us back to the politics of pornography and the sexual gaze.

iii. Freudian Stories, Worldly Mothers, Gendered Disengagement, and Pornography

My reconstruction of patriarchal sexual interactions highlights the importance of both active and passive forms of recognition within gendered social relationships. There remains, however, quite a distance between an understanding of how recognition operates within actual social interactions and an understanding of the disembodied form of sexual "recognition" found in pornography. Pornography, and more generally the ubiquity of objectified images of women surrounding us today, are a feature of modern life that cannot be explained directly by means of the asymmetries of interactive patriarchal sexual agency and power described above. They represent (literally) a culturally dominant, impersonal male sexual gaze that has developed quite recently. In order to comprehend such contemporary forms of sexual recognition we need to investigate what I will designate as "late patriarchal" elaborations upon the earlier sociosexual asymmetries. Our investigation properly begins with Sigmund Freud's psychoanalytic theory of sexual agency and identity.

In the liberal democratic political milieu of late-nineteenth-century Europe, not only radical women but even a few thinkers with the stature of J. S. Mill had begun to challenge the natural as well as the social foundations of patriarchy. Women's demands for economic and political rights threatened to seriously undermine male social authority so long as it seemed to rest upon physiological differences between men and women. Egalitarian doctrines of human potential called into question the moral and political relevance of merely physiological differences.

A universal recognition of male superiority and authority could no longer be taken for granted, despite the fact that patriarchal structures of power remained firmly entrenched. What was needed was a revised explanation of patriarchy's legitimacy, and Freud managed to provide just that. His great achievement was to install a psychological metaphysic of "male

sexual desire" as a new basis for male sexual and social dominance. It became much harder to criticize the social domination of men insofar as
Freud appeared to have demonstrated its psychic necessity, duly linking
his "discoveries" of basic psychic differences with evident physiological
differences of men and women, and explaining both in terms of enduring
myth-laden social and symbolic structures of patriarchy.

The originality and narrative power of Freudian theory has made its
theoretical status highly confusing; controversies over whether it is a
science or an ideology obscure its historical role as both a response to and
a denial of the changing place of women in society. Judith Kegan Gardiner
contrasts radical feminists who condemn Freudian theory "as part of the
ideological apparatus that oppresses women" and psychoanalytic feminists who "agree that Freud was a sexist product of his time and deplore
his belief in anatomical female inferiority but defend the importance of
psychoanalytic thinking."[27] My point is that neither group of feminists
understands patriarchy in sufficiently dynamic terms: Freud creatively extended and adapted patriarchal ideology in an effort (whether conscious
or unconscious) to provide psychological legitimacy for gendered power
relationships whose social base was eroding. The success of Freud's effort
was very much bound up with his ability to make patriarchy fashionable
again by clothing it in new psychic garb. The frequent feminist habit of
identifying psychoanalytic theory as "the unconscious of patriarchal society" is misleading, as this implies it is a report of historically enduring features of patriarchal domination. Freud *invented* this (patriarchal) unconscious, and although it may offer us insights into earlier thinking, it serves
first and foremost as a report on the historically specific concerns of his
late-nineteenth-century Western society.[28] If we focus on revealing the
historical specificity of Freud's late patriarchal narrative we may declare
certain portions of Freudian theory already anachronistic and psychically
implausible, without rejecting the continuing relevance of other aspects of
his psychic worldview.

Having said this, I think that what most distinguishes Freudian theory
from earlier patriarchal belief systems is its singular emphasis upon the
castrated woman, as well as its related obsession with various dynamics
of separation from women. Earlier thinkers, from Aristotle to John Locke,
generally explained women's inferiority in terms of their incompleteness,
or their lesser strength relative to men. Although the image of a woman
as a castrated man was hardly new with Freud, only in his system does
it become the primary characterization of women. The violence and the
instability of this image of women's inferiority is, after all, quite extraordi-
nary. In order to be castrated, a woman must have once possessed the

phallus. This means that her inferiority has been violently imposed upon her through taking from her something originally hers. By contrast with Plato's, Aristotle's, or Locke's complacent conceptions of women's natural inferiority, Freud proffers what is in his own terms a guilt-ridden image suggesting a mysteriously unnatural source of women's inferiority. The castrated woman would seem a cruelly defensive emblem of late patriarchal uncertainty about the legitimacy of male domination.

The separation dynamic that the castrated woman initiates, and which structures the Freudian narrative of sexual desire, is also symptomatic of late patriarchy. In Freud's Oedipal account of boyhood, the child begins by desiring his mother. Having recognized his mother's castration, not only must the boy child break away from his mother to avoid being similarly castrated by his father, but all further contacts with women, and even images of women, are presumed to evoke castration anxiety in boys and in the men they become. It is not the phenomenon of male anxiety when confronted by women's bodies which is new to Freud; rather, it is the dominant place of this desire-based anxiety in his theory of male behavior. Relationships with mothers and wives were taken for granted by earlier thinkers; women were not perceived as occupying the sort of social place that could make them threatening to a man's psychic well-being. Freud, on the other hand, makes the successful repression of the boy's early desire for his mother the foundation for all further relationships, even deriving a man's mature public goals and accomplishments from his successful sublimation of childhood desires for his mother. One of the seductive aspects of psychoanalytic theory for feminists is surely the fact that Freud is the only major thinker ever to take the traditional role of women so seriously, if in a perverse way.

Notice that the Freudian narrative of sexual desire involves a radical turn away from traditional interactive relationships of sexual recognition. Freudian psychoanalysis suggests that each person must seek to discover the psychic origins of their adult sexual desires in childhood relationships. Adult desires, despite their appearance of social immediacy, are always a replay of original Oedipal desires, and in analysis the individual narrates his life story in terms of the significance of the permutations he works upon these original sexual desires. This means that psychoanalysis provides a powerful rhetorical framework for distancing oneself from the psychic give-and-take within adult sexual relationships. As mere replays of the initial relationship of desire and separation from the mother, mature sexual relationships are ultimately about sexual self-recognition.

The sexual objectification of women in the mass media today is a phenomenon highly compatible with this turn away from interactive forms of sexual recognition in adult relationships. Put simply, male erotic pleasure becomes generally problematic insofar as the mere image of a woman is presumed to evoke castration anxiety. One typical solution, according to Laura Mulvey, is "fetishistic scopophilia": the extreme visual beauty of the female portrayed on the movie screen enables men to escape, momentarily, their castration anxiety.[29] Extending Mulvey's analysis to visual representations of women generally, the Freudian narrative explains all too clearly why we are surrounded by idealized sexual images of women in our society, and why women as well as men often find them appealing. With his Oedipal narrative of childhood separation from castrated mothers, Freud emphasized the intrinsically fearful quality of the sexual desire for women, providing a sympathetic perspective on modern alienated forms of erotic desire. Fetishistic representations of women provide men with the occasion for experiencing sexual desire with the least possible anxiety about (castrating) female responses.

Today, however, the social enfranchisement of women, and the advent of what I will refer to as "worldly mothers," throw a bit of a wrench into the Freudian characterization of women and into his story of sexual desire. The image of a castrated mother relied upon the patriarchal opposition between a father whose penis identified him with society's language and laws and a mother whose lack of a penis signified her presocial, bodily existence within the home. Such a binary opposition is increasingly called into question by the new demographics of daily family existence. Mothers today are worldly working mothers, for the most part. Accordingly, it makes increasingly less sense to explain childhood development in terms of an initial bond with a presocial maternal nurturer, and a traumatic break from this primary nurturer in order to enter a social world identified with the father. When a child's mother and father both work outside the home, the presence or absence of a penis will not signify a necessary difference in either parenting roles or in worldly status. When a child lives with a single mother or several women who work outside the home, society's law and language will be personally associated with the lack of a penis. It no longer makes obvious psychic sense to assume that an infant will identify penises with sexual desire or with personhood, and the lack of a penis with castration.[30]

The patriarchal mythology of women's castration represents women as violated and degraded in their female bodily existence. Women cannot afford to accept Freudian versions of a gendered separation dynamic as grounded in a meaningful childhood fear of women as castrated. Having recently acquired the means to control procreation, however, along with expectations of participation in the public sphere, women may have their own interest in narratives of separation from men and children. As women cease to think of themselves as subsumed nurturers and begin to act publicly under their own names, a mythical narrative of female separation from the patriarchal family seems highly appropriate. Despite its troubling implications, a gendered separation dynamic has become historically meaningful to women as well as to men in this late patriarchal moment.

Given the oppositional quality of gender relations during this transitional period, women might be expected to generate a mythology that places the blame for the dynamic of gendered disengagement upon men and their continuing efforts to dominate women. I think it is even possible to interpret the pornography controversy in symbolic sexual terms, as a struggle to define a female mythology of separation from the individual men who have sexually intimidated women. This feminist separation dynamic originates in a male threat of rape rather than a female threat of castration. It will involve the girl child's attraction to, and finally recognition and fear of "the father who could rape her."

In this context, pornography becomes interesting not for its representations of women, which are hardly unique to pornography, but for its attendant phenomenon of "men looking at pornography." It so happens that this "man looking at pornography" provides a nicely delineated image of male sexual desire for the separating, postmodern woman to focus upon. In critically observing this "man looking at pornography" women are able to objectify and delimit the desiring—and thus obviously lacking and incomplete—male sexual being. In thus focusing on the sexual neediness of men, women can experience their own sexual agency of wanting to position themselves as the object of this male desire, while also finally seeing the dangers inherent in the situation. Male fears of castration are supposedly initially grounded in threats of the father, gradually coming to be associated with the very existence of the desirable woman. In a similar way, female fears of rape can be initially grounded in the exemplary fates of oppressed mothers or grandmothers, gradually coming to be embodied in the very existence of the man who desires the two-dimensional women of pornography.

Both sides of the feminist pornography debate can be understood in terms of a female Ur-separation mythology generated in this context. When Laura Mulvey analyzed the male anxiety evoked by images of women in films she suggested two distinct modes of cinematic compensation for male anxieties. She designates one male response to women in films as "voyeurism," involving a male preoccupation with the trauma of the guilty castrating female. In certain films, "pleasure lies in ascertaining guilt, asserting control, and subjecting the guilty woman to punishment and/or forgiveness."[31] In our feminist inversion of this male separation schema, antipornography feminists respond to the rape anxiety produced by the father in a similarly "voyeuristic" manner. They exorcise a preoccupation with the female trauma of rape at the hands of the father by projecting their fears onto the "man who looks at pornography," gaining pleasure and release by asserting his guilt and attempting to punish him.

The second cinematic strategy for allaying the male anxiety of the castrating woman involves the aforementioned "fetishistic scopophilia," whereby the physical beauty of the female body is emphasized.[32] This fetishization of the female body is accomplished within films by focusing attention on the erotic alluring quality of a woman, outside of any particular narrative context, and thus denying the traumatic original story of castration. Pro-sex feminists may be understood as engaging in a similar displacement of female rape anxiety through focusing on the erotic quality of the "man looking at pornography." When Ann Snitow insists, for example, that "men looking at pornography" ought to be seen as engaging in a form of sexual fantasy similar to women's enjoyment of Harlequin novels, she may be seen as choosing a fetishistic response to the anxiety evoked by the original story of male rape.[33] By focusing on the passivity of the man viewing pornography such feminists abstract male desire from its frequent social context of intimidation and hostility. Thus can women fantasize control over the erotic scenario of heterosexual desire, gaining pleasure from this gentler, almost effete representation of male sexuality.

There is incontrovertible evidence today of a broad social phenomenon of *gendered disengagement*. Demographic statistics are compelling, recording trends (in some cases extending back a hundred years) toward later ages of first marriage, greater divorce rates, increasing patterns of unmarried adults and single-motherhood. The figures indicate a separation dynamic of major social proportions. By analyzing Freud's theory of the castrated woman as a late patriarchal separation mythology, and by proposing a corresponding feminist separation mythology founded upon a fear of men as rapists, I have attempted to highlight the historical specificity of this process. The process of gendered disengagement which began a century ago as a defensive male strategy *within* patriarchy has now become a feature of women's struggle for social enfranchisement *beyond* patriarchy.

iv. Jacques Lacan and Women's Desires for Recognition

The social position of women has changed radically in the last quarter of a century. Not only have women achieved unprecedented rights to social participation, but the obligations and burdens that correspond with possessing individual economic and political rights within liberalism have been redistributed with amazing rapidity from men to women. Gendered disengagement, in the form of declining marriage rates, increasing divorce rates, and increasing rates of motherhood outside of marriage, has contributed to this redistribution of social responsibility. *Yet the gendered redistribution of social recognition lags far behind the redistribution of social responsibilities.* Not only are women still looked at as sexual objects in inappropriate situations, but women fail to be positively recognized and rewarded in their new social roles. For example, women who are heads of households are not paid the sorts of wages long apportioned exclusively to men as heads of households. Women who perform as effectively as men in various social capacities are not paid equivalent wages and salaries, nor do they receive equivalent opportunities for promotion. Women, as well as members of various culturally devalued groups, need active strategies for gaining appropriate forms of social recognition.

When patriarchal authority began to be questioned a century ago, Freud could propose a psychic regimen of self-recognition for men as a reprieve from the turmoil and anxieties of changing gender relationships. The superior power of men within a patriarchal society meant that they could defensively maintain their power by ignoring those who would not recognize it. But women begin from a position of social inferiority. Unless women are going to create their own autonomous society, no strategy of self-recognition will do; the social empowerment of women within a patriarchal society requires that men alter their previous beliefs and recognize the new status of women. The antipornography movement was an expression of women's frustration at being denied forms of social recognition appropriate to their new social roles and responsibilities. It was hardly a constructive strategy, however, for attaining the kinds of social recognition women currently yearn for and deserve.[34]

Jacques Lacan, perhaps the most significant theorist of psychoanalysis after Freud, makes the individual's desire for recognition by others the central feature of psychic life. While Lacan had rather conventional assumptions about the social positions women and men were destined to take up, his innovative rearticulation of a still-patriarchal Desire in terms of each person's impossible quest to be socially recognized has interesting feminist implications. In fact, Lacan provides a useful theoretical approach to a global situation in which not only gendered but also racial and ethnic conflict and disengagement have heightened everyone's concerns about social recognition. Moreover, in making language the primary site for our efforts to attain recognition, he posits a complexly interactive social framework for addressing issues of recognition.

Lacan himself never contemplates the critical, interactive strategies of social recognition for which I believe his theory helps to lay the groundwork. He remains firmly committed to the psychoanalytic project articulated by Freud, never questioning the notion that an individual's psychic needs are best addressed through helping him to explore his unconscious desires. Lacan's seminal theoretical contribution lies in his emphasis upon the socially mediated forms, specifically the linguistic forms, which provide the fabric of this psychic drive for self-recognition. The feminist challenge lies in showing how Lacan's vision of desiring subjects constructed within language provides a unique basis for understanding gender oppression, while at the same time suggesting that women and others who are not privileged within a particular symbolic system are likely to develop a critical relationship to it and to those subjects it does privilege.

Freud's theory of sexual desire and self-recognition remained grounded in the male possession of a penis and the female lack of a penis. Lacan's theory of desire and recognition is not linked to the physical possession of a penis, or to any gender-specific biological features. Desire, for Lacan, is grounded in the human baby's physical helplessness and lack of coordination at the time of birth, which he refers to as "the specific prematurity of birth in man." Lacan posits that from the time of birth onward, the infant "magically" experiences "images of castration, mutilation, dismemberment, dislocation, evisceration, devouring, bursting open of the body, in short . . . *imagos of the fragmented body*." This early sense of anatomical incompleteness structures all further psychic development, and from this experience of an inherent "lack" in being comes the lifelong desire to be recognized as a unified self. For Lacan, it is this "narcissistic passion" for recognition that underlies all other forms of desire and most basically fuels human behavior.[35]

His theory of early childhood development also does not differentiate between boy and girl children; it explicates what Lacan considers a basic human fixation upon gaining a unified sense of selfhood through various modes of social recognition.[36] He believed that at about six months of age the child entered what he called a "mirror stage," during which the child first perceived itself as a complete object in the reflection of a mirror, as well as in the gaze of its mother or primary caretaker. The infant's mirror-stage image of wholeness, like all later ones, is only illusory, insofar as the first and most basic body image remains one of fragmentation. At about eighteen months of age, the infant's fascination with its mirror gestalt diminishes, and what has begun as a specular identity gradually becomes a social identity, constituted in terms of language.[37]

Lacan associates the mirror stage with a "natural" consciousness and a primary identification with the mother, and he considers the end of the mirror stage to involve the child's passage into social forms of consciousness, achieved through submitting to alienating patriarchal symbolic structures of law and language. He uses the notion of castration to designate the traumatic end of the infant's primary identification with the mother, and he posits that the actual father functions as a Phallus, or as a symbolic agent of separation making this transition possible.[38] Having made the transition into the realm of the patriarchal symbolic, each individual must forever after seek a sense of his or her unity/identity within language and other social systems of signification, which can, however, only "misrecognize" the self.

Notice that Lacan's perspective on gender relations becomes a bit confusing at the point when the child begins to use language because Lacan adopts Freud's naturalistic sexual categories to explain the process of becoming a social subject. Lacan consciously articulates his theory in terms of patriarchal symbolic structures, accepting "paternal metaphors" inherited from Freud, while at the same time denying the existence of any natural foundations of patriarchy. For example, Lacan emphasizes that all his talk of phalluses is purely metaphorical, having no reference to the male penis or the female lack of a penis.[39] It is for this reason that Ellie Ragland-Sullivan can deny an "a priori Lacanian support for phallocentrism" and even argue that his theory is helpful to feminists in offering "a picture of the place of man and woman within a history of symbolization and meaning."[40] Psychoanalysis was formulated as a social practice, however, a means whereby contemporary women and men attempt to better understand themselves and their desires. In the context of its application, Lacan's psychoanalytic discourse encourages a continuing assumption of patriarchal relationships and hierarchies.

I maintain, however, that Lacan's theory of the constitution of desiring subjects within a patriarchal symbolic system only makes complete sense for those male subjects who have a privileged relationship to the signifying structures of this system. For those subjects who are un-named or otherwise devalued within the dominant signifying systems, we will need to comprehend the logic of their desiring behavior in more complicated ways. Insofar as women have become socially enfranchised today as women within a patriarchal signifying system, we may presume their desires to have been constituted in fundamentally conflicted ways, and expect their relationships with various signifying systems to be contentious. Women's psychic need for recognition will lead them to interact critically with the patriarchal signifying systems that Lacan assumes as foundational structures of psychic desire.

Let us look closely at Lacan's theory of how individuals come to under-stand themselves. Remember that according to Lacan we begin life with a fragmented sense of self which leads to a lifelong effort to substantiate a vision of personal wholeness through social forms of recognition. After the mirror stage has come to an end, we gain our sense of identity within language, becoming a subject of language and in some sense subject to this symbolic order. But language is, for psychological purposes, merely the medium through which we experience the desires and recognition of other human beings. Lacan expresses this social function of language by positing that we gain our sense of identity as a man or as a woman, as well as in other respects, by seeing ourselves in terms of the hypothetical gaze of an Other within signifying systems. Of course, no one signifier, or even many signifiers, can adequately represent who we are. As Lacan says, "It functions as a signifier only to reduce the subject in question to being no more than a signifier, to petrify the subject in the same movement in which it calls the subject to function, to speak, as subject." [41] "Mis-recognition" is thus the paradigmatic dynamic of selfhood for Lacan, the ongoing sig-nifying process within which individuals are necessarily and imperfectly constituted in language and in the gaze of the Other.

As an account of the inevitable inadequacy of language confronted with human particularity, this notion of misrecognition makes sense. It elides the difference between the practical and the cognitive dimensions of recognition rather too quickly, however. It also implies that all forms of misrecognition are equal. Of course they are not, and this becomes evident once we consider that people interact within hierarchically organized so-cial structures in accordance with differential modes of (mis)recognizing one another. As Lacan himself pointed out in a late essay, there are particu-larly deep-seated problems with being misrecognized as a woman. "By her being in the sexual relation radically Other, in relation to what can be said of the unconscious, the woman is that which relates to this Other. . . . How can we conceive that the Other might, somewhere, be that to which one half—since that is roughly the biological proportion—one half of speaking beings relates? And yet that is what is written up on the black-board. . . . Nothing can be said of the woman." [42] Lacan is truly puzzled by the effort to think about how the gaze of the Other can misrecognize something it only recognizes as the Other in the first place. Concluding that there can be "no Other of the Other," Lacan accepts the situation as an interesting paradox created by a patriarchal symbolic system.

For individual women who are recognized in an infinite variety of so-cial roles today, but always *in spite* of being women, it is a rather more serious issue. Until recently, women were indeed subject to an all-too-consistent sense of inferior female identity, insofar as the available social roles for women corresponded with the forms of recognition mandated by patriarchal signifying systems. Today, however, with their social enfranchisement, women experience themselves within radically disjunctive social Gazes. They are expected to position themselves and to participate within various liberal social structures alongside men. And yet, patriarchal signifying systems continue to recognize them in terms of the old modalities of female inferiority. This patriarchal gaze is newly experienced as a denial of female selfhood, however, insofar as women experience *themselves* as full social selves within various roles. Operating within a confusing tangle of symbolic systems that make recognition of women as contemporary social agents both inevitable and impossible, women must contend with repeated instances of what I will call the "anticipatory nonrecognition" of patriarchal signifying systems.

Lacan focused on the desires of male subjects for recognition within a patriarchal symbolic system, which led him to assume that misrecognition was primarily a form of positive recognition. He theorized the desiring behavior of individuals in the context of the symbolic privileges enjoyed by such subjects, not realizing that the desires of women or other subjects not privileged within a particular signifying system would be constituted differently in response to experiences of *nonrecognition*. In fact, with his discussion of the peculiar quality of misrecognition accorded to women in a patriarchal symbolic system, Lacan inadvertently demonstrates that anticipatory nonrecognition is a quite obvious limit form of language-based misrecognition.

Moreover, the phenomenon of misrecognition as nonrecognition is not peculiar to relationships between men and women; it commonly occurs in situations of cultural dissonance as well. At one point, Lacan writes of an episode in which he himself experienced nonrecognition, still managing to avoid noticing its implications for his theory of misrecognition and the constitution of desiring subjects. He reminisces that many years before, he had visited the coast of Brittany for a week's vacation, and each day he had enthusiastically put out to sea in the boat of a local sardine fisherman. As a young intellectual visiting from Paris, Lacan had imagined himself to be sharing a practical, physical experience of work and danger with this fisherman. At some point, however, the fisherman pointed to a small sardine can floating in the water, exclaiming, "You can see that? Do you see it? Well, it doesn't see you!" The fisherman found this "highly amusing," while Lacan did not.[43] Seeking an explanation, Lacan decides that the fisherman's laughter stems from the fact that he, like the sardine can, could reflect light or apparent awareness in Lacan's presence, without really seeing Lacan at all. Lacan uses this incident to demonstrate that cognition is not merely a matter of physical perception but also a matter of subjective desires. We may think and desire to see ourselves as in a particular place, and then find that according to someone next to us who surely ought to be able to perceive our presence, we are not there at all. The fisherman's worldly vision, as reflected in his relationship to the floating sardine can, simply did not include Lacan, even as they were sitting side by side in the boat.

This situation of nonrecognition is for Lacan an exceptional one brought on by his own desires to escape his everyday life. He has very little stake in being properly (mis)recognized by the Brittany fisherman, and despite a moment of personal discomfort at the sardine fisherman's dismissive response to his presence, Lacan can put this instance of nonrecognition behind him, as merely a bizarre experience. His solution to the problem of not being recognized by the Brittany fisherman is obvious; he will simply return to Paris, to the company of people whose desires are compatible with his own. What is significant is that Lacan does not consider the possibility of attempting to engage with the fisherman in such a way as to bring about a greater degree of mutual understanding and thus the cognitive grounds for mutual recognition.

Lacan's example resonates all too intimately with the experiences of women and cultural minorities, typically more close to home. A woman might recollect a hundred instances when she felt like the young Lacan earnestly out to sea off Brittany, brought up short by the fisherman and the sardine can which that glinted at him knowingly in the sun, while explicitly failing to recognize his presence. But a woman invites the alienating experience of anticipatory nonrecognition merely by entering a public space dominated by patriarchal symbolic codes of desire and recognition. It is often within a chosen professional or social group that the startling incident of nonrecognition occurs. Sometimes a woman, or a relevant part of a woman, fails to be acknowledged in any fashion. For example, a woman is not called on when she raises her hand at a meeting, as if female hands themselves became invisible within patriarchal social spaces. At other times a woman will speak in the midst of a discussion, and someone else will immediately take up her point, and somehow it will become his point. Her voice can be heard within a patriarchal discourse, but only if appropriated by a male body.

Everyone is misrecognized within society, according to Lacan. Psychic agency in response to this phenomenon of misrecognition is indefatigable and personally dynamic; we seek out the Other's gaze in a multiplicity of locations, always disappointed, and always hopeful. Yet socially our relationship to the Other and to language is quite static, according to Lacan; we accept each instance of misrecognition as inevitable. We can always move on to another. We do not find it necessary to engage critically with a particular instance of misrecognition—for we do not presume to question the desire of the Other, or the linguistic form it takes. ✗

I have tried to show, however, that women are paradigmatically on a boat off Brittany within their daily existence, not merely misrecognized in the typical sense but frequently unrecognized by male colleagues or lovers for important contributions they make to a shared enterprise. Women cannot simply leave the boat or the boardroom or the relationship and return "home" to be amid people whose subjective desires allow them to include women in their vision. Where would they find such a home? The anticipatory nonrecognition of women is built into the very symbolic codes women grow up articulating their own identities and agency within. For this reason, women can also ill afford to respond to instances of nonrecognition in the passive psychic mode assumed by psychoanalysis. To simply swallow instances of nonrecognition alongside other forms of (mis)recognition is for women to continue to recognize themselves according to a traditional code of female inferiority which their activities and social positions now belie.

Women, in fact, tend to remain on the boat, in the meeting, in the relationship, attempting to negotiate for more viable relationships of (mis)recognition with men. Women are driven by the same narcissistic passions by which Lacan explains the uncritical relationship of men to patriarchal symbolic systems. Their psychic struggle for recognition can hardly leave these patriarchal symbolic systems behind. But for a woman to remain tolerant of the capricious gaze of a signifying system which recognizes her in one instant for her achievements and in the next moment denies her female subjectivity is quite unthinkable if we take Lacan's notion of the narcissistic passion for recognition seriously. A woman will be impelled to engage critically in social discourses where insulting instances of nonrecognition occur. She will find herself proceeding in opposition to such a signifying system, necessarily seeking to rewrite its codes of recognition. In the context of the larger social formation in which women's rights and responsibilities are now being transformed this will not be an idle project; women are potentially capable of transforming retrograde patriarchal signifying structures which no longer correspond sufficiently with social practices.

The personal psychic struggles of women for recognition can thus only be comprehended by acknowledging this immediately political dimension of their desire for recognition. Narcissistic passion will lead women to break out of the self-contained circuits of desiring (mis)recognition when disparities between the patriarchal gaze and more affirmative social gazes become apparent. The normal desire for recognition will lead women to become activated or critical in relation to both the signifying systems as well as in relation to Others utilizing these systems. Lacanian theory can help us comprehend the social trajectory of women's desires if we attend to the current implications of the social enfranchisement of women as signifying agents within patriarchal systems of recognition.

v.   Vital Feminist Glances: Painting Ourselves into the Picture

In pornography the patriarchal gaze of nonrecognition stares with naked hostility out at women today. I have argued that women are psychically constituted as critical in relation to this gaze. The question is: How may women best act to transform it? Antipornography feminists are quite appropriately angry about the demeaning way in which women are represented in pornography. Their solution is appealing, and appalling, insofar as it operates on the same visceral level as does the pornographic image. In effect, the antipornography ordinances would allow women to scratch out the eyes of the pornographer, as traditional Moslem law allows victims the solace of cutting off the guilty hands of criminals. Opposition to the antipornography ordinances presumably springs, in part, from a deep-seated sense of outrage at the presumptuousness of this feminist desire to molest the male gaze in such a fashion. The most important failing of the antipornography ordinances, however, lies in their narrowing of the feminist project. In a yet-patriarchal world order, the demeaning gaze is everywhere, although typically much more repressed than in pornography. An effectively critical stance of women in relation to pornography must be based upon an understanding of the connections between the pornographic gaze and all the other social discourses that perpetuate an oppressive patriarchal gaze in our society.

It is imperative, in the first place, that women be capable of looking at a pornographic image without seeing themselves in it. Lacan interprets the Gospel, "They have eyes that they might not see" as suggesting the capacity of individuals to choose to look at other people in order not to submit to their gaze. Yet he points out that we typically respond to paintings and other visual representations by "laying down our gaze," even sometimes feeling ourselves "caught in the trap" of the artist's vision.[44] From his psychoanalytic perspective, Lacan is not interested in the social power relationships that determine who actively looks, and who passively experiences the gaze of the Other. In fact, a dominant patriarchal gaze is typically embedded in paintings and other representations, as well as in written texts. We are lured into laying down our own gaze and participating in that which is presented to us. It is this seductive quality that is so unnerving about pornography and other sexist texts today. But socially enfranchised women can resist seduction by an overtly patriarchal gaze insofar as it does not accord with the rest of their experiences of themselves in various positions of social engagement and authority today.

Twenty years ago, when the second wave of feminism was just beginning, many women dramatically refused to wear makeup, bras, and other codified symbols of femininity. It was important to publicly express the fact that we refused to identify with sexist images of women. Now that many women, and even many feminists, have returned to wearing makeup and bras, there is a tendency to interpret this as a defeat for feminist principles. In fact, a contrary reading is more appropriate. Feminists can don makeup and other signifiers of femininity again insofar as the point has long since been made that women need not identify with or submit to sexist images of women. June Cleaver (the mother of Beaver) is no longer the norm for women, and Marilyn Monroe is not the feminine ideal. Both have become identifiable as cultural stereotypes of womanhood. As Norman Bryson explains, "The stereotype exists and is known at just those points where it does not tally with the evidence, where it comes away from the surface of practice: it establishes two zones, of enchanted representation and disenchanted experience."[45] Women who wear makeup today participate in both zones of cultural experience.

Feminists can clothe themselves in traditional signifiers of femininity instrumentally rather than ecstatically. Stereotypical modes of presentation evoke positive responses socially, but it is dangerous for a female self to identify strongly with these responses or succumb to the gaze that appreciates her self-consciously codified femininity. Women have the capacity to be self-conscious social actors now rather than traditional passive objects of the patriarchal gaze. Narcissistic passion propels women into signifying engagements and interactions, playing to the expectations of the patriarchal gaze while hoping to rewrite the patriarchal codes which deny women, ahead of time, the quality of recognition they aspire to. Participation in such risky signifying enterprises is increasingly a part of everyday life for women.

Women have no choice but to attempt to rewrite patriarchal codes of recognition. Yet in setting themselves in opposition to the patriarchal gaze, feminist theorists find themselves in a particularly difficult position. The patriarchal gaze is eroding in various spots, but it is still associated with all the dominant social discourses. The theoretical status of any femi-

nist critique is thus necessarily precarious. In attempting to characterize
the status of a feminist theoretical critique in relation to an entrenched patriarchal gaze, it may be helpful to extend our use of visual metaphors, and
contrast the distant ubiquity of the patriarchal gaze with the ephemeral intensity of feminist glances. Norman Bryson has pointed out that by
visually emphasizing the brushstrokes that constitute a particular painting, Chinese art represents the temporal process of producing the picture.
It thus offers us an immediate, shifting, fragile *glance* at the world rather
than the timeless, disembodied *gaze* idealized within modern European
painting.[46] The glance is thus the viewpoint of the actual painter as she
paints or of the writer as she writes; it is the creative envisioning of new
subjects of discursive recognition. The feminist theoretical or artistic
glance is actively signifying meanings that may or may not endure as part
of a disembodied social gaze.

Women are engaging critically and creatively with the dominant theoretical and practical discourses in a diverse array of situations, and there
are signs that their interventions are having an effect. But feminist critiques are glancing blows to a still-patriarchal firmament. We set off momentarily blinding fireworks which cast an eerie glow upon an everyday
life that tends to go on as before. Various commentators have remarked,
for example, that the continuing notoriety of Andrea Dworkin's and
Catharine MacKinnon's views is evidence that pornography does not successfully silence women. Dworkin and MacKinnon would surely reply
that their personal fame/notoriety has little effect on the degradation of
women's daily lives in and through pornography. Ultimately, of course,
we may hope that the many glancing blows of feminist critiques will lead
dominant social discourses to attempt to exorcise their patriarchal features, but it will be a messy process. The hoary old patriarchal gaze tends
to be at once so ambient and so distant that the intense local discourses of
feminism have difficulty connecting with it, despite the fact that they are
structurally constituted in opposition to it.

The pornographic gaze does not seem distant at all, flagrantly exposing
its desires for all to see. Yet it is a desiring gaze which refuses even to flirt
with existing feminist glances, sacrificing carnal immediacy in order to
gird itself against transgressive female sexual agency. From a feminist perspective, it is far easier to disengage from the stark, unyielding porno-
graphics of the patriarchal gaze than it is to reengage with it critically. We
may choose to disengage in the passionate mode of the pornography separation mythologies I suggested above in section iii, recognizing men behind the gaze as "fathers who would rape daughters." Or we may disengage in the calmer practical mode of the contemporary woman who

recognizes the preferences of men for passive, "two-dimensional" women in both professional and personal relationships. In either case, it is difficult to imagine how to constructively recognize the men behind pornography in modes that would require them to recognize contemporary "multidimensional" women.[47]

Pornography finally confronts us with a potentially tragic dimension of the current feminist struggle for recognition. Women can industriously work within and upon the various discourses of social power, attempting to rearticulate them so that women and women's achievements are more likely to be recognized. Feminist thinkers can brilliantly rewrite social theories to put men and women in their rightful places theoretically. But women cannot finally force men to recognize them. Women cannot act directly to dissolve the patriarchal gaze.[48] Some such dimension of existential uncertainty is present in any radical social project, of course. Women need to be both wary and hopeful in recognizing the men behind the patriarchal gaze.

3

Cyborgean Motherhood and Abortion

Abortion has become an important component of family planning practices of women worldwide over the last twenty-five years; as women's reliance upon abortion has grown, political opposition and moral reaction have grown apace. Attacks on women's reproductive freedom have been particularly loud recently within Eastern Europe, where the abortion rights of women are linked with a failed state socialism and threatened by a resurgent Catholic church. In the United States, President Clinton's appointment of Ruth Ginsburg to the Supreme Court makes it unlikely that *Roe v. Wade* will be overturned, allowing states to again make abortion a crime. The millions of illegal abortions in Brazil, or the millions of legal ones in the former Soviet Union, remain, however, potential sites for conservative attacks on what has become a basic procreative practice of women. Abortion controversies today are a multicultural symptom of gender ferment just under the skin of the global body.

It is easy to be weary of, and even bored by, the debate over abortion despite its political significance. In practical terms, abortion exists on a continuum with other procreative powers of women today, a necessary feature of life in the late twentieth century. Laws against abortion will not stem the tide of women seeking abortions; they will only make access to abortions more difficult, and typically most difficult for young, poor, geographically isolated women, precisely the populations of women who already suffer from lack of access to contraception and other aids to procreative choice. Given the moralistic hostility of powerful, conservative men to the unmarried, welfare-supported motherhood of the women whose access to abortion they are most prepared to curtail, the antiabortion movement in this country does not accord with cultural common sense. Furthermore, in a time of escalating urban violence, extreme poverty, drug abuse, and racism in the United States it is shocking to hear philosophers and politicians alike portray abortion as one of the leading moral questions of our times.

We can best understand the intensity of the opposition to abortion by recognizing the success of a campaign to demonize it as a symbolic attack upon traditional families. The battle to take abortion rights away from women has become one of the most popular conservative causes, comparable to the antipornography movement ten years ago in its ability to politicize a population of middle Americans who had shown no previous activist tendencies. Indeed, by stepping back from the social realities of daily abortion decisions for women we can appreciate the conservative drama of maternal goodness against nihilistic radical feminism which the antiabortion movement relies upon. Women who seek abortions are already pregnant, already marked by the "natural" sign of their eternal maternal role. In seeking an abortion, women directly challenge the traditional mandate of good motherhood, daring to renounce the most basic form of female responsibility and one of the only legitimate sources of female significance throughout history.

i. Interpersonal Agency: Rethinking Our Paradigms of Action

The abortion controversy puts the changing quality of women's agency on the line. If there was one social role with which women were universally identified, it was the role of motherhood. It was a sex-specific site of significant social behavior corresponding with diverse sites of significant male behavior. While male public-sphere agency has been associated with notions of rational individual motivation and reward, however, the maternal role of women has been characterized primarily in terms of its onerous obligations and duties. An individual woman might be enthusiastic about becoming a mother, or she might not be. Her generic, womanly desires were inferred from her birth as a woman; her actual individual desires were simply not relevant. She might reap great rewards as a consequence of her performance as a mother, or she might not. Hopes of recognition or reward were not a socially acceptable basis for choosing to mother, as they were a self-evidently necessary basis for male public-sphere activities.

We might be tempted to say that women were denied the most important aspects of individual agency insofar as their desires were not taken into account under traditional patriarchal kinship arrangements.[1] In chapter 1, I compared the status of women with that of slaves, insofar as women were, like slaves, denied independent identities under patriarchy. Women typically lived out their lives as subsumed nurturers, contributing to and participating in the public identities of their husbands and male children. Like slaves, women and their actions were taken for granted, regardless of their actual contribution to the achievements of the master or husband who did gain social recognition. Yet I distinguished the status of women from slaves because women were allowed a qualitatively differ-ent sense of participation in the lives of their husbands and families. So-cially recognized as bearing the children who would carry on the family name, women were not merely human instruments, but were seen by others and by themselves as significant parts of the family whole. In this sense, it is appropriate to say that women exercised maternal and other forms of agency under patriarchy in a way that slaves did not. But the agency of women was not characterized by the individuated choices and rewards accorded to liberal men. It was their individual responsibilities as subsumed nurturers that provided women with a sense of their own im-portance, and in this specific sense, of their agency.

With the social enfranchisement of women, the scope of women's agency changes dramatically, most obviously as they enter the liberal pub-lic sphere as economic and political agents alongside men. But the quality of their domestic agency is altered as well. As I pointed out in chapter 1, it is misleading to think of women today as simply augmenting their tradi-tional female role with what was formerly the male role. Neither of the traditional gender roles of subsumed nurturer or patriarchal benefactor survives for very long in the wake of the social enfranchisement of women. Men and women may continue to go through many of the same domestic motions, and so retain the appearances of their former relation-ship identities. But it is when we evaluate the changing qualities of their still gendered forms of agency that we can mark the magnitude of the transformations taking place.

At this point, it is possible to specify three different *dimensions of agency: individual motivation, responsibility, and the expectation of reward or recognition.* We may attribute agency to an individual if we ascertain that at least one of these dimensions is important in evaluating his or her actions. But not all dimensions are equal in their ability to confer a social identity upon an individual. The oppression of women under Western forms of patriarchy, as well as its current decline, may be tracked quite effectively by taking note of the changing dimensions of agency ascribed to women and men. Under liberal forms of patriarchy, men were understood as the sort of be-ings capable of choosing their individual destiny, expressing basic mate-rial and social desires in individuated ways, and properly seeking particu-lar sorts of social recognition and reward. Women were only recognized for fulfilling subordinate roles in the context of families headed by men; they were not deemed capable of making individuated choices about their own particular destiny or that of their family.

With social enfranchisement, we begin to attribute to women the ca-pacity to make the same sorts of individuated, rational choices about their economic and political destiny as men. Since such choices frequently conflict with traditional maternal obligations, we gradually begin to assume that women will make individuated choices about whether or not to take on the familial responsibilities they were expected to accept unthinkingly under patriarchy. That is, we become interested for the first time in women's particular motivations for becoming wives and mothers. We acknowledge that there may be reasons why a particular woman might choose not to fulfill maternal or domestic responsibilities. And we also become interested for the first time in articulating the particular quality of the rewards and forms of recognition attendant upon assuming the maternal role. A more complete notion of maternal agency begins to come into play.[2]

Despite the fact that we now assume the need to understand individual motivations in taking on family obligations, it is not obvious *how* to characterize women's new modalities of agency in relation to the family — or men's, for that matter. There is a very long tradition of feminist thinkers who have attempted to portray the distinctive quality of women's traditional practices and values within the home.[3] But what we are concerned with here are the practices and values of women and men within the home in a new, quite nontraditional context of individual familial choice. The controversy over abortion arises in this radically nontraditional context of maternal agency.

Both the inevitability and the inadequacy of analogies with public-sphere motivations and choices are evident in current ways of referring to decisions about whether or not to take on maternal responsibilities. We frequently explain an abortion decision by saying that a pregnancy was "unplanned" or "unwanted," suggesting that children produced under such circumstances would suffer from being "unwanted." Of course, many pregnancies are unwanted, and many children do suffer from lack of attention from their parents. But the phrase summons up thoughts of other wanted and unwanted items in daily life: I want green beans for dinner, and I want it to be sunny tomorrow for the picnic. A child is neither wanted nor unwanted in these terms of immediate daily preference. To speak of a pregnancy or a child as wanted or unwanted is to trivialize the issue a pregnant woman faces when she thinks about whether she has the capacity and the will to devote decades of her life to caring for a child.

Those who oppose abortion believe that women continue to have an unqualified responsibility to become mothers. By contrast, those who believe in the legitimacy of abortion insist that women's maternal responsibilities can now only be articulated in a way that allows for the relevance of women's individual sense of social agency, maternal choice being but one component in such agency. Analogies between the decision of a woman to have an abortion and other sorts of individual choice are typically strained and unconvincing because procreative agency is not very much like the economic and political forms of agency we have most experience in evaluating. We need to begin thinking in terms of a distinctive quality of motivations, obligations, and rewards appropriate to procreative and other familial or communal activities. It may even be helpful to construct a category of agency that will make it possible for us to conceptualize the common features of the individuated decisions of women and men alike in relation to contemporary kinship and community relationships.

I will propose a category of *interpersonal agency,* referring to the motivations, responsibilities, and rewards or forms of recognition associated with efforts to create and maintain affirmative connections with other individuals. I see the advantages of a category of interpersonal agency as twofold. In the first place, a notion of interpersonal agency will provide the framework for a new paradigm of procreative relationships, enabling us to radically revise our conception of women's maternal agency, and thereby the quality of women's authority to initiate a process like abortion. Second, a notion of interpersonal agency asserts a relationship between women's maternal agency and forms of agency exercised more generally by men as well as women in creating and maintaining kinship and community connections.

We can, perhaps, imagine a time not too far off when men and women alike will be able to become pregnant, or alternatively when parturition will take place outside any individual human body. Until that time, pregnancy and abortion will remain very much women's issues. I will maintain, however, that currently sex-specific decisions about procreation lie on a continuum with decisions about marriage, friendship, parenting, divorce, and a variety of interpersonal connections within workplace and community which have become salient, and often problematic, nodal points in the lives of men as well as women. In order to understand abortion and the new conception of maternal agency on which it rests, we need to show its relationship to these other issues which are not exclusively attached to women. A notion of interpersonal agency will thus allow us to rethink and revalue an increasingly confusing gender-, race-, and class-inflected texture of everyday relationships and global practices.

ii.   Foundations of the Abortion Controversy

We need to have a clear sense of how the current abortion debate both plays upon and drastically revises historical notions of abortion and maternal agency. Women have been aborting fetuses for thousands of years within Western cultures, and it ought to seem puzzling that abortion has only become controversial in the last fifty to one hundred years. Despite a famous critique by Saint Paul, philosophers and even theologians commonly accepted the practice of abortion until recently. Articulating the viewpoint of classical Greek culture, for example, Aristotle judged abortion, and even infanticide, to be ethical practices when done under the proper circumstances.[4] And for a great many centuries, the Catholic church considered abortion unobjectionable if done within a several-month-long period of gestation prior to fetal "quickening." Societal attitudes toward reproductive issues were primarily pragmatic; abortion and other means of limiting family size were encouraged when times were difficult, becoming less acceptable whenever a higher birth rate was desired. Abortion was a means of population control; it was not a vehicle by which individual women could presume to escape maternal responsibilities.[5]

The meaning of abortion has shifted quite radically within the twentieth century; in the United States this change has occurred primarily over the last twenty years since the Supreme Court decision of Roe v. Wade in 1973. Alongside various technologies of contraception and fertility enhancement, abortion is now a procedure through which women exercise reproductive control. Individual women are increasingly expected to choose when to have children, and even whether to have them at all. While the majority of women, both in the United States and worldwide, continue to bear children at some point in their lives, the number of children born to individual women declines statistically with the availability of contraception. Aided by the various technologies of procreative control, women are focusing more on nonmaternal activities in most Western countries. The naturalistic identification of women with motherhood is seriously undermined by the large degree of reproductive voluntarism evident not simply in the United States, but throughout the world.[6]

Conservatives, and particularly those who feel a stake in maintaining a naturalistic identification of women with motherhood, are understandably upset by these recent developments. While there does not seem to be a great deal that they can do to restore an organic view of reproduction and the family, many have turned to religious narratives of maternal identity as offering potential ideological support for their beliefs. According to Judeo-Christian narratives, for example, the pregnancy of a woman evokes assumptions that some higher power has magnanimously placed a seed of life in her womb.[7] A natural maternal identity associated with womanhood is thus activated by a divine power. When a woman today chooses to say "No" to this gift, as a woman does when she uses contraception as well as when she seeks an abortion, she is transgressive of the higher authority of God. In the context of this patriarchal religious narrative, such a woman takes on a *subaltern maternal identity*, to adopt a term Gayatri Spivak has used to refer to "insurgent" subjects of national forms of colonialism.[8] In the case of the subaltern maternal woman, her womb provides the turf for attempted acts of patriarchal colonization. According to this religious narrative, a woman exhibits a subaltern maternal identity whenever she exercises a form of reproductive control, but it is never so evident as in abortion. With other forms of contraception a woman merely defers the gift of maternity; in abortion she refuses it outright.

Theologians and various other social conservatives in the United States have settled upon abortion as the site of women's new reproductive assertiveness most vulnerable to critique by means of a religious narrative. This strategy has led the Catholic church and various Protestant churches to take a newly absolutist stance according to which human life begins at conception, allowing them to declare that a woman's act of abortion is always an act of murder. In this aggressive and desperate new conservative script, God's authority over women and fetuses is asserted in such a way as to deny a woman's moral right to reproductive determination in this last instance. The involuntary maternal quality of female identity is seemingly resecured—but only tenuously, as there is reasonable doubt among religious believers as to whether the hand of God has been properly invoked in this case.[9]

Many feminists have taken abortion rights to be a fundamental feature of women's program for social emancipation. The naturalistic maternal identity of women has played such a large part in various forms of patriarchal domination that securing control over the procreative process has been deemed both necessary in a practical sense, and symbolically crucial to women's social enfranchisement. Prior to *Roe v. Wade*, and in the twenty years of rear-guard conservative struggle to overturn it since 1973, feminists have viewed the battle over the abortion rights of women as primarily a *political* contest between feminism and worldly structures of patriarchal power. In refusing to respect the rights of women to bodily autonomy, religious narratives of fetal rights fail to take the liberal personhood of women seriously, according to many feminists. From such a political perspective, religious narratives that deny the basic physical and social conditions of women's enfranchisement as liberal agents are woeful anachronisms rather than arguments to be debated.

Since the majority of people would presumably identify themselves neither as feminists nor as conservatives, it can be difficult to assess popular attitudes toward abortion. Kristin Luker offers a sociological interpretation of the abortion controversy that attempts to get beneath the abstractions of religious conservatism and feminist politics, and she begins to capture some of the cultural complexities of the current situation. She presents the abortion debate as a conflict between two groups of people who are devoted to fundamentally different values and ways of life. For prolife men and women alike, she argues, abortion represents an unwonted repudiation of women's traditional role, wherein motherhood was primary and pregnancy was the first stage of motherhood. For prochoice forces, the right to abortion represents a cornerstone of women's new sexual freedom and bodily autonomy, as well as serving as an enabling condition for women's new social and economic responsibilities. Insofar as the abortion controversy has come to stand for the opposition between actual groups of people who either wish to preserve traditional patriarchal family relationships or who reject these as oppressive to women and men, Luker predicts that no theoretical grounds will be found for resolving the debate.[10]

While Luker correctly identifies the ideological quality of the current abortion debates, her analysis is simplified by the fact that the women she studied were activists on either side of the issue with personal identities forged upon unequivocal commitment to an oppositional political position. Other researchers have found that among a more general populace, the attitudes of individuals toward abortion are much more ambivalent. The ideological divisions Luker found characteristic of different groups of people, in fact, seem to be experienced by many individuals as intense and unresolvable *internal* conflicts. Mary Ann Lamanna, for example, concludes on the basis of her research that opposing values for and against abortion are often held by the same individual.[11] Thus both women and men who assert that abortion must be an individual woman's right nonetheless express moral qualms about abortion. Legal thinker Lawrence Tribe assesses the current abortion debate as involving a "clash of absolutes," arguing that most people feel sympathy for *both* the pregnant woman who does not wish to bring a fetus to term and for a fetus which deserves to be protected.[12]

While we may all suffer from a sense of confusion over the morality of abortion, the primary victims of the current cultural ambivalence are clearly the women who experience unplanned pregnancies and must decide whether to have an abortion or carry the child to term. These women occupy a truly unenviable position: they are destined to choose between the ethically tainted freedom of a rational social agent who has an abor-

tion, and the self-sacrificing goodness of a woman who decides to reconfigure the next eighteen years of her life to accommodate motherhood.
The frequency with which women face this traumatizing choice painfully
illuminates the experiential basis for Denise Riley's notion of the "fluctuating identities" of women. Riley suggests, in fact, that since any category
of identity is necessarily unstable, feminism should simply accept
women's "fluctuating identities" rather than seeking to prescribe an appropriate identity.[13] The undesirable qualities of *both* of the identities
available to women who must decide for or against an abortion explain
all too well, however, feminist motivations in formulating positive female
identities. Too many female identities continue to be oppressive. If the
effort to advocate positive female identities is a futile process — and I agree
with Riley that it is — we need to find other means of combating the oppressive quality of women's reproductive positions.

There have been a number of suggestions about how to dissolve the
ideological "clash of absolutes" in the abortion debate. After cogently
identifying the internal moral dilemma experienced by many people today, Tribe himself rather lamely concludes that this clash of moral absolutes can only be resolved through the democratic process of "voting and
persuasion."[14] If such moral confusion is really the product of internal
psychic conflicts, however, it seems clear that the solution cannot occur
on a purely formal political level but must include some more substantive
efforts toward resolving the moral conflicts. The apparent clash of absolutes in the abortion debate surely reflects the fact that the conservative
religion-based narrative repudiating abortion and the feminist political
defenses of women's right to abortion have typically sought to displace
each other without attempting to take each other on theoretically. When
ideological opponents occupy fundamentally different standpoints, the
arguments of both sides can appear persuasive to someone not personally
identified with either standpoint. The goal must be to find common theoretical terrain for resolving the issues.

One such attempt has been made by analytic philosophers who have
responded to the religious claim that abortion is murder by attempting to
formulate criteria for determining whether the fetus has personhood, and
if so, at what stage of pregnancy personhood and a fetus's right to life begins. Unfortunately, no particularly persuasive answers to this question
have emerged.[15] Philosopher Bernard Williams scoffs at such efforts, appealing to the abortion controversy as evidence for his own theory that
ethical conflicts can no longer be resolved by means of philosophically
reasoned solutions. He suggests that the appropriate response to apparently irresolvable moral disagreements is not to seek a principled moral

solution at all, but rather to ask what sorts of "institutions, upbringing, and public discourse" will enable people to feel "ethical confidence" about whatever they choose to do.[16]

Williams is correct, I think, in proclaiming the futility of the metaphysical game of designating the moment at which a fetus attains personhood; and he is perceptive in suggesting that what is needed is a broad-based social reorientation so that women considering abortion can feel confident about whatever decision they finally make. But he is too quick to conclude that we can achieve such a goal without stirring up enduring philosophical questions and challenging some of the old solutions. *The philosophical issue is not about the personhood of the fetus, but about the personhood of women.* Insofar as naturalistic theories of motherhood are inadequate for understanding women's current social responsibilities in reproductive matters, we need to rethink our notions of women's procreative agency.

In *Abortion and Woman's Choice,* Rosiland Petchesky persuasively demonstrates that we lack adequate conceptual and normative frameworks for the reproductive choices we must make. After analyzing with subtlety and compassion the degree to which women and men at all points on the social spectrum are troubled by abortion and related reproductive decisions, she argues that we need a "popular feminist ideology" to provide a social foundation for the legal rights to abortion provided by the Supreme Court in *Roe v. Wade.*[17]

While I agree with Petchesky about the need for a better theoretical framework for making sense of reproductive decisions and justifying abortion, I think the social context in which we operate as feminist thinkers has changed in important ways in the years since she asserted the need for a popular feminist ideology. As Petchesky herself demonstrated, the abortion issue is one that affects women and men in every social stratum. After twenty years of legal abortion in this country, there are few adults who do not have a close friend or acquaintance who has had an abortion. As a consequence of abortion's infiltration of popular culture, what we need in the 1990s is not a feminist ideology so much as simply a conceptual framework capable of enabling everyone to make more confident reproductive decisions. Whether or not women or men identify themselves as feminists, they stand in need of this product of feminist theory.

Because of the breadth of the potential audience, a conceptual framework for thinking about reproductive decisions should not be formulated as a feminist ideology. Along with other reproductive technologies and choices, abortion has become what I will cautiously designate a *postfeminist issue.* The scope of the problem leads us beyond a solution articulated purely in terms of "a female-embodied social subject," to refer to Teresa de Lauretis's recent discussion of the content of any feminist theory.[18] Previous feminist ideologies addressed feminists and all those women, as well as those few men, who were potential feminists. On a topic like abortion, it is evident that this is too narrow a field of address. A contemporary feminist strategy needs to adapt itself to an era in which fewer people are willing to become ideologically identified with any political movement, when at the same time many more people are enmeshed in daily gender-based struggles and conflicts. Feminism is a personal and political origin point for many women today, but for strategic political reasons feminism should be regarded as a theoretical and psychological resource rather than an identifying political uniform.[19]

The many divisions within traditional forms of community in the United States, and the no-longer-absolute authority of structures of kinship and community taken for granted a generation ago, mean that responsibility for the making and breaking of interpersonal connections increasingly falls upon the shoulders of individuals. In decisions about marriage, child-bearing, child-rearing, divorce, remarriage, and job changes involving large geographical moves, women and men of all social backgrounds are confronted daily with choices and responsibilities for the construction, maintenance, destruction, and reconstruction of relationships of kinship and community that were previously secured by mandates of divine, historical, customary, or natural authority.

The antiabortion movement has opportunistically mined what is perhaps an inevitable vein of cultural fear in reaction to the increase in individual responsibility and control over interpersonal relationships. Once we have recognized the surplus moral value they would have us vest in abortion, however, we can attempt to distribute our moral concerns more evenly over a broad spectrum of significant interpersonal decisions engaged in by both women and men. This is a process that will be encouraged by a concept of interpersonal agency, but we must first clear a pathway through various confusing attempts to rationalize abortion by means of current theoretical models.

iii. Traditional Maternal Narratives Compromise Abortion Justifications

In order to explain and finally disperse the odd cloud of social obviousness and moral wrongfulness that hovers over discussions of abortion, we will need to investigate several layers of liberal political theory that currently provide the basis for defending the abortion rights of women. The practice of abortion on demand in Western countries was made possible by values associated with a liberal paradigm of individual agency. The present technology of contraception and abortion was developed in the context of a capitalist market interest in supplying services for which there was correctly presumed to be a large potential demand. Abortions have become one of an array of gynecological health services that individual women within developed Western countries have come to rely upon pursuant to leading a normal adult life.

Yet the quality of the social choices exercised by women and men making procreation decisions is quite different from that presumed by economic and political conceptions of autonomous individual agency. Indeed, the Supreme Court's *Roe v. Wade* decision disappointed many feminists by refusing to defend abortion as a matter of each individual woman's right to the autonomy of her body. Justice Blackmun instead emphasized the personal and private quality of the decision to have an abortion, making a woman's constitutional right to abortion a consequence of the constitutional right to privacy. One of the weaknesses of Roe's defense of abortion, particularly evident since the Webster decision in 1989 allowing increased state regulation of abortion facilities, is that the public space in which abortions are provided and utilized is rather at odds with the Supreme Court's characterization of abortion as a private decision.[20]

Both the laissez-faire vision of abortion as merely another commodified medical service and the legal vision of abortion as an aspect of the individual right to privacy involve formal attempts to extend liberal frameworks to shield abortion from public review. Neither goes very far in explaining or morally justifying individual acts of abortion.[21] If we lay aside these formal legal and economic frameworks, there remain two substantive possibilities for conceptualizing women's grounds for choosing an abortion within liberalism. On the one hand, we may make a rights-based argument for *the right of a woman to the autonomy of her body*. To make this argument stick, we must assert that an individual's right to an autonomous body "trumps" any countervailing rights that a fetus may have to develop within a woman's womb.[22] On the other hand, we may construct a more utilitarian defense of abortion as a desirable social policy. In this case, we will maintain that the social situation today is such that it is in *the interests of society* that individual women be allowed to choose to have an abortion when they feel it appropriate. I will briefly assess why rights-based and consequentialist approaches both fall short of offering an acceptable contemporary vision of abortion.

Judith Jarvis Thomson makes perhaps the strongest argument for basing a political right to an abortion upon a woman's right to the autonomy of her body. She goes so far as to argue that even if we believe the fetus to be a person, it has no fundamental moral or political right to demand that a woman donate her body as a life support system to enable its survival. A fortiori, in the first months after conception, when our sense of the fetus as a person is least strong, a woman's right to assert the autonomy of her body by means of an abortion becomes even more compelling.[23]

Thomson's analysis notoriously begins with a bizarre comparison between a woman who finds herself pregnant and a woman who awakes one morning to find herself hooked up to a famous violinist who will die if she denies him the use of her kidneys for nine months. Her analogy between the demands of an importunate fetus and those of a famous violin player wishing a woman to serve as his life-support system for nine months dramatically conveys the idea that a pregnant woman may experience herself as hostage to a fetus. Thomson characterizes the traditional maternal role of women as that of a Good Samaritan, required to sacrifice everything on behalf of a needy fetus. This standard of obligation does not seem fair today. We do not require men to make such sacrifices; there are even occasions when we allow men to kill another person in self-defense. Thomson thus argues that a woman has the right to deny the demands of a fetus-person by aborting it, in self-defense.

The problem with Thomson's political rendering of the relationship between a pregnant woman and a fetus is that it rests upon, and actually exaggerates, a traditional image of pregnancy as involving the implantation of another living being in a woman's womb. The needy violinist, like a needy fetus-person, will be sustained or denied in its already begun life by a woman who will decide whether or not she will grant its importunate request. Even if one is persuaded by Thomson's argument that a woman has a right to defend herself against any such request, Thomson's pregnant woman is not in an enviable moral position. Somewhat better off than Lawrence Tribe's pregnant woman who finds herself attempting to resolve an absolute conflict between the values of personal liberty and fetus life, Thomson's pregnant woman is still in a morally compromising position. Not too surprisingly, Thomson points out that in certain circumstances we might judge a woman "self-centered and callous, indecent in fact, but not unjust" if she decided to have an abortion. An analogy with a celebrated defense of the freedom of speech by Oliver Wendell Holmes may provide the most apt perspective on this defense of abortion. Justice Holmes declared that the most important function of the First Amendment lay in its protection of "the thought that we hate." In Thomson's account of abortion, the principled quality of our commitment to a woman's right to the autonomy of her body is proven by our recognition that this right protects abortions we may personally deem morally unsavory.[24] If women are ever to become morally confident in their abortion decisions, we will have to replace the traditional images of maternal responsibility which undermine Thomson's revisionary theory of a pregnant woman's rights with a substantively different vision of procreative agency.

We might initially rest our hopes for a different vision of procreative agency upon those moral and political philosophers who assert that the rights of fetuses are not at issue in discussions of abortion. Rights are presumed to adhere to persons, and while fetuses may be characterized as future-persons, they show a degree of unformedness and dependence that may render them nonpersons in any meaningful legal or political sense. According to such thinkers, the personhood status of the fetus is so peculiar that we should not attempt to assess the moral obligations of a pregnant woman toward a fetus in terms of its rights. Instead, we may take a utilitarian approach, according to which we evaluate the consequences for society as a whole of allowing individual women to have abortions. It is not difficult to make the case for abortion in terms of a straightforward cost-benefit analysis. We may toll the immediate misery and suffering to mother and child alike that are the frequent consequences of forcing women to bear children they are unprepared to love and care for, as well as the long-term costs to society in both economic and noneconomic terms. Whether we emphasize the size of the welfare rolls or the statistics on educational performance or crime, it is not difficult to show the social disadvantages when women lack sufficient economic, social, or psychological resources to care for their children properly.[25]

While consequentialist approaches effectively make the social case for allowing abortion, they do no better than rights-based arguments in providing individual women with a sufficient basis for ethical confidence in deciding to have an abortion. It is quite possible to believe that society, the pregnant woman herself, and even the fetus benefit from abortion without ceasing to believe that an individual act of abortion is morally wrong.[26] As in utilitarian moral arguments generally, the point is to determine the act that promotes the most beneficial consequences. The individual action that best promotes the social good is justified instrumentally, even if it may be judged an intrinsically evil action. Many people reason about abortion in this way, taking Lawrence Tribe's clash of moral absolutes for granted and judging abortion to be a "necessary evil" within our society.[27]

Utilitarian arguments often rely upon an analogy between production and reproduction, or between workers and mothers, each person contributing to the social good through their role in the productive or reproductive process. This production analogy might at first sight seem a good strategy for reconfiguring our image of maternal agency in such a way as to give women moral confidence in their authority over all procreative decisions. If women are seen as reproductive entrepreneurs, then it is their social obligation to make all decisions about starting and stopping fetal production. The problem, however, has been that women have not been envisioned as reproductive entrepreneurs, but as mere workers within a reproductive process initiated by God or Nature. Whether the reproductive woman is presumed to be laboring in the service of God or nature, the traditional model of involuntary maternity has hardly been jettisoned.

Thus when a pregnant woman decides to have an abortion, it is as if she is choosing to destroy an Ur-product as it begins to progress along the womb stages of child production. Such destruction is most readily justifiable if the Ur-person is malformed, as with the involuntary "abortions" that occur naturally in the first months of pregnancy, as well as in therapeutic abortions. But if the original fetus is well-formed, destroying it after it has begun to move through the production process does not make sense on any standard model of social production. In fact, a worker who destroys such an Ur-product can be prosecuted by his or her employer for a crime against valuable property. Moreover, in accepting this analogy between parturition and other materially productive human activities, we are caught up in a logic that implies that the significance of abortion involves determining the value of what is being destroyed. Since what a woman destroys is an incipient life, a fetus on a path toward birth, analogies between abortion and murder inevitably enter the picture at this point, rebutted only by emphasizing that the fetus does not have the legal status of a person. An abortion becomes all too readily a sort of reproductive tort, an act of violence justifiable under special social circumstances.

Attempts to justify the abortion decisions of individual women have either emphasized potential conflicts between a woman's political rights over her person and traditional maternal obligations, or they have juxtaposed macroscopic social interests against the traditional maternal obligations of individual women. They have succeeded in making us more sympathetic to the concerns of women who seek abortions and have even made some of us self-righteous about believing that women should have abortions in certain circumstances. But they have not provided a sufficient basis for respecting the moral authority and the procreative agency of individual women who choose to abort a fetus.

The problem with both utilitarian and rights-based justifications of abortion is that they attempt to qualify traditional maternal narratives instead of replacing them. Whether a pregnant woman is a willing host or an unwilling hostage, a natural maternal coproducer or an oppressed pregnant laborer, the involuntary quality of her initial participation in maternity is still taken for granted, just as it is in religious narratives that emphasize her absolute maternal responsibility. The problem with justifying a woman's act of abortion today lies with a naturalistic vision of motherhood still implicit in all these narratives. We do not yet conceive of women as procreative agents in a postmodern world.

iv.   Carol Gilligan: Rethinking Gendered Categories of Moral Agency

A feminist/postfeminist theory must attempt to explain abortion in the context of the changing social agency of women, responding to the fact that the diverse social roles of women today make previous notions of maternal agency misleading in a number of ways. A woman within various traditional cultures had the obligation to produce children and to care for them, and her most basic motivations were presumed to accord with the frequent need for sacrificing her own interests on behalf of those of her children. In order to be recognized as a successful person, a woman had to fulfill a maternal role, and she could expect to be supported in this role by some specific form of kinship structure, wherein her spouse and more extended family members shared the economic and social burdens of maintaining and raising her children.

Women today have neither such a straightforward obligation to produce children nor such a definite structure of kinship support. China's one-child policy is only the most extreme example of a global transformation of the earlier concern with producing more children to a goal of producing fewer children. Consequently, individual women have become responsible for contraception and for limiting their production of children. In addition, structures of kinship support have waned considerably. A woman may often find herself the sole supporter of her children, economically and otherwise. At the same time, we no longer assume that a woman will be or ought to be motivated to sacrifice herself totally on behalf of her husband and children. We frequently attribute to women motivations for individual achievement in the larger world similar to those attributed to men. Recognizing that women have taken on a role outside the family, we assume that a woman's public responsibilities may conflict and compete with whatever maternal responsibilities she may have. And liberal standards of universal justice are now interpreted as saying that if a woman accomplishes what men have accomplished, she should be recognized and rewarded for these nonmaternal achievements, regardless of whether she has fulfilled a maternal role.

Although Carol Gilligan does not conceptualize her work in these terms, I think she makes a serious contribution to the feminist process of rethinking maternal agency. She also frames the moral drama in such a way as to prepare us for a conception of interpersonal agency that would apply to both women and men. It is significant that she developed her theory of an alternative form of moral reasoning in part through evaluating the process by which a number of young women arrived at a decision as to whether or not to have an abortion.[28] She was interested in discovering the various immediate motivations as well as long-term goals and forms of responsibility these women articulated as bearing upon their decision about having an abortion. In terms of the dimensions of agency I delineated earlier, Gilligan was concerned with understanding *the woman's experiences of moral agency* in the context of an unexpected pregnancy.

Gilligan came to the conclusion that the most complex and mature examples of ethical thinking about abortion could be understood in terms of a model of individual responsibility and care. Her findings provided a welcome alternative to those of Lawrence Kohlberg, who had suggested a theory of moral development according to which the highest forms of moral reasoning involved appeals to abstract principles of justice. On Kohlberg's model, persons who had attained the highest stage of moral thinking would apply either utilitarian or rights-based theories to abortion decisions, insofar as these are the primary forms taken by abstract principles of justice in liberal society. As I suggested in section iii, however, neither utilitarian nor rights-based theories provide an adequate way of morally resolving issues of abortion. Gilligan's studies of women's moral reasoning suggested that Kohlberg's conception of moral development was incomplete and inadequate not only for abortion but for women and men alike within a variety of situations.

Did Gilligan discover a notion of moral agency capable of making sense of abortion? She proposed that the morality of abortion could be explained by taking seriously a form of moral reasoning that she discovered was common to many of the women she studied. It is important to be very clear on the fact that Gilligan does not consider traditional female forms of altruistic caring an adequate basis for women making decisions about abortion. She explains and criticizes traditional forms of self-sacrificial caring as based upon women's lack of a sense of self within patriarchal relations of domination. In the context of her analysis of women's abortion decisions, she suggests what she terms a "post-conventional form of caring" in which the individual woman attempts to balance out care for others and for herself.[29] I will refer to this postconventional form of caring as "fair-caring," to distinguish it from the altruistic or self-sacrificial caring expected of traditional women.

It is also important to recognize that Gilligan does not intend this notion of fair-caring to apply solely to women. She goes on to apply her postconventional standard of moral care to the case of Mohandas Gandhi. An earlier biographer found it puzzling that Gandhi, a man renowned for his commitment to abstract principles of political justice, had nonetheless, on his own admission, mistreated his family. Gilligan uses the case of Gandhi to show that there are circumstances in which men as well as women need to act on the basis of a postconventional notion of caring, rather than assuming that abstract principles of justice will provide adequate moral direction in their lives. Gilligan maintains that both men and women face some circumstances in which abstract principles of justice are appropriate, and others in which postconventional caring is ethically called for.[30]

Both advocates and critics of Gilligan have frequently interpreted her work as relying upon an essentialist distinction between a stereotypical male concern with abstract principles of justice and an equally stereotypical female concern with caring / not hurting others. Gilligan's critique of gendered conceptions of moral agency is often simply taken as a celebration of a female moral identity, with a corresponding critique of the moral ideals associated with men.[31] Far from advocating such a gendered moral essentialism, however, Gilligan ventures a normative critique of prevailing male *and* female moral standards. She criticizes conventional female sacrificial caring, insofar as it seems grounded in patriarchal relationships that deny women an adequate sense of themselves, and she criticizes ideals of abstract justice for failing to address moral responsibilities of a personal sort in the lives of men as well as women. Gilligan is neither celebrating nor criticizing gendered identities, but is instead deriving a new conception of moral agency from investigating the ways in which women currently struggle to live within a female identity. While Gilligan does not develop her notion of postconventional caring as fully as one might hope, her distinction between conventional altruistic and postconventional forms of fair-caring is very clear.[32]

There are at least two reasons why her suggestions for understanding the morality of abortion decisions have not had more impact on the abortion debate. In the first place, her postconventional category of caring never received sufficient attention. It was as if people could not intellectually process the distinction she was making between traditional and postconventional forms of caring. In Gilligan's interviews, various women articulated their sense of moral obligation in the face of pregnancy in terms that did not necessarily commit them to motherhood, and Gilligan appeals to these women's voices to first explain her postconventional notion of caring. Gilligan also insists that the moral terms of a fair-caring agency are not intrinsically gendered; her moral assessment of Gandhi's behavior was meant to show its applicability in the lives of men. An ethic of care is so firmly embedded in a maternal identity in our society, however, that Gilligan's readers frequently ignored her efforts to construct a postconventional category of caring that would apply to women and men who were not engaged in "mothering" as well as to women who were. Those such as Nel Noddings who followed up on her ideas tended to read Gilligan's transgressive concept of fair-caring back into a conventional maternal mode.[33]

There is also a second reason Gilligan's theory has not had more impact on the abortion debate. Her notion of postconventional caring, no matter how generously read, does not finally offer a sufficient rubric for understanding the moral agency of women choosing abortion. Gilligan is surely correct in insisting on the importance of an ethic of care, and also in formulating a critique of a conventional altruistic care ethic in favor of a postconventional notion of fair-caring that includes care for oneself in the basic moral equation.[34] This is an ethic of care that takes account of liberal norms of equality while also suggesting the need for a greater emphasis on individual motivations and responsibilities for making and maintaining connections with others in contemporary society. But to suggest that a just balancing out of care for oneself and for others can resolve a woman's doubts about abortion is to beg the question of what a notion of fair-caring is for a pregnant woman.

Even when a woman adds herself to the equation of care, the question remains whether and why care for herself or for others would indicate an abortion. The *quality* of caring is at stake here, rather than merely the distribution of care. For a woman who still believes in a traditional sense of female obligation toward a fertilized egg in her womb, care for herself and for the fetus are not easily separated. Only when a woman has already begun to assume personal authority for deciding upon the future of a fertilized egg can Gilligan's notion of fair-caring become helpful in a woman's reflections upon the morality of abortion in her particular situation. Gilligan's analysis of the actual abortion decisions of various women provides anecdotal evidence for a qualitative shift in our sense of legitimate female caring motivations and responsibilities. Her brief discussion of Gandhi suggests a possible shift in our assumptions about male familial responsibilities as well, such that personal caring concerns would become a greater priority for men. Gilligan's work thereby implies a complex set of alterations in our understanding of the moral agency of women and men. Not surprisingly, such changes cannot be adequately dealt with simply by adding an ethic of care to an ethic of justice.

Ad hoc combinations of previous conceptions of agency will not enable us to make sense of the lives of contemporary women and men. In deciding to raise children while pursuing a career, in resorting to a vast array of new reproductive technologies, in deciding to divorce or to remarry, in deciding to be a single adult with or without children, men as well as women face a transformed set of life choices and obligations. We may expect that in the case of men and women both, individual motivations will need to be reinterpreted, obligations reapportioned, and forms of recognition and reward altered as societies grope to make sense of these new social practices.

v. A Cyborgean Theory of Procreative Agency

In daily life, women increasingly find themselves with both the technical capacity and the social responsibility to decide whether and when and how to have children. As a purely practical matter, they have primary authority for procreative decisions. Yet once a woman becomes pregnant, whether voluntarily or not, religious and naturalistic conceptions of maternal agency imply that she has a moral obligation to bear a child. Whether as host or as hostage or as reproductive laborer, a pregnant woman is imagined to be a participant in an organic process that requires her continued cooperation. As a pregnant woman she already has a maternal identity, and her moral authority appears inseparably bound up with her responsibility within an organic process of human reproduction. Insofar as it appears fundamentally *unnatural* in relation to this process, a pregnant woman's desire to opt out of further maternal participation can easily seem capricious and irresponsible. While abortion may be legally defended either in terms of a woman's right to bodily self-defense or in terms of society's interests, it cannot be understood as an act of individual moral agency so long as pregnant women are seen as organically implicated in motherhood.

I think that a "cyborgean" analysis of persons will provide the radical shift in perspective we require in order to explain the morality of abortions. Such an analysis will also provide a foundation for the broader effort of re-thinking postmodern procreative decisions in such a way as to connect them with other forms of interpersonal agency. Donna Haraway has suggested that we borrow from science fiction the cyborg image of "creatures simultaneously animal and machine, who populate worlds ambiguously natural and crafted," as a means of portraying some of the peculiarities of women's lived experiences in the late twentieth century.[35] One of the most peculiar of these experiences, while also one of the most transformative, as I have tried to show, is women's experience of resorting to various reproductive technologies in order to exercise individual control over the processes of bodily procreation. It may be startling to think of adopting a cyborgean perspective on pregnant women. Yet once we acknowledge the force of Mary O'Brien's argument that the contraceptive revolution makes organic motherhood a thing of the past, we require some radically new conception of maternal agency. I will attempt to demonstrate the advantages of a cyborgean analysis of motherhood.[36]

A cyborgean image of persons emphasizes the contemporary breakdown in our once-firm sense of the boundaries between our own organic selfhood and the nonorganic machines we increasingly call upon within our everyday activities. Until very recently, we have taken the alien and even alienating qualities of the machinery and technologies we rely upon for granted, their usefulness always bounded by their metallic, clanking lack of ensoulment. The most staunch advocates of the machine age have yet stressed the need to vigilantly maintain human control over whatever artificial intelligences and robotic wonders we may create. And in the view of critics, from Luddites and utopian socialists in the nineteenth century to the deep ecologists of today, we must fear for technology's ability to ride roughshod over those aspects of our humanity that we most value.

Yet technology has ceased to be an alien presence in our lives. We wake up to the insistent beeping of digital clocks and amiable microwave ovens, slide behind the wheel of a car accompanied by more interactive electronic beeps, and typically maintain intimate aural and physical contact with various technologies throughout a normal day. Moreover, we regularly choose to undergo operations in which our hips, knees, and other organic body parts are removed and replaced with artificial ones. And for most of us who write as a way of life, our personal computer has become our favorite means of accessing our ideas and harnessing our creativity. We describe our relationships to these machines in very peculiar terms, by earlier standards; but these terms express the degree of technological penetration into our personal lives. We gratefully say that artificial hips and knees make us feel "like our old selves again." And after becoming accustomed to writing on a computer, we may express horror at the idea of returning to previous writing practices which may now seem both less effective and less enjoyable.

Are we still in control? Does our dependency upon these machines make us less human? The point of the cyborg image is to suggest that these questions have lost their meaning. These machines make us better able to do the things we most value as individual human beings, and were we to be forced to give them up we would feel diminished as human beings. This does not deny their quality as machines and technologies. It does imply that we need to rethink our relationship to machines quite radically so as to expunge antitechnological biases that have become hypocritical and misleading at this point.

The feminist relationship to technology is particularly fraught with confusion, and important to work out in the context of the new procreative decisions women and men are called upon to make. Reproductive technologies play an extremely important role in the social enfranchisement of women today. Our relationship with technology is nowhere more intimate or more significant than in our sexual lives. Individually, we may rely upon various sorts of contraceptive technology on a daily basis for decades, abortion providing a safety net for those who find themselves involuntarily plunging toward maternity. We increasingly call upon more esoteric forms of reproductive technology as well, whether as means of enhancing fertility, or as means of ensuring the well-being of fetuses prior to birth. Reproductive methods that take place partially or wholly outside the womb, or in alternative wombs or womblike structures, are developing quite rapidly.

Our cyborgean dependency upon technology as a normal condition for reproductive decisions has serious implications for how we think about the procreative process. Insofar as the organic conditions for producing a child are interpenetrated with technological and social considerations, children become products of our social decisions in a thoroughgoing sense. In Haraway's political myth, "cyborg replication is uncoupled from organic reproduction."[37] Were this the case for us, it would simplify the analysis a great deal. The problems we encounter in this real-life cyborgean moment are often a result of the perplexing entanglement of our old organic relationships with postmodern technological ones. In the case of procreative situations, it seems inappropriate to speak of replication insofar as that implies mechanical multiples of an initial prototype. But the old organic quality of human reproduction is surely dominated today by recent technological procedures and the particular social decisions they make possible and necessary.

If we emphasize the *social mediation* of both natural and technological processes, I think we have a basis for appropriating Haraway's cyborg mythology for everyday use. One important implication of cyborgean

Two independent claims:
(1) Technology will change our moral/emotional linkage between child bearing and women
(2) Claim: a necessary condition for a moral birth is decision

112   Cyborgean Motherhood and Abortion

Q: what if it's not there?

reproduction is that children come to be seen as "social offspring" of many possible procedures and practices in which technology and nature are intermixed inseparably. Unlike Haraway's science-fictional replicants, who may do without origin stories altogether, our social offspring are historically specific children, and will surely continue to ask from whence they have come. But our answers will refer to the various social decisions that led to a child's birth. It will no longer make sense to think about children in terms of their natural origins. A pregnant mother, for example, will no longer be seen as the natural origin of a child. Even if a particular child is the product of a pregnant mother, she or he will be the social offspring of a decision by this woman, and perhaps others, to produce a child in this fashion. *Mere pregnancy will not be a morally or socially adequate basis for producing a child. A social offspring must have a properly social point of origin in the conscious decision of one or more persons to raise a child.* Mythologies of natural fetal origins remain quite strong today, and antiabortion arguments rely upon them heavily. Such arguments will no longer make sense from a cyborgean perspective. Social offspring are born of acts of interpersonal agency, and only incidentally of women's wombs.[38]

Notice that a cyborgean analysis makes the special parameters of women's reproductive agency quite explicit. So long as the gestation process takes place in a woman's womb, she must have final authority over deciding if and when a gestation will take place. She must be motivated to take on that initial responsibility. An individual woman may choose to give a particular man a role in her decision-making process, of course, particularly if he is willing to commit himself to parental responsibilities after a child is born. Should there come a time when gestation occurs outside a woman's body, the initial interpersonal decision will be shared by those taking responsibility for the development of the child at that point.

I think a cyborgean understanding of reproduction makes a lot of sense today, and I do not see any other way to secure the ethical confidence of women who choose to have abortions than to adopt this postmodern view of procreation. Yet it will not be easy for many people to give up cherished personal visions of natural fetal origins. I suspect that many feminists may find this cyborgean narrative troubling as well. Feminists have accepted contraceptive technologies quite readily; their potential contribution to the sexual empowerment of women is indisputable. But the organic capacity of women to bear children has provided a sentimental core for an impassioned feminist maternalism.

Twenty-five years ago, a brash young Shulamith Firestone suggested that artificial reproduction was "not inherently dehumanizing" and that it might be part of the solution to women's oppression within the patriarchal family. She pointed out that "at the very least, development of an option should make possible an honest reexamination of the ancient value of motherhood."[39] Indeed, this was not the sort of examination many second-wave feminists had in mind. A furious outcry arose against Firestone's unsympathetic attitude to motherhood, as well as against earlier feminists, such as Simone de Beauvoir, who were not overly appreciative of women's capacity to bear children. While the unsubtle romanticization of maternity may have abated recently in feminist theory, there has been no effort to recuperate Firestone. At the point where technology undermines the bodily uniqueness of female procreation, feminism tends to balk.[40]

A skeptical response to various modes of reproductive technology is firmly grounded in feminist political analysis. Within patriarchy, women have been oppressed as mothers; patriarchal institutions of motherhood have transformed a potentially wonderful experience into an unbearable one for many women. In *Of Woman Born*, Adrienne Rich articulates her intense anger in the face of her recognition that she has been alienated from her children and from her own body by patriarchal thinking that has "limited female biology to its own narrow specifications." She emphasizes that women must "repossess their bodies" and struggle for new relationships to their children by destroying patriarchal institutions of motherhood.[41] Reproductive technologies are highly suspect as a recent product of a scientific establishment that may defeat this feminist project by extending and strengthening patriarchal control over women's bodies. Barbara Katz Rothman indicts recent medical practices, from sonar womb scanning to surrogacy, for their literal ability to separate a woman from her body and from the body of her child.[42]

Furthermore, many feminists believe that motherhood has been and continues to be such an important site of female praxis that feminism must extricate it from the patriarchal grasp which has crushed and perverted it, reinstating it as an institution uniquely capable of affirming the social and historical significance of women. In *Maternal Thinking*, Sara Ruddick expresses hope that men will eventually come to participate fully in the "maternal work" of caring for children; and yet she is resolute in her belief that the maternal work of "protecting, nurturing, and training" children should continue to be termed "mothering." Desiring that this historically feminine work may finally transcend gender, Ruddick yet "wants to recognize and honor the fact that even now, and certainly through most of history, women have been the mothers."[43]

Rich, Katz Rothman, and Ruddick provide insightful and provocative responses to the current situation of women; such thinkers represent feminist identity politics at its best. Poststructuralists such as Judith Butler explain very well the dangerous ground such theorists tread in articulating their notions of maternal thinking and motherhood, insofar as such texts are invariably read as imparting universalizable truths (thus falsehoods) about motherhood.[44] Yet the feminist politics of the poet Adrienne Rich and the philosopher Sara Ruddick reflect the experiences of women traumatized by a historically specific institution of motherhood in this country. For much of this century, upper-middle-class women were allowed to pursue the same intellectual preparation as men, yet upon completion of their studies men became poets and philosophers, while women became mothers, with the understanding that as mothers they were disqualified from becoming serious poets or philosophers. Rich and Ruddick, and many other second-wave foremothers of the contemporary era, struggled successfully to demonstrate that patriarchy can no longer dismiss mothers or fail to recognize mother-poets and mother-philosophers. If women in the 1990s decide that it is necessary to develop a politics that conceptualizes the struggle of women somewhat differently, it will be because the experiences of women today, as poets, philosophers, and mothers, are different in significant ways from those of this previous generation of feminists—in large part due to the efforts of these powerful foremothers.

vi.   The Interpersonal Agency of Cyborgean Parents

A postfeminist theoretical position attempts to capture the changing quality of our procreative experiences in the context of the more general process of women's social enfranchisement. Certainly reproductive technologies such as contraception have historically played a contradictory role, at best, in efforts to emancipate women.[45] For so long as we live in a patriarchal society, we will need to remain vigilant against a continuing tendency for medical techniques to be utilized in ways that deprive women of control over their sexual and reproductive lives. Yet there is something very right about Mary O'Brien's bold enunciation of the world-shaking historical force of a Contraceptive Revolution today. The experiences of women coming of age in the 1970s, 1980s, and 1990s, after contraception and abortion became socially and politically accessible modes of reproductive choice for women, are in some ways radically different from those of women coming of age in the 1950s and 1960s, when female sexuality and heterosexual love were fraught with the dangers of pregnancy and motherhood. Despite the fact that reproductive choice is not yet distributed equally or fairly among women in our society, the reproductive lives of all women increasingly involve new sorts of responsibilities and decisions.

I would suggest that my own experience of my body and my procreative agency is both peculiarly contemporary and also rather common among women coming of age in the 1970s or later. I have a cyborgean sense of my personhood, insofar as I have felt sexually empowered for the last twenty years by taking the pill, and can imagine nothing that would make me feel more alienated from my body than to be deprived of this technological means of reproductive security. Were I to become pregnant, I would feel ethically confident in obtaining an abortion because I have the cyborgean belief that children are social offspring, and can be morally conceived only by acts of interpersonal agency, wherein one or more individuals consciously commits themselves to a future parenting relationship. Unlike Firestone, I am not recommending a cyborgean attitude toward motherhood as a radical option, to be judiciously evaluated for its possible emancipatory effects on women. I am maintaining that we can hardly avoid a cyborgean sense of our personhood today, reproductive and otherwise.

Attitudes toward abortion and other procreative decisions are only the tip of a postfeminist iceberg, according to this narrative. As interpersonal agents, we are responsible for creating and maintaining, and ending when appropriate, a sometimes terrifying array of relationships and connections within both domestic and public arenas. We may be expected to change jobs, careers, marriages, and geographical venues with the same resignation or optimism as we switch channels. We may be described, without undue exaggeration, as operating within a tangle of motivations, responsibilities, rewards, and forms of recognition unmoored from traditional male and female, public and private identities. Given the chaotic state of individual motivations and responsibilities in this scenario, it may be wholly unrealistic to expect anyone to worry very much about establishing firm social identities — feminist, feminine, maternal, or otherwise.

The neediness and dependency of children imply that relationships between parents and children must remain a site of relative stability in this chaotic moment of cultural transformation, however. Insofar as traditional notions of maternal and paternal identity are no longer either available or appropriate as foundations upon which to ground relationships between cyborgean parents and children, we need to rethink parental roles as fundamentally as any others. Moreover, as in the case of other interpersonal renegotiations, this inquiry will typically take place in the context of an ongoing parent-child relationship. Unlike other interpersonal relationships, however, this is a situation in which a basic asymmetry is a dominant factor in the bond between the parties. Because of the dependency of children, neither party can readily put an end to a relationship that goes bad; and because of the intense emotional and cognitive interactiveness of children, parents and children tend to develop psychic connections that endure for a lifetime. The dependency of children places constraints on parental freedom, and suggests definite, if now indistinct, parameters of parental responsibility. Parents require new criteria for assessing their actions and the quality of the bond they are creating with their children, often in spite of themselves.

A notion of interpersonal agency provides cyborgean parents with a framework for attempting to achieve ethical confidence as parents. It encourages individuals to attend to their own particular motivations, while attempting to reconcile these with a reasonable sense of obligation toward children. It also suggests the need to evaluate the particular forms of recognition or reward they seek as parents. A concept of interpersonal agency highlights relevant dimensions of women's and men's changing experiences of parenting in the face of women's social enfranchisement and all the consequences it may have for kinship relationships. It can help individuals reformulate parental relationships in the direction of mutually desirable divisions of labor between men and women, as well as between persons within wholly non-traditional parenting communities.

One of the most important functions of a notion of interpersonal agency may lie in its ability to decisively confront and disperse a powerful but antiquated aura of moral rectitude that continues to surround motherhood. In many societies in which motherhood is deemed a necessary and natural role of women, a mantle of unqualified Goodness descends upon a woman who produces a child. The moral valence of maternity functions like a bribe; it is grounds for a woman to reconcile herself to the burdens of a maternity she cannot refuse in any case. Such a normative privileging of maternity is operative in our society in capricious postmodern forms, with sometimes cruel and frequently inappropriate results. For example, Ann Snitow has diagnosed a "pervasive pronatalism" afflicting various privileged strata of our society.[46] Among couples and single women who have devoted themselves exclusively to careers and worldly possessions, it can suddenly seem necessary to have a child to fulfill a vague sense of unmet desires. Forty-something women who have proven themselves successful at every other aspect of life become prone to feelings of inadequacy for not having fulfilled their maternal potential. Childless women of means resort to extensive and expensive fertility treatments with only the faintest hope of finally bearing a child. Given the maternal obsessions of women who have so many other sources of personal affirmation, we should hardly be surprised when teenage girls from impoverished back-grounds imagine that motherhood will provide them with a sense of per-sonal significance and make their lives more bearable.

The mantle of maternal goodness not only leads people to want chil-dren for the wrong reasons; it also puts obstacles in the way of redistribut-ing parental responsibilities. The sex-specific quality of maternal good-ness forces men who participate extensively in parenting to operate in drag, as it were. We are likely to be critical if such men admit to motiva-tions, senses of obligation, or feelings of reward which the privileged maternal identity does not sanction. Moreover, many women still jealous-ly guard their claim upon the unqualified goodness of the maternal iden-tity, even when they are drastically overburdened by its responsibilities.

This anachronistic valence of unqualified maternal goodness is diminished by thinking of motherhood as simply one mode of interper-sonal agency. It allows us to concretely discuss the motivations, obliga-tions, and rewards appropriate to child-rearing, distinguishing them from the motivations, responsibilities, and rewards possible in other sorts of in-terpersonal relationships. It helps us to suggest alternative forms of inter-personal agency more appropriate to most teenage girls, for example, or to career-driven women and men. It enables us to persuasively suggest why there is a whole spectrum of meaningful nonparental personal con-nections that may better satisfy the psychic yearnings of a particular in-dividual.

On the other hand, by regarding parenting as a subset of interpersonal agency, we also become better prepared to accept and constructively re-spond to the fact that contemporary parents are likely to exercise qualita-tively different forms of parental agency than those associated with tradi-tional mothers of any sort. Women who work outside the home today may have quite different motivations for becoming mothers, different no-tions of maternal responsibility, and derive different feelings of reward from their parental role than did women fulfilling maternal roles in the past. And we may expect men to begin articulating parental motivations, obligations, and rewards in ways that sound quite novel or even strange to a conventional maternal ear. Yet if such reformulations of parent-child bonding make parenting less foreign to men while fulfilling the needs of children, we should encourage them.

vii. Postfeminism and the Waning of a Maternal Identity

I have attempted to show that previous notions of maternal identity, whether religious, naturalistic, or humanistic, whether dismissive or celebratory, fail to adequately represent the procreative agency of women today. Inspired by Mary O'Brien's hopeful proclamation of a Contraceptive Revolution, I have sought to articulate what might come after organic motherhood. Donna Haraway's "blasphemous image of the cyborg" is one of those rare political metaphors with immediate metaphysical resonances. For many of us today, our dependency upon technologies, whether upon computers, or artificial knees, or contraceptives, is such that we would feel "less ourselves" without them. This I take to be a condition of cyborgean personhood, and indeed more particularly a condition of cyborgean motherhood.[47]

Our ubiquitous and intimate dependency upon reproductive technologies means that children may reasonably come to be seen as "social offspring" of various possible practices and procedures in which organic conditions are thoroughly interpenetrated with technological ones. It will no longer make sense to think of a pregnant mother as the natural origin of a child, and pregnancy will not be seen as a sufficient ethical condition for producing a child. Children will be born of acts of interpersonal agency: conscious decisions by one or more persons to take on the social responsibilities involved in raising a child. A cyborgean paradigm of motherhood will provide women with the discursive grounds for ethical confidence in choosing abortion, as well as encouraging women and men both to exercise personal responsibility over whatever procreative technologies become available to them in the future.

I refer to abortion as a postfeminist issue because, in practical terms, it pushes us to reach beyond the boundaries of a feminist audience, providing an occasion for us to address a mainstream that is beginning to discover the impact of gendered transformations on its everyday life. More controversially, I also suggest that abortion is a postfeminist issue in theoretical terms. Cyborgean mothers eschew the sort of maternal identity that has often seemed to lie at the heart of feminist theory. They accept with equanimity the idea that the bodily uniqueness of female procreation may be a historically limited phenomenon, and they locate their sense of maternal agency on a continuum with many other forms of interpersonal agency in which men participate on potentially equal terms.

With the social enfranchisement of women and the erosion of patriarchal kinship relationships, we need a notion of agency capable of delineating the heightened level of individual choice and responsibility for creating and maintaining various significant forms of personal connection. I suggest a concept of interpersonal agency as the basis for articulating the particular qualities that will allow us to distinguish this form of individual agency from dominant liberal economic and political notions of agency.

Decisions about if and when to become pregnant, like decisions about parenting and all the contemporary permutations of intimate domestic cohabitation, will only begin to make sense once we recognize the vastly different quality of the motivations and notions of obligation as well as recognition and reward appropriate to such forms of individual agency. While our initial understanding of interpersonal agency will draw heavily upon the various practices and norms of traditional notions of mothering, the abstract quality of the concept of interpersonal agency is meant to encourage a reconfiguring of parenting that will enable women and men both to participate in a broader range of relationships with children than prescribed within patriarchal families.

A category of interpersonal agency will provide women and men alike with a basis for achieving ethical confidence in procreative decisions, as well as in renegotiating parental connections. In later chapters, I will explore its applications in nonfamilial contexts. I will demonstrate that interpersonal motivations, responsibilities, and rewards constitute an increasingly significant component of public as well as personal forms of individual agency.

4

A Genealogy of Individualism

There are periods in history when a whole community . . .
finds itself in the presence of new issues which its old customs
do not adequately meet. The habits and beliefs which were formed
in the past do not fit into the opportunities and requirements
of contemporary life.

—John Dewey

Writing in the early decades of the twentieth century, John Dewey was already speculating that "vast social changes" associated with the machine age were making previous conceptions of morality and politics inadequate.[1] As we make our way through the last decade of the century it is difficult to avoid an even clearer sense that changes in dominant social narratives are afoot. Processes of social transformation within global structures of economics and nationhood as well as kinship have led to widespread practical and theoretical confusion. In the first three chapters of this book, I investigated sites of gendered conflict in the United States that lead us beyond available models of individual identity and agency. In this chapter I will attempt to demonstrate, more generally, that an analysis of changing gender relations provides a necessary foundation for comprehending our chaotic postmodern era, much as an analysis of economic relationships was necessary for understanding major developments of the modern era.

i. A Gendered Genealogy

Underlying my theoretical approach lies an assumption that notions of individualism provide a basic and enduring framework for social analysis in this society. Although I am highly critical of liberal forms of individualism, I have focused on individually experienced problems of identity and agency, and suggested that a new category of individuated action — interpersonal agency — will contribute to a postmodern theory of social transformation. In this chapter, I present a historical account of several devel-

120

opmental phases of individualism. My goal is to rearticulate the complicated underpinnings of liberal individualism, and to explain the emergence of a successor form of individualism which I call "engaged individualism," resulting from the reorganization of everyday life brought about by the social enfranchisement of women.

What makes this a *genealogy* of individualism? The OED defines a genealogist as one who traces the descent of persons or families, much as I wish to trace the descent of notions of individualism. Friedrich Nietzsche famously borrowed this term to refer to his own investigation of moral values, complaining that everyone "has taken the *value* of these 'values' as given, as factual, as beyond all question." In order to engage in his moral critique, he argued, "*the value of these values themselves must first be called into question*—and for that there is needed a knowledge of the conditions and circumstances in which they grew, under which they evolved and changed." [2] A genealogical analysis showing the conditions under which particular values or categories of individualism arose enables me to suggest the circumstances under which these values or notions of individualism may decline and need to be replaced.

Karl Marx made a powerful genealogical critique of liberal individualism a century ago, castigating the "theological" dogmatism of nineteenth-century political economists who presumed to "demonstrate the eternity and harmoniousness" of capitalist social relations.[3] Having shown the conflict-ridden origins of Adam Smith's "economic man" in capitalism, however, Marx also predicted the historical demise of individualism in the development of class consciousness and the overthrow of capitalism.[4] Although class struggle did provide a powerful vehicle of collective political opposition to capitalist forms of exploitation, we are now faced with the fact that capitalism has not been overthrown and individualism remains a potent category of social analysis and behavior in our society.

Contra Francis Fukuyama and other conservative theorists excited by the recent downfall of communism, it is no more defensible today than it was in Marx's day to consider bourgeois social relationships an ultimate historical achievement.[5] Indeed, it is becoming important to distinguish notions of individuated desire, responsibility, and recognition or reward important within liberalism from qualitatively different notions of individuated behavior which are appearing with ever-greater frequency. As I argued in chapter 3, for example, efforts to make sense of practices related to developing reproductive technologies will not go forward until we begin to recognize and appreciate new forms of individuated reproductive agency. The time is thus ripe for a renewed genealogical analysis of individualism.

At this juncture, however, attempts to make sense of such emergent forms of social interaction have stalled. Ironically, Marx's historical narrative tracing the relationship between liberal individualism and capitalism has attained a naturalized status analogous to that of the idealized bourgeois theory Marx set out to criticize. Conservative and radical social critics alike associate all individuated forms of agency with liberal individualism, and assume the desirability of forms of social organization that deemphasize individualism. Condemning the selfishness encouraged by capitalist competition, as well as the "ghostly individualism" wrought by the loosening of traditional kinship and community bonds, conservatives advocate a return to traditional forms of community.[6] Critical of the hierarchies within traditional forms of community, but uncomfortable with the egoistic consumerism of capitalist culture and still inspired by Marx's "communitarian" perspective, radicals champion utopian forms of socialist or egalitarian community.[7] It is easy to criticize liberal individualism from a feminist perspective as well, and various theorists have disparagingly contrasted liberal values of abstract autonomy and choice with traditional maternal values of connectedness and care for others.[8]

Yet notions of individual autonomy and choice have become quite important to women involved in extricating themselves from oppressive patriarchal relationships over the last few decades.[9] Even radical communitarians have a tendency to tolerate exploitive or hierarchical sexual relationships when these are intrinsically bound up with the historical integrity of an ethnic or religious group.[10] From a perspective of socialism, feminism, and postmodernism, Iris Young has recently criticized the assumption that we must choose between liberal individualism and communitarianism. She proposes an "ideal of city life" in which group differences are affirmed and there is "an openness to unassimilated otherness." While her multicultural ideals of urban living are appealing, however, she herself acknowledges features of contemporary liberal democracy that seem to make these virtues of urban living unlikely to be realized any time soon. Racial, sexual, cultural, and class hierarchies and injustices are so thoroughly embedded in the social structures of the liberal state as to severely constrain an openness to unassimilated otherness. Few individuals are so privileged as not to have experienced being threatened by those who are different from them.[11]

In her attempt to formulate a postmodern politics of difference, Young goes further toward addressing the new issues raised by contemporary cultural conflicts than other political theorists who trace their origins to the new left social movements of the 1960s. Yet Young remains mired in the socialist idealization of collective forms of agency, emphasizing the political goal of respecting the agencies of heterogeneous groups. While injustices are assignable to groups of people, the appreciation of diversity and the friendly interactions between members of different cultural groups which Young aspires to will not occur unless individuals are motivated to affirmatively construct and maintain relationships with "others." Young evinces little concern, however, for changing modes of individual agency. Indeed, she seems to assume that liberal notions of individual autonomy and political empowerment can be adapted to the ends of a politics of difference.[12] Yet her political ideals remain utopian unless we have grounds for thinking that very basic strife-producing aspects of liberal agency and identity are capable of being transformed within contemporary multicultural scenarios.

There are, in fact, indications that such changes are possible today, but in order to explain the quality of these changes we will have to recognize the centrality of gender relations in the construction of liberal forms of agency and identity as well as in their reconfiguration. While he showed little interest in gender, Michel Foucault used a notion of genealogy to emphasize that discursive constructions of the self occur in the context of a multitude of different social power relationships, and not merely economic ones. Contrasting notions of reason and madness in the classical age with very different notions of sanity and insanity in our age, he suggested the surprising degree to which individual experiences of rationality are subject to social manipulation. Even more radically, he investigated the history of sexuality and maintained that what we currently experience as natural forms of sexual desire have been constructed as part of a complex set of discourses and practices enabling "bio-political" forms of surveillance and social control.[13] While Marx unmasked the origins of bourgeois forms of rationality and desire in capitalism, Foucault showed that individual experiences of reason and desire are quite typically produced within historically variable discourses involving complicated social power relationships.

I think that a genealogy of individualism can demonstrate that public as well as private experiences of desire, responsibility, and recognition have been constructed within liberal society by means of discourses in which gendered forms of power figured as significantly as economic power. Liberal individualism has functioned as a result of an intimate relationship between the familiar economic and political discourses articulated by philosophers and the less familiar patriarchal kinship practices that feminism has begun to articulate. As patriarchal kinship relationships begin to unravel with the social enfranchisement of women, the familial inscribing of gendered forms of identity and agency becomes less and less easy to reconcile with public discourses of liberal individualism. Public as well as private experiences of individual agency and identity have begun to change dramatically. The social enfranchisement of women will transform familiar modalities of individualism into radically new shapes.

Our understanding of what Dewey termed "the opportunities and requirements of contemporary life" is obstructed by continuing attempts to explain individual actions and identities according to the old patriarchal parameters of liberal individualism, and will improve only when we begin to articulate a new form of individualism which I will term "engaged individualism." While liberal individualism is primarily associated with public forms of economic and political agency, and with various masculine norms of social identity, engaged individualism will be associated with the breakdown of strict divisions between public and private spheres of activity, as well as with the dissolving of firm gender identities. Freed to some extent of the historical and patriarchal baggage of liberalism, a concept of engaged individualism can provide an organizing umbrella for individuals combining economic and interpersonal forms of agency, and experimenting with various identities as well as diverse familial and community relationships.

ii.   Reenacting Individualism after a Second Unmooring

We are familiar with stories about the emergence of liberal individualism from feudalism in the sixteenth and seventeenth centuries. In this section I will explain my reasons for thinking that there are important historical and social parallels between the development of liberal individualism following upon the decline of feudalism, and the current development of engaged individualism corresponding with a decline in the kinship structures of patriarchal liberalism. As serfs left the estates of feudal landowners, material forms of human neediness were unmoored from stable agricultural communities, and today as women leave the home to enter the workplace, psychic relational forms of human neediness are coming unmoored from patriarchal kinship relationships. In each case, individuated notions of meaningful activity, and social relationships supportive of these forms of individual activity, evolve to address forms of neediness previously satisfied in the context of prescribed community roles and hierarchies — *in both cases, the emergent forms of individualism and agency may be explained as consequences of the unmooring of particular forms of neediness from traditional community structures, and can be seen in the resulting transformations in the organization of everyday life.*

The origins of liberal individualism are not controversial. For hundreds of years under European feudalism people lived in towns and on the estates of landowners in complexly hierarchical social relationships, each person's position in the community indicated at birth by the status of his or her parents. At the beginning of the sixteenth century, according to Marx, "a period of vagabondage arose," caused by "the abolition of the feudal bodies of retainers, the disbanding of the armies consisting of a motley crowd that served the kings against their vassals, the improvement of agriculture, and the transformation of large strips of tillage into pasture land." These vagabonds resisted efforts to force them into the towns to work, and Marx reports that at one point Henry VIII of England had 72,000 of them hanged. With the rise of manufacturing, however, they were eventually prevailed upon to settle in the growing urban centers and to work as laborers in the factories and shops. The great industrial cities of Europe and the various structures of modern society developed subsequently.[14]

The significance of the modernization process is read somewhat differently by liberal and by Marxist theoretical traditions. For classical liberalism, this was the birth of modern freedom, as grounded in individual economic and political rights. The industrial development and market competition associated with capitalism gave every man an equal opportunity to succeed, the effort and achievement of the individual rather than social status at birth now determining the material rewards a man could expect in life. For Marxism, on the other hand, this was the birth of the urban proletariat, a massive group of wage workers born into industrial slavery. Evicted from the lands that had served as their historic means of material production, this urban proletariat was subject to exploitation by the class of men who now controlled the means of production and administered capitalist relations of production. Liberal individualism was a political ideology that made men compete against each other and value material possessions over the good of the community. In the Marxist worldview, capitalist relationships were a vehicle of economic and political oppression, while for liberalism they were the foundation of freedom and equality.

Central to both these accounts, however, is the fact that the individual's relation to his or her daily requirements for material subsistence changed dramatically in the transition from feudalism to capitalist forms of society. Both political narratives also emphasize the change in the status of the individual as a consequence of the development of modern economic and political discourses. Under feudalism, everyone was born into a nexus of relatively well-defined and fixed communal practices and relationships which determined the ways in which their various social and material needs would be satisfied. With the end of feudalism and the peasants' eviction from the lands of their ancestors, their material neediness for food and shelter as well as for the other elements of what Thomas Hobbes referred to as a "commodious life" were suddenly a matter for differential individual resolution. As material forms of human neediness became unmoored from stable feudal community relationships, they fell in a newly unmediated fashion upon the shoulders of individual men and women who then became recognized by their efforts, and particularly in terms of their successes, in meeting these needs. Previously undifferentiated or closely related aspects of material neediness in an agrarian setting were transformed into multiple discrete needs for units of food, shelter, and amusement, necessarily satisfied within numerous distinct market relationships of production and exchange.

The encompassing stratifications of feudal communities came to an end. Yet the new social formations of liberal individualism were not wholly unmediated by previous social structures. The gendered hierarchies of patriarchal kinship relations survived the transition to liberalism, despite changes in the organization of family life. Even when men and women performed the same economic functions, they experienced their positions in the emergent liberal society very differently, due to their different identities and roles within patriarchal kinship structures.[15] As the social and intellectual structures of modern capitalism developed, and as new modes of individuated "economic" responses to material forms of human neediness replaced the former communal relationships, social assumptions about individual identity and agency changed dramatically to accommodate and naturalize the new patterns of behavior. Yet the public discourses about individual motivation, responsibility, and reward that developed in the context of capitalism and liberal democracy delineated male norms of individual behavior. Despite the universalist rhetoric of liberalism, gender was tightly woven into the practical and categorial fabric of modern society in ways that have only recently become subject to critical analysis.

The origins of engaged individualism lie in the social enfranchisement of women in the twentieth century. In fact, we tend to interpret this process primarily in terms of the dramatic changes in women's status that occur when they are finally allowed unrestricted participation in the public sphere of liberal individualism. But such an analysis has led to great frustration and disappointment; women have hoped and expected to attain some measure of "equality" with liberal male individuals and no such equality has been forthcoming. The cruel fact is that no matter how successfully women mimic the public agency of liberal men, they lack the crucial social support system of the patriarchal family. The public lives of liberal men have always been premised upon the extensive personal services of wives, and women today could only attain equality with such liberal men were they to acquire "wives." The depressing new forms of inequality created by the large-scale participation of women in the liberal public sphere have led to bitter debates within feminism over the best political strategy for empowering women; while many still argue that the situation of women will be improved most by enforcing standards of formal equality, others believe it is important to emphasize the different needs of women. The issue has never been resolved, and it is increasingly evident that it has no solution in these terms.[16]

The solution, or the beginning of a solution, is only possible when we analyze the gendered social dynamics of the current situation more broadly. As masses of women begin to leave the home each morning along with men, it is not just the status of women that changes but also that of men. Indeed, when men lose their positions as heads of patriarchal families, a major foundation of liberalism is undermined. It is not simply that men lose various services provided by wives who devoted their efforts exclusively to raising children and maintaining the home. There have always been some women who worked outside the home, and their activities did not necessarily call their husband's identities as liberal individuals into question. Moreover, there is evidence that working women today go to great lengths to continue to perform many of the domestic and personal services men have relied upon.

The changes set in motion by the social enfranchisement of women are both more radical and more subtle than can be revealed by studies of the re-distribution of labor in the workplace and the home. In chapter 1, I focused on the behavioral implications of an erosion of familial identities of men and women alike. And in chapters 2 and 3, I began to articulate gendered parameters of individual agency which would be transformed by changes in kinship and workplace relationships. I pointed to distinct *dimensions* of agency in terms of the motivations, responsibilities, and recognition or rewards corresponding with particular social roles, and I distinguished between the different *qualities* of economic, sexual, and interpersonal forms of agency. The social enfranchisement of women has led to the disengagement of women, men, and children from the patriarchal families which were the foundation of liberal individualism. We may expect that the gendered experience of the motivations, responsibilities, and rewards of both family life and public life will change dramatically during this period for women and men alike, and that new family and workplace relationships will eventually have to reflect and allow for these changes.

In accordance with values and assumptions of liberal society that we all take for granted, however, we are only prepared to recognize the significance of the economic and political agency of women in the public sphere. Our appreciation of women's new public role is accompanied by questions as to how we may best ameliorate the chaotic familial effects of this role. Yet if the historical parallel I have drawn between the end of feudalism and the end of patriarchal liberalism holds true, then in the long run the social enfranchisement of women will necessarily involve broader issues of community reorganization. When masses of serfs were pushed off the landed estates of the feudal lords, they immediately became roving vagabonds unmoored from stable agricultural communities. Eventually vagabondage declined and individuals became embedded in new social structures that allowed for the individuated satisfaction of material forms of neediness. In a like manner, the social enfranchisement of women has immediately resulted in what appears to be a massive unmooring of individuals from stable family communities. Only one quarter of all households now conform to the traditional heterosexual family structure; one out of three families is headed by a single man or woman; 50 percent of all children will spend time in a single-parent family, and the number of children in foster care has risen by 50 percent in the last seven years.[17] If the parallel with the end of feudalism is valid, however, people will eventually become embedded in new social structures that allow for more individuated means of satisfying the psychic relational forms of neediness once met within patriarchal families. Women, men, and children who find themselves disengaged from each other with the decline of patriarchal family bonds will gradually experience their psychic needs as reconfigured and capable of satisfaction in various new public and private venues. A more complex understanding of individual agency, and a regulative ideal of engaged individualism, will provide a framework for developing postpatriarchal forms of identity and community.

The erosion of stable kinship relationships is self-evident today. Yet because there was previously no theoretical recognition of the agency of women attending to psychic relational forms of neediness within traditional families, the unmooring of psychic neediness from these structures may be less obvious. Moreover, since the interpersonal labor of mothers and wives ministering to these forms of neediness was not specified in terms of individuated motivations, responsibilities, or rewards it is difficult to imagine how psychic forms of neediness might be delimited and addressed through individuated efforts to satisfy specific needs. Because we are accustomed to taking the interpersonal labors of women in families for granted, a notion of interpersonal agency may seem at once very obvious and very vague. Yet we have a developing social need for effective individuated efforts, by men as well as women, outside of families as well as inside them, to create and maintain various sorts of affirmative connections between persons. We require a more adequate conception of what acts of interpersonal agency may entail.

Our imagination may be stimulated by considering recent public manifestations of psychic neediness unmoored from patriarchal kinship structures. Perhaps most discussed are unmoored childhood needs for developmental nurture. The psychic relational neediness of children is so urgent that strategies for reconfiguring child-care structures to better accommodate the responsibilities of mothers in the public workplace constitutes one of the major political issues of the day. Alternative forms of child care, more flexible work schedules, expanded responsibilities of fathers, extended school days, as well as an increased concern for encouraging socially responsible decisions about reproduction, all become issues of public concern. All entail choreographing the interpersonal agency of various individuals so that the developmental needs of children are satisfied.

Traditional modalities of domestic intimacy and affectional bonding between adult men and women have also become subject to critical public review. In the context of the social enfranchisement of women, psychic relationships based upon familial forms of patriarchal power have been called into question. Domestic violence, for example, is an oppressive form of interpersonal agency long sanctioned under patriarchy. In saying X that domestic violence must end, we are demanding that men find ways of expressing and satisfying their psychic neediness that are not oppressive to women or children. Domestic violence often indicates psychic needs for individual empowerment and respect that must be addressed in nonfamilial forums. By recognizing the breadth of interpersonal forms of agency, we can better analyze relationships between male behavior in diverse settings.[18]

The expression of psychic relational forms of neediness in the workplace is also open for discussion today. Psychic neediness has always existed within the workplace, and accepted forms of professional interaction, such as mentor relationships, may be best understood as modes of interpersonal agency. With the greatly expanded presence of women in the workplace, however, there are new issues to be dealt with. Sexual harassment cases illustrate the potential for patriarchal expressions of psychic neediness to migrate from the private into the public sphere, casting a lurid light upon workplace hierarchies and potentially upsetting standard notions of economic and political agency. Insofar as psychic relational forms of neediness remain an unrecognized presence within economic and political interactions, they will destabilize the grammar of social behavior presumed within liberalism. We will not achieve an adequate understanding of economic and political relationships until we acknowledge the positive as well as the negative significance of interpersonal factors.

A broad spectrum of intangible yet profoundly significant forms of psychic relational neediness is thus acquiring a salience in people's lives analogous to that which forms of material neediness have held since the end of feudalism. Material forms of neediness and the necessary individual struggles to see that they are met have long been accepted as a basis for personal anxiety as well as individual achievement within liberalism. I think we must begin to recognize the fact that various modes of psychic relational neediness are similarly becoming occasions for both personal uncertainty and individual ingenuity. We see the fissioning of traditional family and community relationships, and we hear the public outcries it evokes. If we look, we also see women and men experimenting, in some cases deliberately and in other cases quite unconsciously, with new permutations of work, domesticity, parenting, and intellectual and political forms of community. Psychic relational forms of neediness are acquiring social definition in terms of the qualities of needs experienced by individuals in particular circumstances, and also in terms of the modes of psychic connection by which people attempt to address these needs.

Significant social theorists from Sigmund Freud to Carol Gilligan have attempted to interpret human motivations and desires in terms of psychic forms of neediness. I believe, however, that a fundamental paradigm shift will be necessary before we can properly comprehend psychic forms of neediness as organizing principles of individual behavior. The social paradigms of liberal individualism assume the dominance of economic and political forms of individual agency, existing in a symbiotic relationship with patriarchal kinship structures within which psychic forms of neediness are satisfied according to prescribed familial practices. As patriarchal kinship roles decline, psychic needs must instead be met in the context of newly voluntary and contingent interpersonal relationships, in many ways comparable with economic and political relationships. Yet the motivations associated with psychic neediness, and the responsibilities and rewards associated with pursuing interpersonal relationships will often be very different from those within economic and political relationships. Once we recognize the growing centrality of interpersonal forms

of agency in our daily lives, we can self-consciously participate in this
postmodern moment of reenacting our individualism.

iii. Public Dimensions of Liberal Agency

In this section and the following one, I will present a revisionary account
of the liberal individual. A gendered analysis of the forms of individual
agency within liberalism reveals what I will call an "incorporated family
self" in the place of the so-called liberal individual. This concept will provide a basis for understanding important continuities as well as contrasts
between liberal and postmodern forms of agency and individualism. If the
familial moorings of the liberal individual are properly emphasized it becomes much easier to construe liberal and postmodern forms of agency
and individualism as successive historical moments in a two-stage process
of community unmooring and regrouping. The analysis of the incorporated family self will enable us to understand the sort of fundamental
reconfigurations of agency and individualism that become a necessary
consequence of the social enfranchisement of women and the dissolution
of the patriarchal family-self.

Any contemporary theory of gendered social relationships must ultimately contend with a long history of theoretical pronouncements about
the place of women in society. In the *Republic*, Plato advocated the communal upbringing of children apart from their parents, and the presence
of women alongside men within the ruling "guardian" class; yet the frequent refrain of "women and children and slaves" in the *Republic* is probably a more reliable guide to his gendered worldview. Aristotle was
explicit about the biological "incompleteness" of women, and drew analogies between the natural "aristocracy" of men and women in the household and that between men of different abilities in the polis.[19] It became
typical in modern discourses to emphasize public forms of male economic
and political agency and to ignore the household, designating the latter a
natural and therefore theoretically uninteresting background of male activities. Since the nineteenth century, however, it has been common to
counterpoise the self-interested activities of "economic man" in the public
sphere to the complementary altruistic activities of wives and mothers in
the private sphere of the home.[20] Socialist and feminist theorists alike have
criticized the reductiveness of this bourgeois and gendered model of social
behavior. Yet these gendered ideologies of liberal individualism are extremely tenacious, and it remains difficult to explain individual actions —
be they economic, ethical, or political — in terms that escape the binary opposition of self-interested and altruistic behavior.[21] My two-stage theory

of individualism points to the sources of this dualistic vision of agency within liberal individualism and demonstrates the basis for a new orientation to social behavior today.

By exploring the implications of the incorporated family identity of the liberal individual we can comprehend the complex dimensions of economic and political forms of liberal agency, gaining a more socially nuanced view of what has often been too simply dismissed as self-interested behavior. By closely reexamining the quality and dimensions of agency within patriarchal liberalism, it becomes possible to locate the familial origins of the interpersonal forms of agency that begin to manifest themselves explicitly only after the social enfranchisement of women and the decline of the incorporated family. Most important in this process of rethinking liberal agency is theorizing the connections between the public and private spheres of liberal individualism more adequately, articulating various repressed relationships of agency within the incorporated male family self.[22]

In this section, I will investigate how individuated responses to material forms of neediness became intertwined with economic and political ideals, operating as "recognition and reward factors" in public forums of individual agency. In the following section, I will analyze the complementary dimensions of responsibility associated with male and female agency within the incorporated family self. Dimensions of both recognition and responsibility were fundamental to male agency under liberalism. Yet political ideals of freedom and equality were not wholly compatible with the basic relationships of dependency and hierarchy within patriarchal families. The different qualities of the public and private agency of men were thus difficult to reconcile within liberalism. A reductive economic model of self-interested behavior gained much of its appeal by virtue of its ability to provide a least common denominator for comprehending the public and private behavior of the liberal individual. The competitive market behavior of economic man segued very nicely into the personally interested behavior of the incorporated male family self.

Let us first consider how the seminal philosophers of modern individualism, living in the conjunctural era between the end of medieval feudalism and the beginning of the early modern state, strove to articulate human motivations and relationships in terms of the central place of material forms of neediness in organizing and disorganizing individual lives. Thomas Hobbes was the first great theorist/storyteller of modern forms of material agency, articulating the power of material desires and their anarchic implications within a society in which market-based economic structures had not yet developed. In the *Leviathan*, Hobbes asserted a continuum between basic physical motions within the human organism and the social motivations of individual men, such that complex social motivations could be understood in terms of the simple categories of "appetite" and "aversion." According to Hobbes, "That which men Desire, they are also sayd to Love: and to Hate those things, for which they have Aversion. So that Desire, and Love, are the same thing." Even the most general social norms could be understood as based upon individual desires and aversions. "But whatsoever is the object of any man's Appetite or Desire; that is it, which he for his part calleth Good: And the object of his Hate, and Aversion, Evill." While the Greeks assumed that the use of the concepts of desire and aversion for these more complex social aims was merely "Metaphoricall," Hobbes denied that *his* terminology was metaphorical.[23]

Hobbes's radically physicalist conception of human agency is one of the basic sources for our modern belief in social equality. Individual men are obviously not equal in mental or physical abilities according to any absolute rendering of these capacities. Hobbes argued, however, that men *should be considered equal* insofar as each could imagine having, and getting, whatever any other man had. "Nature hath made men so equall, in the faculties of body, and mind; as that . . . when all is reckoned together, the difference between man, and man, is not so considerable, as that one man can thereupon claim to himselfe any benefit, to which another may not pretend, as well as he." Of course, this competitive conception of individual desire and equality was a prescription for conflict between individual men in a world in which any form of material scarcity prevailed. "From this equality of ability, ariseth equality of hope in the attaining of our Ends. And therefore if any two men desire the same thing, which nevertheless they cannot both enjoy, they become enemies; and in the way to their End . . . endeavor to destroy, or subdue one an other." Men were not motivated purely by desire for material gain, even in Hobbes's state of nature. A competitive desire for "glory" or "reputation" was also "a principall cause of quarrell . . . and warre of every man against every man."[24] Self-interested conflict was thus a basic feature of a modern society in which men, along with their various forms of material neediness, had been freed from the hierarchical moorings of feudal communities.

Fifty years later, John Locke modulated Hobbes's fierce image of human nature and contributed another fundamental component of the liberal conception of individual agency by articulating the political significance of the materially productive capacities of all men. Locke pointed out that by "mixing his labor with nature," each man could both improve the world and create for himself as much as he needed without taking anything away from his neighbor.[25] The liberal individual is equal not merely in his acquisitive orientation to the world; he is also to be understood as endowed by his maker with a common capacity for self-expression through productive labor. A Lockean man individuates himself through his ability to produce novel and useful material goods which benefit others as well as himself.

We may think of Hobbes's theory of anarchic, acquisitive agency as a "preeconomic" understanding of modern man. Hobbes could hardly assume developed structures of competitive exchange in seventeenth-century Europe; he was theorizing the egalitarian potential of "sandbox-grabbing" behavior between grown men in the absence of socially prescribed behavioral hierarchies. Locke was also preeconomic in abstractly focusing on the inborn capacities of all men that would predispose them to respond productively to material forms of neediness as individual agents. Locke chose to ignore the gritty social issue, already evident in his time, of how the unequal division of land would affect relationships of production on a day-to-day basis. Indeed, after explaining the *metaphysical* origins of private property as based upon the productive capacity God had bestowed on all men, he averted his theoretical gaze from further consideration of the material level of lived social inequalities. His radical contribution was to link individual productive capacities with democratic ideals of equality and personal achievement.[26]

For the social contract theorists—Hobbes and Locke as well as Jean-Jacques Rousseau—the ideal of freedom within the modern democratic state was guaranteed by the presumption that each individual could refuse to be part of any social relationship that was coercive or unfair. Whatever the apparent inequalities within lived social relationships in the seventeenth and eighteenth centuries, the individual's capacity to live, as in a "state of nature," outside of any formal relations of social dependency was idealized as the basis for a freely contracted society of political equals.[27] By the late eighteenth century, however, urbanization and industrialization had developed to a point where this romantic vision was not terribly convincing. It was becoming apparent that, as Adam Smith put it, civilized individuals were utterly dependent upon their relationships within a vast community of others, and could not imagine living outside such a community.

It was accordingly Adam Smith who first articulated the social component of our present notion of economic and political agency: "The propensity to truck, barter, and exchange one thing for another . . . [is] common to all men, and to be found in no other race of animals, which seem to know neither this nor any other species of contracts." Smith emphasized that this propensity to exchange allowed us to explain the seemingly paradoxical fact that men within civilized society "stand at all times in need of co-operation and assistance of great multitudes" while yet each operates primarily out of "self-love" rather than benevolence.[28] Unlike two dogs with bones, when two men discover that each desires something the other possesses, each will quite naturally offer up what he has in exchange for the satisfaction of his own desire, and there lies the basis for productive communities organized around the institution of the marketplace.

Smith retheorized the basis for individual equality and freedom in terms of *the reciprocal voluntariness of individual exchange relationships and the relative autonomy of each individual within exchange relationships.* Although we depend upon their services, "it is not from the benevolence of the butcher, the brewer, or the baker, that we expect our dinner, but from their regard to their own interest. We address ourselves, not to their humanity, but to their self-love, and never talk to them of their own necessities but of their advantages. Nobody but a beggar chooses to depend chiefly upon the benevolence of his fellow-citizens."[29] Smith articulates the social identity of the liberal man in terms of his disposition toward self-love versus benevolence, and independence versus dependency. Only the beggar relies upon benevolence and falls into public dependency upon others. Yet while the respectable liberal individual may not rely upon the benevolence of others, he must rely upon their disposition to exchange. Each exchange relationship is a contingent conjuncture between the personal desires of two people; either person within an exchange relationship may terminate the relationship of exchange if his desires change or it becomes unfair. The equality and freedom of individuals is ensured by this now quite specific notion of social autonomy. Only the beggar must accept what others give him (and Smith was anxious to assure us that even the beggar engages in exchange relationships on the basis of the funds provided him by charity). But every man depends upon the general disposition of others to exchange goods with him.

Narratives of individual freedom, equality, and achievement have been articulated with economic notions of material neediness and self-sufficiency in various ways over the several hundreds of years of supervening Western cultural history. In the United States, the myth of the western frontier gave priority to the Lockean "state of nature" story, emphasizing basic material forms of achievement and freedom. A man could personally express himself through building a house for his family and tilling his fields, at once proving his self-sufficiency and his civic equality with others. This romantic narrative has gradually given way to a twentieth-century scenario of massive corporate institutional relationships within which individual forms of economic and political agency struggle to survive. Immediate desires rule once more in an anarchic Hobbesian sense, and yet we are ever more dependent upon exchanges with others and thus, ironically, more "civilized," in Adam Smith's terms. Ideals of liberal freedom and equality reside ever more tenuously in the abstract capacity of each person to buy and consume whatever he or she desires. It is particularly difficult to give personal achievement, the important Lockean recognition-and-reward factor within liberal individualism, substantive embodiment within this contemporary life story. Marx's notion of the alienated worker is taken for granted as a problematic aspect of the modern workplace, as wage-based freedoms of consumption are increasingly disconnected from productive forms of self-expression.

As this brief account demonstrates, liberal individualism has involved a distinctive interweaving of public dimensions of economic and political agency. A striving to satisfy material forms of desire has been linked with a goal of achieving equality with and autonomy from other individuals. An ineradicable kernel of material dependency upon others has been articulated in relation to goals of individual achievement and mechanisms for achieving relative autonomy from others. The liberal ideals of freedom, equality, and individual achievement have functioned as powerful recognition-and-reward dimensions of individual agency within a historically and demographically varying liberal democratic public sphere. At their best, these public dimensions of liberal agency have encouraged not merely self-interested competition but also creative and productive forms of social cooperation. The critique of these public dimensions of liberal individualism necessarily involves rethinking the social bases for creative and productive forms of public agency.

iv.   The Incorporated Male Family Self

Feminist theorists have bitterly reproached male philosophers for failing to recognize the significance of women — and more generally, the family — within liberal society. Political thinkers such as Hobbes and Locke could not have been unaware of the importance of the family in daily life, in some quite literal sense. They referred to the relationship of men to their wives and children, upon occasion; but they said very little about women or life within the family.[30] The prosaic reason for this, I think, is that they believed that they could continue to take patriarchal kinship structures for granted. Philosophers, as Gilles Deleuze says, are people who create concepts.[31] They respond to the necessity for rethinking categories when social institutions are undergoing radical change and people require new ways of understanding themselves and their world.

Social philosophers during this period were focused on the project of articulating new economic and political relationships in response to the demise of feudal hierarchies. Modern political theory had to make sense of radical upheavals in power relationships between men as previous social hierarchies lost their legitimacy. While historians now describe significant and even dramatic changes in kinship relationships and families over the several hundred years of developing liberalism, *kinship hierarchies* within families were not fundamentally challenged during the transition from feudalism to modern society. The quality of patriarchal relationships changed substantially during this period, but the legitimacy of the patriarchal power of men within families was not fundamentally called into question.[32] Thus philosophers were not compelled to rethink kinship power relationships as they were driven to examine economic and political relationships.

The family was discursively constructed during this time as a "natural" entity, the apparently transhistorical givenness of kinship obligations now contrasting with the artifice and rationality that social contract theorists were proclaiming as the basis for civic responsibilities within the democratic public sphere. Nevertheless, as the social foundation upon which the new public sphere was erected, the meaning and significance of kinship relations could hardly remain unaffected by the developing economic and political categories of liberalism. Though the family was never explicitly articulated as an institution of liberalism, a *familial shadow image* of the liberal individual developed over time. Extended kinship relationships contracted, and the family was articulated as a penumbra of activity surrounding and supporting the dominant figure of liberalism: the public male individual.[33] As we map the relationships and agency of persons within this familial shadow image it should become clear why I have said that the public agency of the liberal individual presupposes an incorporated male family self, and why the various agency dimensions of individualism are likely to change dramatically after the social enfranchisement of women.

It has been a common practice of political thinkers to use terms of liberal theory metaphorically to refer to relationships within the family. John Locke and Immanuel Kant, for example, made superficial efforts to explain marriage as a form of contractual exchange between a man and a woman.[34] Since neither of these theorists considered women to qualify as independent economic and political agents capable of entering into contracts in other contexts, their references to a marriage contract were more a matter of rhetorical convenience than rigorous analysis. Feminists, as well as some nonfeminists, have judged such references quite harshly.[35] As

As with Plato: why?

Hegel tartly reminded such thinkers, the marriage agreement was as likely to begin as a "contrivance of benevolent parents" as with "the inclination of the parties" to the actual marriage. In either case, it hardly fulfilled the conditions of a contractual exchange, insofar as the contingent contractual quality of the agreement had to disappear once the parties consented to and became conscious of what Hegel called their "ethical unity" with one another. The traditional marriage bond, once consummated, was presumed to become unconditional, for at least the period of time when children were being reared.[36] While Kant and Locke made casual references to the marriage contract, it is significant that none of the liberal political philosophers made the further "category mistake" of discussing private-sphere family relationships in terms of public-sphere ideals of individual achievement, freedom, or equality.[37]

As a site of hierarchical power relationships, the patriarchal family was not an entity that liberal political theorists could justify, except very superficially, in terms of the democratic principles of social contract theory. Carole Pateman has recently suggested, however, that the patriarchal family within liberal society is indeed the consequence of a social contract, but it is a "sexual contract" among men as a fraternal group, rather than between a man and a woman. She proposes that "the sexual contract is a repressed dimension of contract theory, an integral part of the rational choice of the familiar, original agreement."[38] Her idea is a striking one; if the modern patriarchal family is a construction of liberalism, corresponding with the creation of the liberal democratic state, then the personal sphere is immediately rendered a political one, as feminists have long maintained on less theoretically explicit grounds. There is also an undeniable social logic to Pateman's claim. The subordination of women within patriarchal kinship relationships is clearly to men's advantage, and thus it is abstractly conceivable that men might have consciously chosen patriarchal families. Furthermore, Pateman is correct in maintaining that the freedom enjoyed by men within liberal society has depended upon the continued patriarchal subordination of women.[39]

Yet patriarchal kinship relationships were a fundamental aspect of medieval feudalism, and were thus social background conditions for modern contract theory, hardly a product of it. Social contract theory was formulated in the context of fundamental political upheavals and a quite real framework of economic and political alternatives within the public sphere. Such a context of radical structural change was simply not present in the eighteenth-century family. In the seventeenth and eighteenth centuries, when social contract theory was being enunciated as the basis for individual freedom and equality in the liberal public sphere, men and women both accepted gendered, hierarchical family roles as natural and necessary social identities designated at birth. Even those rare women and men who questioned the tyranny of men in their family roles offered no vision of alternative roles for men and women.[40] The modern liberal categories of individual voluntariness and choice so basic to notions of contract are inappropriate in formal analyses of men's relationships to their families, until recently.[41] While patriarchal domination assured men of certain advantages within marriage, it hardly implied their ability to choose whether or not to be in such a relationship. As Foucault has emphasized, persons who dominate within a particular social relationship may yet wholly lack the power to change the structure of the relationship.[42] Feudal patriarchy was the context for the relatively unself-conscious development of modern patriarchal families. The quality of relationships within the patriarchal family of liberalism is therefore obscured rather than illuminated by projecting upon it a contemporary vision of self-conscious patriarchal agency.

The family of liberalism was neither a natural nor a contractually constituted entity. It was at once a hierarchical community held over from medieval feudalism, and a modern construct of liberal discourses and the silence of liberal discourses. The modern patriarchal family was created by the simple maneuver of excluding women from participation in the new public spheres of liberal agency. Although women were quite active entrepreneurially at the beginning of the modern period, as manufacturing developed and capitalist structures were articulated in the eighteenth century, women were legally excluded from most forms of economic participation.[43] As the constitutions of modern democratic states were created, the presumption was that only men of property could show the independence of mind required for exercising political citizenship.[44] Women were written out of the public sphere of economic and political agency and out of the constitutive discourses of liberal individualism. Juridically denied the right to participate in the public spheres in which modern individual agency was embodied, women could have no identity within liberalism as social selves. A woman was regarded as a private extension of either her father's or her husband's public self, and her activities were conceptualized in terms of the reproductive needs of the incorporated family self. Since only the male head of the family participated in the public spheres in which modern selves were constituted, each adult male was, in an almost literal sense, the visible social head of a socially invisible family body. Women and children could have significance in the discourse of the liberal public sphere only as represented by a male familied self.

It is possible to make various analogies between the incorporated fam-

ily within liberalism and a modern corporation.[45] Like the modern corporation, the modern family acquired the legal status of a single person
within liberal theory.[46] The role of the economic corporation is one of
production, while that of the incorporated family is social reproduction.
No matter how many employees a corporation has, their relationships and
their labors are all subsumed by the corporate entity. The corporation
makes a profit, or declares bankruptcy; the employees never do. So too
with the incorporated male family self; married women, for example,
were not allowed to own property. The corporation has a clear authority
structure; so too the patriarchal family. The agency of men as well as
women in the family involves mutual but asymmetrical hierarchically organized relationships of duty and obligation.

Of course, the modern corporation is finally a product of contractual
relationships. Employees must accept the hierarchical structure so long as
they choose to work there, but they may always decide to break their employment contract. The responsibilities of the employees to a corporation
are always finally limited, in the last instance, by each individual's ability
and right to decide to end the relationship. This element of liberal autonomy or personal freedom is not present in the patriarchal family, at least
prior to the social enfranchisement of women. Only by exploring this final
disanalogy with liberal forms of incorporation can we gain a full understanding of the patriarchal family. The familial obligations of men and
women were very different from each other, but inherent in both were
qualities of givenness and absoluteness that have become difficult to comprehend today.

For men, familial duties were conceptualized as "special obligations,"
presumably to distinguish them from the normal, more limited sorts of
obligations incurred in contracts in the public sphere.[47] These familial obligations were explained in ways that allowed them to be compatible with
public categories of individual agency. The theory of the incorporated
male family self is important for understanding how the frequently quite
onerous breadwinner responsibilities of an individual man could intensify
his public sense of economic "self" interest, without compromising his
sense of freedom and autonomy. Insofar as a man experienced his wife and
children as extensions of himself, his obligations and concerns for his family become an aspect of self-love. Indeed, his incorporated family self was
an important background condition for his striving to attain autonomy
and self-sufficiency in relation to other men.

Men were citizens and workers, and their familial obligations were
limited in various ways by their public roles. Unlike men, women's identity was constituted within the family, through fulfilling the obligations

of motherhood, wifely care, and domesticity. In a liberal context of individuated agency we often think of the unceasing labors of women on
behalf of husbands and children as "self-less." Yet once we grasp the context of women's agency within the incorporated family self, we will realize
the limitations of this concept with regard to women's activities. Prior to
the social enfranchisement of women, liberal discourse did not acknowledge the individual achievements of women or their pursuits of
freedom. Regardless of their *actual* activities and achievements, the recognition factors of the liberal public sphere were not available to women.
Women were recognized, almost exclusively, for their familial activities;
to toil in the fields or to minister to the needs of a sick child were all part
of women's familial duties. Such familial obligations were potentially
limitless, as limitless as the demands made upon a slave. But unlike the
slave, who was treated as a mere instrument of another's needs, a woman's
labors were basic to her identity as a wife and mother. What we find oppressive and demeaning from a liberal perspective is that a woman had no
individuated identity within the patriarchal family. Once we acknowledge the corporate identity of a wife and mother, however, we realize that
acts on behalf of family members were also acts on behalf of herself.

The incorporated male family self has provided the social foundation
for male and female kinship relationships and agency, as well as for public
forms of male agency within liberalism. Remarkably, these hierarchical,
gendered relationships continued to appear natural and necessary to most
people until very recently, despite the possibilities for criticizing them
afforded by the doctrines of liberal political theory.[48]

*In fact, any thoroughgoing critique of patriarchal relationships within the family
compromises liberal society, as well as any socialist variation upon it that assumes
an incorporated family as a primary means of satisfying psychic relational forms of
neediness.* Only when the social enfranchisement of women and the attendant unmooring of psychic relational forms of neediness from traditional
kinship structures has reached a certain quite advanced stage does the
necessity of envisioning societies in which these forms of neediness are
met in new ways become unavoidable.[49]

v. Familial Unmooring: Individuals Reengaging

Having firmly anchored the liberal individual in the patriarchal family, we
are better prepared to witness the pathos of his unmooring, as the social
enfranchisement of women proceeds. I will analyze three phases of the
current process of social unmooring of persons and forms of neediness
from the incorporated family of liberalism. In the first phase, as women

take on public forms of liberal agency they and their material needs are unmoored from the male family self of liberalism. In the second phase of this process, men come unmoored from the family, as their patriarchal identity as its head is challenged and loses its legitimacy. In the third phase of generalized unmooring, the quality of the family unit as a site of social anchorage even for children comes into question. It is at this point that "family values" become an open subject of debate.

Consider the features of the first phase. After the Civil Rights Act of 1964, there was a heady decade and more during which the employment rights of women expanded dramatically; past exclusions of women from various job categories were declared unconstitutional, and there were statutory and regulatory mandates to provide women with equal opportunities for promotion and job compensation. At the same time, the economic responsibilities of women as family members, and increasingly as heads of families, grew rapidly. The contraceptive revolution also occurred during this period of time; in the context of this chapter its relevance lies in the instrumental role of contraceptive technologies in the transformation of women's agency and identity in both the public and the private spheres. As massive numbers of women were propelled into the public workplace, female obligations with respect to reproduction began to become articulated in unprecedented ways.

The first phase is most identified with the fact that, within a shockingly brief span of time, the "natural" dependence of women upon the economic and political agency of fathers and husbands came to an end. Conservative and progressive men alike were persuaded with surprising ease that women, or at least the women they were personally involved with, could shoulder the economic obligations of maintaining what had been the patriarchal family. Women have not let their husbands or their former husbands down. Upon being allowed and encouraged to leave the family domicile each morning along with men, women soon began to demonstrate all the psychological features of economic and political agency that had been presumed biologically and/or psychologically exclusive to men. With astonishing speed, women have proven their capacity for public forms of liberal agency: from motives of material self-interest and even greed to calculating unemotional forms of rationality, women have shown the ability to master all the iconically masculine forms of competitive behavior. This recent history strongly supports the idea that women's previous failure to manifest many of the traits of economic and political agency associated with liberal individualism was more a consequence of their exclusion from liberal economic and political structures than a matter of natural deficiencies. Longstanding assumptions of gender essentialism with respect to the motivational structures of liberal agency simply look foolish today.

Most dramatic, however, has been the transformation in our social assumptions with respect to the responsibility dimension of women's agency. Within a period of no more than twenty-five years, social norms about the economic responsibilities of women within marriage have been turned inside out. The economic dependency of women upon men, which had long been idealized within liberalism, rapidly became tinged with moral illegitimacy once the social enfranchisement of women began. Because traditional female domestic and maternal duties did not decline very much as women's economic obligations outside the home grew, women's overall burdens have increased substantially, as discussions of "the double day" of women bitterly chronicle. Ironically, while kinship obligations no longer have the absolute, unqualifiable hold over women that they had within the incorporated patriarchal family structure, the familial responsibilities of women have frequently become more onerous.

Moreover, liberal recognition-and-reward dimensions of agency have proved singularly rigid; the continuing masculinity of the social gaze during this period has become increasingly frustrating. As women have enthusiastically sought equality with men in economic and political relationships, basic forms of liberal recognition have been denied to them. Women now make approximately 70 percent of what men make in wages and salaries; there is still a "glass ceiling" in many corporate structures above which women have difficulty rising; sexual forms of recognition continue to operate in highly asymmetrical ways that contribute to women's subordination, and even invisibility, in various public contexts.

It is important for women to remember, however, that "equality" within liberal political theory has always signified a particular dimension of recognition relationships rather than anything of deep metaphysical import. Thomas Hobbes presupposed mental and physical differences between men, discounting them in the context of the greater significance of equality based upon the common ability to imagine having and getting glory and material goods. However different women are from men physically and mentally, what is socially significant is the fact that they now participate fully in the economic, political, and familial responsibility structures of liberal agency, and may thus be presumed to participate in liberal appetites for material goods and glory. According to such an analysis, women are currently suffering the effects of a lag between their rapid induction into liberal structures of motivation and responsibility and the relatively slow pace of change within liberal dimensions of recognition and reward.[50]

The disheartening disparity between the gender mobility of the motivation and responsibility dimensions of liberal agency, and the gendered immobility of liberal dimensions of recognition and reward has inspired recent feminist theories of a "backlash" against feminism.[51] While the effects of the lag in recognition and rewards have been extremely oppressive to women, I think we can best struggle against these effects by understanding this disparity as a structural problem rather than by reacting to it as rationally motivated political behavior. Certainly a great many men have reason to wish that the social enfranchisement of women had never begun, and correspondingly, they have reasons for attempting to obstruct women's achievements and to impede their attainment of proper rewards. But deep-seated problems of recognition and reward today are a consequence of changing modalities of agency and individualism, and will increasingly affect men as well as women who choose to act in ways not readily identifiable according to the recognition-and-reward structures of liberal individualism.[52]

The second phase of this process—the unmooring of men from their patriarchal family selves—begins soon after the social enfranchisement and unmooring of women, and overlaps with this first phase. When women take on liberal forms of economic and political agency, the patriarchal identity of men as the head of an incorporated family self ceases to be legitimate insofar as it assumes the subsumption and subordination of women in a male-headed family. The notions of agency associated with an incorporated family identity cease to make sense in the same way. Even for men who remain conscientious fathers and husbands, "self" ceases to have an incorporated familial meaning and comes to mean "mere personal self." The "special obligations" of a man to his family are no longer quite so special, and definitely not so absolute.[53]

It is not much of an exaggeration to say that all dimensions of male familial agency are cast into disarray once the unmooring of men from patriarchal kinship structures has been set in motion. Economic self-interest, freed from an absolute familial ballast, becomes more discretionary. The recognition and rewards men could count upon as primary breadwinners of the family have become less available to them. Even twenty years ago, men were praised for being the sole providers for their families, and frequently looked down upon for allowing their wives to contribute to the family income. They could enjoy without guilt the pleasures of returning home at night to the ministrations of a traditional wife. Today, by contrast, men are respected for marrying women capable of sharing economic responsibilities, and may even be criticized for allowing a wife to take advantage of them by refusing to work outside the home. The familial dominance of a sole male provider is never secure, as the potential economic agency of a woman is always evident to both husband and wife.

As in the case of women, it is the responsibility dimension of male familial agency that has been most drastically transformed in the wake of the social enfranchisement of women. A quarter of a century ago people expected marriages to last for the duration of their lives. Male familial responsibility was defined in terms of a lifetime duty to provide for, and therefore to remain domestically connected with, a wife. Male responsibility for children was more temporally limited, of course, requiring material maintenance and connection for only the first sixteen years, approximately, of each child's life.

When women began regularly sharing in the economic maintenance of the family, the day-to-day familial economic responsibilities of men immediately declined in intensity. Men of previous generations were forced to work overtime or take on second or third jobs when their families required more income, but today much of the pressure is off men. Even women fully occupied with raising children in the home will readily take on a paying job when family finances become difficult. It is the lifetime extent of male familial responsibilities that has been most dramatically qualified, however, by the enfranchisement of women as economic agents. The obligation of men to their wives and their children had an absolute quality in the past; divorce or abandonment were censured by all relevant social institutions to a degree that enforced lifetime responsibility codes. Once the economic and political independence of women had been sufficiently asserted, however, male duties to wives and children took on an increasingly discretionary quality. Without coming to approve of divorce, society has come to accept it as necessary and reasonable in many cases. The responsibilities of men and women to previous spouses have been difficult to agree upon. The responsibilities of men to children they have fathered but whom they do not live with have proven surprisingly difficult to define, and even more difficult to enforce. Male familial obligations have oscillated from relative absoluteness to relative voluntariness in this period of loosening familial bonds.[54]

Men are likely to be increasingly dissatisfied with public-sphere forms of recognition and reward as a direct result of familial disengagement. The privileged gender status of men as heads of incorporated family selves was a basis for experiencing equality with other men, and without this social privilege the great inequalities sanctioned by the institutions of the public sphere become more evident. The liberal ideal of individual achievement was also propped up to some extent by the incorporated male's implicit sense that his family was a personal achievement he could be proud of,

A man alone can do any of the [for non-family things he could do with a family, no? So where is the "autonomy /freedom - liberty)" [used family" link?

146   A Genealogy of Individualism

even if his job did not fulfill that ideal. Marx's alienated worker was yet an incorporated male family self. The psychic comforts provided by his family distracted him from public injustices and presumably diminished his commitment to class struggle in ways Marx failed to recognize. Workers today are more likely to lack familial substitutes for workplace meaning. Even the liberal ideal of personal freedom is unlikely to be enhanced more than momentarily by male familial disengagement, as it rapidly becomes evident that the old familial regime was an important condition for attaining a satisfying sense of liberal male autonomy. The second phase has undermined the social identities of men in all spheres of their lives.

The third phase of familial unmooring commences when patriarchal kinship structures have declined to such an extent that the problems of unmoored children become salient. As women increasingly leave home each day to take on responsibilities within economic and political institutions, as men abandon and feel themselves abandoned by patriarchal kinship structures and family roles, the importunate needs of children remain, and become newly visible within the public domain. The previously absolute, "natural" responsibilities of women and men in relation to patriarchal kinship structures have undergone various liberal and postliberal mutations. We have no narratives or frameworks adequate for understanding the current mushrooming of ad hoc accommodations to parental responsibilities in a time of accelerated familial disengagement.

What were previously experienced as natural responsibilities are now intertwined with technological as well as economic and political forms of agency, in the experiences of women as well as of men. The social grounds for believing that parental responsibilities are natural or absolute have declined. This is the context in which I suggested in chapter 3 that motherhood is a cyborgean identity today, and proposed that interpersonal agency must be a component of any reproductive process such that cyborgean reproduction is not presumed to begin until potential parent(s) have committed themselves to the project of creating and maintaining developmental connections with a future child. In this chapter, I am suggesting that a notion of interpersonal agency is also necessary in order to begin rechoreographing day-to-day domestic relationships between individuals within postmodern families in which neither male nor female forms of agency can any longer be construed as absolute. Individuated decisions to create, maintain, and when necessary break off affirmative connections to others must somehow add up to forms of intimate community sufficient for the raising of children and the psychic well-being of adults.

Current debates over "family values" can seem rather bland; everyone believes in some sort of family values. But these discussions have revolutionary implications. Prior to the social enfranchisement of women, there could be no fundamental debate over family values; hierarchical heterosexual relationships were constitutive of patriarchal families. Relationships within post-social enfranchisement families are on a newly voluntary basis for both men and women, and to some degree even for children.[55] Families are limited partnerships now, created and maintained according to the daily decisions of the adult partners. Discussions of family values signify the arrival of a plethora of "grass-roots" alternatives to the patriarchal family. These familial permutations are perhaps united only by the fact that all are constituted and reconstituted each day by discretionary individual motivations, notions of obligation, and concerns for social recognition. Presumably as interpersonal modes of agency play a greater part in our lives, the quality of individualism will become more sociable. Just as practices within the incorporated patriarchal family prepared children to participate as adults in the structures of liberal individualism, egalitarian postmodern families will raise children who have learned how to develop and maintain close relationships in which no one's identity is sacrificed to that of another.[56]

The efforts of adult men and women to satisfy their psychic neediness within relationships based upon individuated forms of interpersonal agency may result in relatively institutionalized structures of intimate community evolving over a period of time. It is the urgency of children's physical and psychic forms of relational neediness, however, which ensures that the dissolution of the incorporated patriarchal family will inspire immediate efforts to generate new "familial" configurations capable of meeting the needs of children and parents. The neediness of children not only forces us to rethink our gendered, heterosexual notions of familial responsibility, but it also leads us to question previous boundaries between private family communities and more public communities, such as schools and workplaces, which are increasingly called upon to play a part in child-rearing.[57]

The third phase is upon us, and as we struggle to deal with the unmooring of children from patriarchal kinship structures, we are likely to be most conscious of the structural and institutional changes necessary to accommodate cyborgean motherhood and postmodern reproductive relationships. But it is already clear that the transformations resulting from disbanding the incorporated male family self will hardly end there. In chapter 1, we investigated major upheavals in male and female identities, and ensuing confusions in our most basic notions of rational agency. In chapter 2, we considered gendered recognition relationships and the dramatic alterations in public as well as private narratives of achievement required by the social enfranchisement of women. The most confusing aspect of phase three, however, involves the fact that as familial structures undergo fundamental changes, and as male and female identities and notions of public as well as private agency are transformed, *public structures of power continue to appear relatively unchanged*. Surely these structures will eventually show the effects of the decline of the culture of liberal individualism. A multitude of indirect and currently dispersed effects will manifest themselves gradually as the culture of liberal individualism wanes, and women and men develop new public and private relationships in a culture of engaged individualism. The last chapter of this book explores contemporary sites of micropolitics in which public-sphere relationships are beginning to be renegotiated and reigning institutional structures challenged.

vi. Beyond Liberal Notions of Agency

Here an overview of the two-stage theory of individualism presented in this chapter is in order. Afterwards, I will briefly speculate upon the character of this unfolding postmodern moment. I have argued that it is reasonable to think of the dominant paradigm of agency under liberalism as "economic" insofar as it developed in response to the unmooring of individuals and their material forms of neediness from the landed estates of medieval feudalism. As we saw in section iii of this chapter, however, the public agency of the liberal individual was typically understood in relation to complex political ideals of equality, freedom, and individual achievement. Complementing the public dimensions of liberal agency were various gendered familial dimensions of agency. In section iv, we investigated how the motivations and responsibilities of the liberal man and his wife were jointly articulated within the incorporated family self in relation to the public dimensions of his agency.

In section v, I sought to demonstrate that a second historical stage of individualism is currently beginning; an unmooring of women, men, and children and their psychic forms of neediness from the incorporated family selves of patriarchal liberalism is occurring. Just as the need to respond to material forms of neediness in newly individuated ways explains the development of economic forms of agency and liberal individualism, I maintain that the need for individuated responses to unmoored psychic relational forms of neediness fosters the development of interpersonal forms of agency. The importance of interpersonal forms of agency in the lives of women, men, and children who find themselves newly disengaged from traditional family structures will gradually lead to a culture of engaged individualism.

I envision engaged individualism, at least in the early phases of this process, as an amorphous umbrella-like "identity" harboring multiple, often conflicting forms of agency that are operative in the daily lives of contemporary individuals. The distinctive quality of engaged individualism will be produced by a subtle shift in emphasis away from paradigms of agency that ultimately refer back to material forms of neediness, and toward agency paradigms in which actions and decisions may equally well originate in psychic forms of neediness. Neither economic nor interpersonal modes of agency will be hegemonic. Yet all the different dimensions of agency, from recognition-and-reward factors to notions of desire and responsibility, will reflect this basic shift in the social parameters of agency.

At least they will reflect this shift insofar as we are successful in articulating a postmodern theory of individual agency. There are powerful social currents tending to undermine our belief in individual agency today. As previous liberal notions of agency make less and less sense in contemporary society, an explanatory vacuum is created. When we criticize and forecast the decline of the gendered kinship relationships that have undergirded liberal notions of agency, we call into question our most basic assumptions about the sources of individual agency. Patriarchal notions of sexual agency, and of economic and political agency as well, have rested their conceptions of desire, responsibility, and recognition and reward upon specific gendered relationships between men and women. As our vision of society comes to rest less and less upon distinctly binary gendered relationships, our sense of individual agency loses its patriarchal foundations. Individual agency will appear to wane insofar as it is strongly identified with its previous binary, gendered content.

Scientific efforts to comprehend behavior in causal terms quickly move into the breach. In addition to longstanding efforts of natural scientists to explain human actions in terms of physical causes, social scientists now explain our behavior in terms of various sociological and linguistic structures of causation. If narratives of individual agency are to regain not merely plausibility but social and theoretical significance in the postmodern milieu, we will need to articulate the motivations, responsibilities, recognitions, and rewards of individual agency in ways that explain egalitarian relationships between women and men, as well as between persons from different cultures. I believe that discourses articulating interpersonal agency will provide the social fabric for more egalitarian relationships in our milieu. In the concluding chapter of this book I investigate different ways in which micro-political forms of individual agency are already transforming relationships within particular institutional contexts today.

It is important, however, to understand the current vulnerability of the concept of individual agency in more specific terms. Feminism and the civil rights movements of blacks and other minorities initially defined their basic political projects with reference to liberal political ideals of individual achievement, freedom, and equality. For a number of reasons, these recognition-and-reward dimensions of liberal agency elicit an increasing amount of skepticism. Because they are fundamental components of individual agency today, our ideals of freedom, equality, and achievement must be reconfigured in relation to the projects of currently engaged individuals. The social enfranchisement of women has fundamentally upset gendered liberal assumptions about the origins and distribution of desire and responsibility as well. Given the decline in liberal forms of individual agency, we can fend off claims that the explanatory frameworks of the physical and social sciences make notions of human agency unnecessary only if we can point to new modes of individuated behavior embedded in currently evolving public and private relationships.

The disillusionment with liberal ideals of political agency on the part of marginalized groups is reflected in the bleak title of black law professor Derrick Bell's recent book, *Faces at the Bottom of the Well: The Permanence of Racism*.[58] After twenty-five years of antiracist, antihomophobic, and feminist battles for equality and justice, there is a clear sense that the liberal ideals that fueled these struggles initially are inadequate or even empty. Feelings of social impotence are strong among women and minorities whose social position has not improved very much by many objective measures. The postmodern theories of Jacques Derrida and Michel Foucault have been criticized for encouraging this sense of impotence, insofar as they blithely deconstruct liberal categories of political agency, analyzing the ubiquity of power relationships within everyday life, and implying that any theory of progress or emancipation will be vulnerable to similar deconstructive unmasking.[59]

Yet it seems clear that with the decline of the incorporated patriarchal family and liberal individualism, we are faced with a historic opportunity to rearticulate political ideals to address the concerns of women and cultural minorities, as currently disengaged but potentially engaged individuals. Notions of freedom and individual achievement, for example, will have very different associations for the engaged individual than for the incorporated family man. Some theorists are beginning to recognize the conceptual challenges at hand. The political economist Amartya Sen contrasts a typical liberal emphasis upon the quantity of resources a person is allotted with what he sees as a more important concern with ensuring that each person possesses capabilities of acting. What Sen criticizes as liberalism's "well-being" standard of freedom might previously have been justified, of course, in terms of the incorporated male's primary responsibility for maintaining the physical well-being of a family. Sen advocates that we instead adopt what he calls an "agency" standard of freedom, emphasizing the ability of individuals to act in diverse ways, pursuing well-being in some cases and in other cases pursuing goals that may adversely affect their well-being.[60] Sen's proposal rightly responds to a situation in which women and various Others are newly participating in the public sphere and bringing with them needs and goals that must be encompassed within a more flexible and dynamic concept of freedom. Given the various problems faced by unmoored individuals today, concerns with increasing material well-being may not always have the highest priority.[61]

Notions of individual achievement and freedom are extremely conflicted today as a consequence of social transformation. Economist Juliet Schor points to polls showing that most Americans would prefer more leisure, even at the price of reduced material living standards. She also observes, ruefully, that shopping has become the chief leisure-time activity of many, resulting in a work-and-spend cycle that dominates people's lives. People might prefer more leisure and less emphasis on material goods when offered this as an abstract choice — yet they continue to opt for longer work hours in order to pay the bills their leisure-time habits generate. Longer workdays, perversely, will be associated with greater freedom for so long as our notion of freedom is dominated by material sources of satisfaction.

Schor suggests social incentives that might encourage people to "reclaim" leisure time.[62] The very term "leisure time" suggests the dominance of economic agency in our self-understanding, however. What does leisure connote other than time when we are not working? We need constructive accounts of the important activities that occupy our so-called leisure time in order to justify turning away from the work-and-spend cycle and the well-being notions of freedom dominant within liberal culture. If we learn to think of ourselves as engaged individuals with various interpersonal relationships and activities that are just as important as economic activities we may begin to structure our lives quite differently. We may come to think of ourselves as *requiring* a balance between economically driven activities and various community and familial activities.

Indeed, as men and women have come to share economic responsibilities, there are signs that they both have inclinations toward regarding familial duties as alternative sites of meaningful achievements and free-dom. Yet postmodern narratives of parenting must portray familial activi-ties in a whole new light if they intend to alter current representations of child care as a site of socially devalued labor. Only a dramatically new story of child care and related activities, supported by changes in institu-tional practices that allow child care to become a site of personal em-powerment and freedom will make it possible for women and men to justify decisions to forgo work or leisure-time shopping in order to care for or play with their children.

This is only the most obvious example of how narratives as well as in-stitutional norms of recognition and reward must change in order to revitalize a sense of individual agency in a postmodern world. At the mo-ment, there are not grounds for immediate optimism with respect to this project of redefinition. Yet our sense of agency is relatively well-devel-oped around the dimensions of recognition and reward in this society, and it is possible to concretely project the sorts of changes required to make individual ideals of freedom and achievement meaningful goals once again.

When we turn to the dimensions of desire and responsibility, the very tenuous status of any contemporary theory of agency becomes more evi-dent. Liberal notions of obligation and desire are increasingly unable to make sense of contemporary behavior, but postmodern conceptions of in-dividual responsibility or desire are difficult to enunciate. The self-other dualisms so fundamental to the discourses of liberal individualism inhibit understandings of relationships in which individuals act out of interper-sonal agency to create egalitarian bonds of desiring intimacy or responsi-ble dependency. The sorts of postmodern bonds that will make sense be-tween engaged individuals are construed as unlikely and compromising when envisioned between liberal individuals.

Consider first the dimension of responsibility. Liberal theory delineates determinate and distinct forms of public and private responsibility for in-dividual men. Obligations in the public sphere are defined in terms of con-tractual relationships; each individual is presumed to act in response to a rational (welfare-maximizing) conception of his self-interest. The parties to contracts are presumed, in the words of John Rawls, to be "mutually disinterested," or "non-tuistic." The moral philosopher David Gauthier elaborates: "The market requires only that persons be conceived as not taking an interest in the interests of those with whom they exchange . . . my preferences do not involve you, although they may involve some third person not party to our interaction."[63] Indeed, the economic individual's public responsibilities are purely contractual, but his special obligations to his family are also taken for granted. As Gauthier's specification of the theory of non-tuism demonstrates, economic theory explicitly distinguishes between the mutual disinterest of parties to a contract, and the fact that each man's individual preferences are likely to include concerns for his family. The man's special obligations to his family are, of course, complemented by the rather more absolute set of duties of women as wives and mothers within the incorporated patriarchal family. In other institutional contexts as well contractual responsibilities have typically been supplemented with variously defined "special" obligations.

While contractual notions of responsibility remain operative today, the special duties and obligations generated within many traditional contexts, from religious and familial bonds to pedagogical and civic associations, have ceased to function with any reliability. In this third phase of patriarchal unmooring, men, women, and children are all relatively disengaged from kinship as well as from other communities within the liberal polis, and it frequently looks like there is an epidemic of irresponsibility infecting people today. If postmodern permutations of responsibility are in fact taking the place of prior notions of duty, they may be overlooked or discounted until we begin conceptualizing the interpersonal commitments appropriate between engaged individuals. The theory of cyborgean reproductive identities I propose in chapter 3 addresses this issue by suggesting grounds upon which we might reformulate parental responsibilities. In chapter 5, I discuss the redistribution and redefinition of gendered forms of responsibility in the context of various contemporary political controversies.

Consider finally the dimension of desire. When we judge whether a person possesses agency or not, notions of desire or motivation are typically uppermost in our minds. While patriarchal liberalism had little concern for the individual desires of women, I have maintained that women were nevertheless familial agents based upon the social recognition they received for their reproductive responsibilities. Yet to be recognized only in relation to one's responsibilities is oppressive, and one of the most important trajectories of social enfranchisement involves women's struggles to have their desires recognized and respected. While radical feminists once predicted that when women's desires were finally unleashed they would transform the world, such utopian visions are no longer so compelling. It is not clear how different women's interests will be from those of men once women are full social participants. It is also not likely that women will all share the same motivations and desires. The postmodern desires of women, and of men as well, are just now beginning to develop in discernible ways.

The social positioning of women and men in our present conjuncture remains asymmetrical, however. Insofar as the social agency of women has been denied under patriarchy, they are just now beginning to articulate their actions in terms of their own personal desires, responsibilities, and expectations of recognition and reward. As women newly experience the rich "three-dimensionality" of social agency enjoyed previously by many men in our society, their actions exist upon a social trajectory of hope, even when their daily efforts are not wholly successful. Men, on the other hand, may frequently experience their personal agency as declining, or even as painfully subject to attack. For as women, as well as members of other previously discounted cultural groups, acquire a status of formal social equality within the dominant culture, various everyday desires of liberal individual men become suspect.

In chapter 2, I argued that if individuals act out of a desire for recognition, as Jacques Lacan asserts, women are compelled by repeated experiences of patriarchal nonrecognition to interrogate and challenge the desires of men with whom they interact. I have shown in this chapter that the subordinate status of women is a basic feature of public as well as private familial motivational structures within liberalism. In chapter 5, I investigate some of the micro-political engagements now developing within institutions previously structured in terms of patriarchal notions of desire. Current frameworks of motivation also become subject to critique and reformulation in a multicultural context. The contemporary scenario of conflicting desires involves us in various critiques of liberal individual notions of agency, and in efforts to reconfigure the qualities and dimensions of agency within particular institutional contexts. A culture of engaged individualism will evolve as notions of agency are reworked as a consequence of micro-political struggles within diverse social institutions. With the greater social salience of interpersonal forms of agency following upon the unmooring of psychic relational forms of neediness from the patriarchal family, we will come to expect and appreciate substantively different forms of individual agency in all social spheres. As interpersonal modes of agency become a greater part of our lives, the quality of individualism will become more sociable.

Liberal social scientists and political thinkers have long assumed that the interests and the very existence of women and children were identifiable with those of the male head of household, a theoretical practice that testifies to the ideological reality of an incorporated male family self. As the social enfranchisement of women has proceeded, feminists have strenuously protested that such a theoretical perspective denies the significance of women and children and makes relationships within the family invisible. Despite increasing acknowledgements of the legitimacy of such complaints, this practice remains widespread in disciplines such as sociology and political theory.[64] It is one thing to formally recognize the new social agency of women. It is quite another to work out the theoretical implications of this new social agency with respect to liberal discourses. I hope that my theory of a second stage of individualism provides us with the analytic capacity for appreciating the truly cataclysmic implications of the social enfranchisement of women for contemporary social and political institutions—and for our ways of thinking about them as well.

5

Agency and Politics in a
Postfeminist Decade

Looking back, one of the most powerful components of Marx's theory
was his conception of class struggle. It was a vehicle of change, linking
individual consciousness of capitalist oppression to a macro-political conception of the actions that would destroy it. By the 1970s, when I came
to Marxist theory, the notion of class struggle was easy to criticize for its
romantic simplifications of the problems of revolution, as well as for its
failure to address gendered and other forms of oppression embedded
within proletarian existence. The idea of an alternative female revolutionary subject was worth entertaining, but only briefly, its limitations even
more readily evident.[1] In giving up the hope of a world historical revolutionary subject, however, we give up a great deal. For many disillusioned
radicals, it has meant becoming skeptical of the very idea of constructive
social transformation.

Postmodernism eschews traditional unitary, linear notions of progress,
yet many of its adherents remain intensely opposed to relationships of
domination. We find ourselves struggling with desires for progressive
forms of change for which it has become difficult to provide a theoretical
framework. The problem for postmodern radicals is to formulate new visions of struggle and social reorganization, to explain all over again the
quality of events and transactions that are likely to produce significant
changes in our lives. The universalizing macro-politics of class struggle
have come to seem as retrograde as purely abstract liberal ideals of dis-
tributive justice in this time of global ethnic fragmentation and local
familial unmooring. My theory of agency is intended to provide the social
fabric from which a postmodern micro-politics may be fashioned, and in
this chapter I will focus on several recent gendered controversies in which
this conception of political action proves illuminating.

i. Toward An Embodied Micro-Politics

The embodied quality of contemporary forms of political agency is an important feature of postmodern and postfeminist politics. Liberal notions

of political agency have typically emphasized the disembodied quality of political rationality, as in the Rawlsian theory of justice in which political agents place themselves behind a "veil of ignorance" which keeps them from remembering anything about their own concrete social circumstances, thus enabling them to legislate with *disinterested fairness* toward others.[2] Marx disputed the disinterestedness as well as the fairness of liberal politics, suggesting that political actions are always a product of some form of *interested (class) consciousness.* By contrast, my postmodern theory of action assumes that *politically engaged individuals will act in contextually interested ways, while frequently lacking any overarching consciousness* of the social implications of their actions.

Various institutions and discourses provide the material and symbolic parameters of micro-political motivations, responsibilities, and expectations of recognition and reward. Individuals become agents of social change as they engage in social relationships in ways that leave a particular mark on these institutions and discourses. While my account does not deny the possibility or even the likelihood of some degree of individual political consciousness, such consciousness is no longer the dominant feature of political agency. A postmodern political theorist is concerned with changing patterns of individual actions and transactions as manifested within particular institutions and discourses. She or he is concerned with tracking the complexly changing motivations, responsibilities, and notions of recognition and reward which characterize micro-political forms of agency today, and which will eventually bring about differently configured institutions and communities. We may continue to take individual "consciousness" for granted, as a basic feature of human experience; but we are aware that individual consciousness may have idiosyncratic and unpredictable relationships with actions and events, particularly in times of confusion and change. Psychologists will continue to study relationships between consciousness and action, while political theorists may now shift their focus away from this disembodied "interiority" of individual agency and toward the manifest actions of an embodied micro-politics.

The embodied quality of postmodern politics also has a second, less metaphysical reference point. The physical bodies of women, as well as of peoples possessing non-European skin colors and features, have come to signify a bottom line of social prejudice and oppression in our late-twentieth-century North American society. While grandly espousing principles of universal brotherhood and equality, liberal societies have always had difficulty in living up to their ideals of justice and democracy. Nevertheless, the United States has proudly maintained a tradition of religious and ethnic assimilation which has prevailed over various internal divisions for more than two centuries. Current multicultural problems, however, are beginning to indicate deep fissures in the American way. The variously sexed and colored bodies of women and minorities are coming to have an unexpectedly potent political presence.

The embodied social differentials of race and sex have finally exposed some very ragged edges of liberal universalism in the United States. When confronted with large numbers of heterogeneously gendered and colored participants demanding fair treatment, the vaunted inclusionary dynamic of our liberal system visibly chokes up. Those of us who are not physically assimilable stand upon previously unremarked boundaries of liberal universalism, representing its de facto exclusionary capacities for all to see.[3] There are a great many less visually stimulating grounds for oppression and unfairness in this society; but it is the visible physical markings of gender and race that allow us to represent our political agency most vividly. And should we forget for a moment our embodied political status, some unlooked-for confrontation, small or large, is likely to intrude upon our forgetfulness and return us to the struggle.

The embodied quality of our postmodern political agency can prove misleading, however, if we are not careful. There is a temptation toward reductive narratives of agency based upon sex or race. Patriarchal forms of oppression, for example, have acted directly upon the sexed bodies of women, and feminists have responded with various notions of how women must act in order to reappropriate female bodies. From the anti-pornography movement's literal-symbolic attempts to take back from men sexualized bodily images of women, to the "sexual-textual politics" of French *écriture féminine* proclaiming that women must reinvent language through "writing the female body," to the many theorists intent upon articulating the maternal identity of women, second-wave feminist politics has often relied upon a recuperation of the female bodily self as a source of alternative knowledge and power. Insofar as a focus on the bodily aspects of women's oppression under patriarchy is understood as justifying a politics of "sexual difference," oppositions between women and men provide the dominant rubric for political analysis.[4] In fact, feminists in the 1970s often saw their political struggles in terms of binary oppositions between women and men. For different reasons, Black Nationalists often saw their politics purely in terms of race.

Such reductive forms of "identity politics" have been criticized at length in the last few years. Black, Latina, Asian, lesbian, and working-class feminists have protested the exclusionary quality of a middle-class white feminist politics that did not take account of the cultural differences in women's experiences of oppression. As a consequence of this critique, many feminist theorists today distance themselves from universalistic positions that fail to acknowledge differences between women based upon age, class, sexual preference, race, and culture. We recognize the "multiple subject positions" of each individual.[5] The problem is that this more descriptively adequate notion of political positionality threatens to compound the consciousness of oppression while removing any clear sense of group-based political agency. Instead of identifying women in relation to a single form of patriarchal domination, we recognize the racial and cultural complexity of domination suffered by women. In the place of a reductive identity politics of feminist solidarity against male oppressors, we sympathetically create subjects of multiple forms of oppression who are likely to experience themselves as politically alone and impotent. In projecting multiple oppressed subjectivities onto each social actor as a way of not privileging any one notion of oppression, we risk privileging all of them! Without a well-defined conception of a multicultural politics, there is a very real danger that the poststructuralist critique of identity politics will encourage cultural relativism and political passivity.[6]

We need to find the terms to represent a struggle that is not only without a unitary political subject but also without a unitary political opponent. Legal theorist Kimberlé Crenshaw articulates very powerfully the ways in which black women disappear as political subjects by virtue of the fact that they have no unitary and constant opponent. White women can set themselves in opposition to the category of men. Black men can set themselves in opposition to whites. The black woman who is oppressed by black men thereby loses her sense of political solidarity with her own race, and when oppressed by white women she loses solidarity with her own gender. Suggesting the notion of "intersectionality" to identify the social phenomenon of multiple dimensions of oppression, Crenshaw examines the ways in which race, sex, and frequently class as well, intersect and typically intensify the problems of rape and domestic violence experienced by women of color. She demonstrates how white feminists and black male nationalists both disregard the particular features of black women's situation, with the result that they often contribute further to black women's difficulties, as each pursues a race- or gender-based agenda.[7]

We require a conception of political struggle that builds upon the facts of cultural intersectionality. Previous models of oppositional politics fail to recognize the fact that class, race, and sex, as well as other differential grounds for action, interact today in site-specific ways, requiring a more dynamic and flexible model of political agency. The concepts of interpersonal agency and engaged individualism that I began to develop in chapters 3 and 4 can help us investigate the *multiple agency positions* of individuals today, designating the diverse and conflicting practices, pressures, and possibilities that provide the context for political struggle and social transformation. If we assume the conjuncture of multiple dimensions of both oppression and agency within concrete institutional settings, we can seek to construct a fluid micro-politics embracing diverse forms of intersectional agency and struggle.[8]

In this chapter, I maintain a gendered perspective while analyzing three intersectional sites of micro-political struggle which emerged in 1991, and which have since proliferated into further conflicts. In each of these cases, multiple agency positions come into play as women seek to renegotiate the terms of female participation in legal, political, economic, military, racial, and sexual discourses. From the soldier-mothers who went to the Persian Gulf leaving military spouse-fathers at home with the children, to Anita Hill's Senate testimony of sexual harassment by Supreme Court nominee Clarence Thomas, to the date rape claims of Patricia Bowman against the Kennedy family scion William Kennedy Smith, and of Desiree Washington against the world championship boxer Mike Tyson, 1991 was a year of unprecedented public gender controversies, as women began challenging the constricted and exclusionary narratives of patriarchal institutions on many new fronts.

Philosopher Christina Hoff Sommers contrasts what she calls the "equity feminism" of the first wave of feminist struggle (which continued from the late eighteenth century up through the achievement of suffrage in 1920) and the "gynocentric feminism" of the second wave (which began in the late 1960s). She maintains that the majority of American women sympathize with equity feminism's demands that women receive fair treatment, while remaining skeptical of gynocentric beliefs that women are oppressed by the patriarchal qualities of social discourses and practices.[9] As a social philosopher and as a feminist, I find it difficult to imagine how any intellectually robust woman or man today could fail to recognize the fact that women have been oppressed by institutions and relationships that have privileged male agency over female agency, and that equity for women will require major transformations in these institutions. In this postfeminist moment, however, I think we have the opportunity to reach beyond both the superficial universalism of equity politics and the reductive sexual binaries of gynocentric or purely gendered politics, and to articulate our demands for change in more complex and constructively focused ways. For example, as women enter the military in large numbers and assert their individual (equity) rights to full participation, a postmodern political analysis emphasizes potential transformations in the symbolic structures of both military and kinship institutions. An intersectional micro-political analysis looks at how both the symbolic and material parameters of parental and military agency are changing in relation to race, class, and sexual-preference dimensions.

There is a third, purely metaphorical way in which a micro-politics of agency may become embodied. Second-wave feminists rightly emphasized the domination of and contempt for women's bodies under patriarchy, and the need for bodily notions of emancipation. Yet when feminists seek to reappropriate either the maternal body or the sexual body of women, they become enmeshed in binary gender narratives which are no longer adequate to women's and men's dynamically evolving notions of parental and sexual agency. We need an embodied metaphor of struggle that does not embroil us in previous kinship narratives and social identities. A postmodern micro-politics addresses individuals inducted through their participation in a variety of conflictual institutional discourses into politically significant struggles. Despite the fact that these public and private battles often seem thrust upon us out of nowhere, we tend to become personally invested in them to a very high degree. We need an image that can express the lived and bruising quality of these conflicts as well as their contextually variable institutional contents.

I think a sports metaphor may often provide a good way of thinking about such micro-political forms of struggle. A sports metaphor suggests the rich array of possible institutional and domestic arenas, as well as the many different regulations and game plans that may inform a particular fight.[10] It captures the odd combination of immediate seriousness and intensity, even bloodiness, of the gendered, racial, and economic struggles in which we find ourselves embroiled, while at the same time suggesting the temporal and conceptual limitations of our efforts and goals on any particular day. We grapple with confusing people and situations, participating to the best of our abilities in processes whose significance may not become clear until long afterwards, in distant places. Anita Hill's Senate testimony, for example, was a courageous and persuasive individual performance whose immediate resonances for those watching it were often overpowering. Yet its impact became dramatically overshadowed for the remainder of the hearings after Clarence Thomas's claim that he had been "lynched." The long-term significance of Hill's testimony only became evident over the succeeding year as women across the country spoke out in growing numbers against sexual harassment and became galvanized to greater political participation in the 1992 elections, in the name of Anita Hill. A sports metaphor counsels us to maintain our social bearings by focusing on our footwork and our jabs, so to speak, attempting to make the best of each round. When the bell sounds, we return to our corners and our friends, reassessing strategies, marking the differential abilities and tactics of colleagues in neighboring rings, often sharing information and learning from them. It allows heroines like Anita Hill to emerge from particularly fierce battles as symbolic figures of strength and leadership in future confrontations.

A metaphor of the female athlete also provides an alternative to the prevailing image of women as victims. Marx's model of capitalist exploitation and proletarian struggle to overcome capitalist forms of oppression has provided the basic rubric for twentieth-century political movements, from anticolonial movements to feminism. Accordingly, second-wave feminist politics have been organized around the project of overcoming patriarchal forms of oppression, and women have been portrayed as victims of various forms of male domination. The image of women as victims, however, is beginning to be experienced as overly confining in activist feminist contexts. As Nan Hunter, a Brooklyn Law School professor, recently explained, "Women-as-victim is a cultural script that evokes sympathy without challenging the hierarchical structure. It's a kind of melodrama that doesn't lead to any change in the conditions that cause the victimization."[11] Victims are perceived as passive and subject to further abuse unless protected by society. Athletes are perceived in opposite terms, as necessarily aggressive and capable of taking care of themselves. They must be strong in order to undertake their particular physical struggle, and while they may become bruised and lose in a particular engagement, they are prepared to train harder so as to have a better chance of winning in the next scrimmage. While the victim enters the struggle in order to put an end to the pain of oppression, the athlete places value in the struggle itself, and therefore has less immediate need to win. Patriarchy has endured for thousands of years and will surely not be defeated in merely a few decades of struggle. In the battle against patriarchy we must learn to love the struggle itself, as athletes rejoice in achieving a certain level of performance, regardless of whether it earns them a medal of victory.[12]

A sports metaphor is flexible enough to provide a rubric for many different processes and tactics of struggle and for the substantively diverse social goals of people who find themselves in very different institutional settings. It can make sense of spontaneous individual political acts as well as cooperative struggles extending over time, and allows for a dynamic rethinking of struggles from within the field of action. After analyzing several celebrated date rape trials we may begin to wonder, for example, if the criminal category of date rape is the best legal vehicle for renegotiating intimate relationships between men and women. A civil procedure grounded in the legal equality of the parties rather than in the victimization of the woman might be better suited to bringing about the redistribution of sexual desire and responsibility that many women are seeking. A sports metaphor encourages oppositional thinking grounded in constructive practices and goals. It recognizes that each of us will be sometimes a participant and at other times an observer or an advisor on the sidelines of these engagements. Finally, a sports metaphor provides a properly abstract framework for thinking about many different conflictual processes and relationships that all rely upon an interface between a material level of immediate struggle and a symbolic plane of projected and changing social meanings.[13]

A sports metaphor can also help us escape from the inevitable conservatism of our own visions of possible change through focusing upon the immediate field of action. Several scientists have recently compared the improvement rates of men and women in various running events over the past seventy years, and have concluded that women should be running marathons as fast as men by 1998, and rivaling men in all running events before the year 2050.[14] Of course, these startling predictions are scoffed at by other scientists. To imagine women besting men in an athletic competition is beyond comprehension for most of us. But the present level of female economic and political participation outside the home was surely beyond the wildest dreams of most people a century ago. The allusion to physical competition rightly suggests that there are measurable patterns of change to be evaluated, and that we might do better to rely upon statistical projections of current social trends than upon our own sense of how things are or of their potential for change.[15]

While I believe that the social enfranchisement of women and the resulting processes of social unmooring are the basic foundation upon which contemporary social changes are constructed, a micro-politics for the twenty-first century is a multicultural politics embracing issues of race, ethnicity, and sexual preference, as well as gender. Our differential sexual and racial embodiments are socially and politically significant facts that a micro-politics of agency can make sense of better than any identity-based politics.

ii. An Intersectional Analysis of Military Mothers

A cross-section of 1991 shows a pattern of publicly transgressive female activity from start to finish. In January the Gulf War occurred, and the media presented us with narratives of soldier-mothers who had voluntarily forsaken their domestic obligations in order to fulfill their military duties in the Persian Gulf. These women were not only trespassing on the primal male territory of combat, but they were openly violating cultural assumptions regarding the binding commitments of women within the family. Women participated in the Gulf War in greater numbers and more significant capacities than ever before, and in its aftermath Congress repealed a 45-year-old law prohibiting female pilots from combat duty. Although the military has resisted acting upon this go-ahead, a number of senior generals now support the right of women to participate in ground as well as air combat according to their abilities, many having become concerned that their daughters are not receiving equal treatment as they train for positions as pilots and other combat-related roles.[16] With Bill Clinton as the president of the United States, it may only be a matter of time before sexually discriminatory combat restrictions are rescinded, yet divisions exist even among feminists as to how we should interpret this possibility.

The symbolism associated with women's military participation is potent. The military is a final limit-case of the gendered division of social roles. Women have been allowed to take on the motivations and responsibilities of agency in most other workplaces, with only the recognition-and-reward dimension of agency still commonly withheld from them. In the military, however, women have not yet been allowed to take on the defining duty of soldiers; the activity of fighting and killing enemy forces is still deemed by many a sacrosanct male obligation/privilege. If women are accepted as military combatants, a last remaining essentialist distinction between men's and women's work will have been erased. The symbolic significance of military combat in our culture far outweighs its practical import, of course. It might be argued that gendered hierarchies will only have been truly routed when a woman's obligation to defend her country supersedes that of defending her own honor.[17]

Overseas military deployment of women also represents an unmatched apogee of female unmooring, and potential male remooring within the family. When women leave young children at home in the care of husbands and other caretakers for an indeterminate period of time, as they did in the Persian Gulf build-up, they are accused of cruelly deserting their children. In fact, their children may be loved and well cared for by others in their absence. It is the traditional maternal model that these women are deserting. In doing so, they are dramatically expanding the possibilities for redistributing parental responsibilities to fathers and others willing to share in child-rearing duties. The soldier-mothers who accepted their sudden deployment to the Persian Gulf demonstrated that in the right circumstances radical changes in familial roles may occur quite unexpectedly.

How did the Persian Gulf War happen to raise these issues, and what was the popular response to women's heightened military role? Women made up between 6 and 7 percent of the approximately 500,000 American troops eventually sent to the Persian Gulf in response to Iraq's invasion of Kuwait in August 1990. The presence of women in the American military was foregrounded in the Gulf crisis by the size and relative spontaneity of the U.S. operation. A large percentage of the forces deployed in the Middle East were called up suddenly from the reserves; and it turned out that a great many women with children now belong to the military reserves. A male military bureaucracy had failed to consider the kinship logistics involved in mustering the current mix of men and women reservists to report for active duty. A number of mothers of young children responded to the call-up without complaint, explaining that their primary duty was to serve their country, and that they expected their husbands to care for their children while they were away.[18] Other women, and a few single fathers, had more difficulty in responding to the call-up, particularly if they had no one immediately available to assume responsibility for their children. Ironically, both the desire of soldier-mothers to go to the Persian Gulf, and the desire of soldier-single-parents of both sexes not to go, upset many people. What became evident is that conflicts between professional and parental obligations constitute a growing institutional issue for the armed forces.

The military was caught short in this instance; it had avoided confronting the institutional ramifications of the growing percentage of women in its ranks. In the past, the military, like any other employer, could assume that its workforce would be made up of incorporated male family selves, wives and children forming a relatively autonomous kinship unit in the background. As long as servicemen were paid enough to support their incorporated family selves, the military could assume that its soldiers would accept deployment far from their homes in times of national need. The economic and political agency of the enlisted man or the officer was presumed dominant, overriding domestic obligations for the duration of the national emergency. But as a consequence of the social enfranchisement of women, the military finds itself employing male as well as female parents who have primary responsibility for their children. The call-up of reservists for duty in Saudi Arabia only highlighted a more general problem with the military's patriarchal workplace assumptions. The Gulf build-up demonstrated that the military cannot continue to assume the absolute dominance of its demands in the lives of enlisted personnel and officers. The armed services need to rethink the whole concept of military obligations, as well as their institutional responsibilities for the children of military personnel.

Neither the institutional obligations of the armed services to children nor the primacy of military duty over domestic duties was a major focus of public debate, however. The patriarchal logic of liberal individualism encouraged public discussion to focus on whether women, and particularly women with children, should be in the military at all. After all, the argument went, since a soldier must always be prepared for active duty in a national emergency, female soldiers with children would regularly be faced with divided responsibilities at such a time. Would it not be wise to ensure that the children of soldiers would not be endangered by every national emergency by simply barring women with children from serving in the armed forces? Of course, this argument assumes the gendered division of kinship responsibilities associated with the traditional incorporated male family self. It is ironic that male economic agency and female domestic agency is still implicitly assumed in public discussions, even now when the lives of the majority of people do not support such a gendered vision of responsibilities. In many ways, the issue of women in the military is no different than the issue of women in the public workplace generally. These problems will only be resolved on an institutional basis when employers accept the new reality of single mothers and fathers, and of parents within two-wage-earner families whose sense of daily obligation is divided between home and workplace.

Many feminist thinkers, however, would not readily accept this sanguine perspective on women in the military. When active mothers were called up for active duty in the Persian Gulf, many feminists found themselves troubled by conflicting allegiances to "feminist free choice" and equally basic commitments to a "feminist different voice." One of the long-standing political positions of feminism has been the insistence that women have the right to equal employment opportunities, even in such supremely male-identified institutions as the military. The visibility of women on the military front in the Middle East was very encouraging to those seeking to force the military to change its policies on combat duty and become a nonsexist employer. Yet when feminist thinkers reflect upon the "different voice" that women potentially contribute with their entry into positions of social power, many hear a voice of care and nurture, a voice raised in opposition to the violence and war associated with male notions of international justice. Sara Ruddick has even argued that women's bodily relationship to children within maternal practices provides a basis for challenging traditional justifications for war.[19] Women who choose to become soldiers, and particularly those soldier-mothers who place a priority on fulfilling their military obligations, may be accused by some feminists of succumbing to oppressive male values.

I believe, however, that such ideological commitments currently blind feminists to the intersectional micro-politics within the military. It is primarily working-class women and women of color who enter the armed services today, and their participation in the military undermines normative gendered binaries which have become comfortable and quite limiting within feminism. By thinking of women soldiers as engaged individuals struggling to make sense of their lives in relation to multiple conflicting structures of agency, we can begin to appreciate the complexities as well as the possibilities associated with their actions. It is appropriate to remember that as they renegotiate the gendered, raced, classed, and sexed meanings of their parental and military agencies, they are potentially contributing to a much broader social and symbolic reorganization of families and public institutions beyond the military.

A postfeminist analysis must assess the significance of women's military participation without being distracted by the traditional normative characterizations of male and female activities that continue to dominate the discussion of these issues. Above all, we must see our way beyond the reductive "good mother" versus "good soldier" dichotomy. As discussed in chapter 4, the public achievements of liberal men, including those deemed "good soldiers," were premised upon an incorporated family self, whose demise is signaled by the social enfranchisement of women. Workplaces in our society have hardly begun to adjust to the unmooring of women, men, and children from incorporated family units, however. It is primarily women performing the responsibilities of liberal men by day and fulfilling the obligations of subsumed nurturers by night who allow the patriarchal organization of the workplace to continue. When the mother-reservists were called up for service in the Persian Gulf, the far-reaching implications of the unmooring of women from the incorporated male family self were briefly exposed for all to see—although not too many people wanted to consider them. In the minds of even some feminists, the old gendered binaries continue to function as cultural blinders: a good soldier would accept deployment to the Middle East for the duration of the emergency, while a good mother would not consider leaving her child for such an extended period of time.[20] Instead of acknowledging the need to change the structure of public institutions to correspond with changing kinship institutions, they transform the daily frustrations of all working mothers into an existential choice for soldier-mothers.[21]

A postfeminist analysis insists, however, that soldier-mothers as well as soldier-fathers are engaged individuals who place all previous conceptions of parenting agency as well as military agency into question. The Persian Gulf military scenario provides a good occasion for reaching beyond our present conceptions of both the "good mother" and the "good soldier," bearing in mind the more general applications to other sorts of "good workers." Few feminists would take issue, presumably, with my earlier arguments for how the military must institutionally rethink the professional responsibilities of soldiers so as to give greater weight to male as well as female familial obligations. Yet contemporary feminists, along with the culture at large, frequently show a sentimental attachment to visions of good motherhood which would preclude the degree of parental role rethinking suggested by the potential military commitments of women.

While these normative feminist notions of motherhood may seem surprising in light of the great changes in "good motherhood" requirements over the last twenty-five years, it is precisely the trauma of these changes that may psychologically account for feminist rigidities. In *Of Woman Born*, Adrienne Rich dramatically articulates the pain of educated, middle-class women who were confined within a life of unrelenting maternity as recently as the 1950s, entrapped by psychologists and a culture that insisted that a good mother would not leave her children to work outside the home each day. Yet Rich also chronicles the intensely felt momentary joys of such a practice of motherhood.[22] Today, as feminist and non-feminist mothers alike leave the home each morning for workdays alongside men, many are surely waylaid by conflictual Rich-like images and personal memories of a generation of mothers who stayed at home with them, for better or for worse. Frequently placed on the cultural defensive about forsaking the maternal practices of their mothers and leaving their children with strangers each day, contemporary women may understandably have difficulty in imagining even greater changes in mothering practices. For those raised within an ethos of full-time mothers and incorporated patriarchal families, the military deployment of a mother to the Persian Gulf for six months may seem beyond the pale of any reasonable notion of maternal responsibility.

This is precisely the point at which an intersectional analysis becomes both politically and theoretically imperative. There are alternative cultural models of child-rearing according to which maternal responsibilities may be transferred for extended periods of time to others. Such alternative patterns are not only present in foreign cultures but are even available in our own society, in American black culture as well as various ethnic subcultures. While it is psychologically understandable that white middle-class feminists do not readily identify with such alternative patterns of child-rearing, it is neither politically nor theoretically justifiable to overlook the viability of these alternative models.

Black women in our society, for example, have long borne a larger share of economic responsibility for their families than white women, insofar as racism has hindered black men from economically incorporating as family selves. Not incidentally, the concentration of kinship and economic obligations on the shoulders of black women has reinforced alternative patterns of child-rearing. Extended familial responsibility for children is not uncommon in this culture, mothers sending their children to live for long or short periods of time with other family members. Since a relatively high proportion of women and men in the military are people of color, it would seem blatantly racist for white middle-class feminists to overlook or discount the fact that black women soldiers might have perfectly sound conceptions of mothering genuinely different from their own and more compatible with military combat duties.

For white middle-class feminists to impose their judgments of good mothering upon women of color whose experiences validate quite different child-rearing practices is not only politically offensive but theoretically foolish. The responsibilities of many white "middle-class" mothers today, particularly those who are single mothers, are more like those of black foremothers who were compelled by racism to find ways of economically maintaining their families than like those of white foremothers gently suffocating within incorporated male family selves. Women's relationships to their children are being transformed by the unmooring of men, women, and children from incorporated family selves, and we have little choice but to gradually relinquish previous liberal images and norms of motherhood. As we begin to reconceptualize parental agency, it is a great advantage to have historical models of black women's economic and parental agency to appeal to.[23]

A socially conscious feminist today is quite likely to accept the argument I have made for multicultural awareness. This argument requires that she accept the possibility of other viable conceptions of motherhood, but does not finally make substantive claims upon her own normative understanding of motherhood. The greatest challenge for an intersectional analysis of military mothers lies in the effort to rearticulate the dimensions of parental and military agency in ways that bring the lives of soldier-mothers closer to home, so to speak. By imagining the ways in which women may rethink the agency involved in both mothering and soldiering, we may achieve a more sympathetic conception of their actions. And we may also begin to recognize the vast potential for real and symbolic changes in our understanding of social activities such as mothering and soldiering which we have come to take for granted.

A soldier-mother is fulfilling roles once inhabited by traditional male and female agents, but insofar as she must integrate several sites of agency not previously conjoined, we may expect her understanding of her actions to be different at many points. For example, female soldiers may obviously be motivated by the same economic desires and obligations to provide for their children and spouses as men have been, as well as by the perception that the military offers greater chances for minority career advancement than the private sector. Women soldiers may also have the same patriotic motivations as men. But at this moment in time, it seems likely that service in the military, and particularly service in a war zone, may have intense personal rewards for women of a specifically gendered quality. As one of the primary political symbols of citizenship in a democracy, and as one of the last symbols of equality withheld from women, female combatants are pioneers and may be expected to be motivated by this fact. To be one of the first women to achieve this sort of symbolic recognition, to do so on behalf of oneself and also on behalf of other women who identify with your unusual achievement, is surely a very significant honor, an honor that may conceivably override individual considerations about the social justifications for military ventures.

Furthermore, soldier-mothers are also likely to have complicated and, at first sight, surprising interpersonal narratives explaining their actions.[24] It seems quite possible that a woman who chose to leave her child when she was called up for duty in the Persian Gulf war was motivated, at least in part, by a quite particular sense of responsibility to her child. Faced with an unusual opportunity to provide her child with a model of womanhood she or he would otherwise be deprived of, she may have felt obligated to suppress her more conventional maternal desires in order to fulfill this symbolic possibility. Can we really afford to say that this woman's sense of parental duty is not as rich or possibly richer than that of a more traditionally motivated mother who gives priority to remaining in physical proximity to her child? As I argued in chapter 3, our responsibilities as cyborgean mothers have a much greater social scope than those of organic mothers, and soldier-mothers provide a good illustration of an expanded conception of parental obligations.

It is also important to constructively explain the agency of the male military spouses who found themselves the primary caretakers of their children when their soldier-wives left for the Persian Gulf. These were men who were left quite suddenly, in some cases involuntarily, with an intense level of parenting duties for which they had little previous preparation. Moreover, as single fathers they presumably experienced the oppressive "double days" women typically bear, as they sought to combine the roles of chief nurturer and economic provider. Surprisingly, not only did a number of fathers satisfactorily fulfill the primary nurturing role required of them in their wives' absence, but some claimed to be grateful for having had the experience.[25] These military spouses are extreme examples of men in all walks of life who accept some increased degree of domestic and child-care obligations as an ongoing part of their contemporary kinship arrangements. While a great deal of attention has been focused on men's resistance to taking on the onerous domestic obligations of cooking and cleaning, little concern has been shown for investigating the ways in which men are actually beginning to make sense of new domestic and kinship duties.

We may infer from our intersectional analysis of the resistance shown by many feminists to different cultural practices of motherhood that feminists may be equally ready to reject men's articulations of parental agency insofar as these differ appreciably from those approved by feminists. Yet if we want men to participate more fully in parenting and other domestic tasks we must be willing to accept some changes in these practices. At the end of chapter 1, I used Donald Davidson's analysis of surd and meaningless behavior to explore the psychological effects upon men of currently declining patriarchal family identities. If men are not to experience their new parenting activities as surd and meaningless, they must be encouraged to articulate the quality of their motivations, senses of obligation, and of reward, regardless of how much these differ from women's previous conceptions of maternal agency.

With the erasure of gendered dichotomies such as those of the "good mother" and the "good soldier," the work of reconstructing postmodern forms of agency has just begun. New social narratives and fleshed-out subject positions are unlikely to emerge with any great speed, and to assume their necessity will only discourage individual efforts to reconfigure agency on a more immediate basis. It is misleading, for example, to refer to the "multiple subject positions" of a soldier-mother, insofar as this implies that there are several traditional subject positions that such a woman can attempt to combine. This route leads us back into a thicket of binary oppositional characterizations of the roles of mothering and soldiering. It is more politically compelling, as well as more analytically precise, to think in terms of the "multiple agency positions" we occupy. Each engaged individual must attempt to integrate and reconcile a confusingly varied set of motivations, obligations, and desires for recognition or reward on a day-to-day basis, and over time. Within broad institutional boundaries, individual creativity plays an important part in this process of reconfiguring social roles.

The Persian Gulf war dramatized, of course, the disparity between Western treatment of women and the continuing efforts of various Moslem cultures to deny women basic forms of civic recognition or participation. In such a context, liberalism is all too ready to congratulate itself upon its universal commitment to individual rights. Perusing the situation of women in the former Soviet Union and Eastern Europe, not to mention the Arab world, feminists must acknowledge the benefits of a liberal tradition of human rights. Yet a postfeminist micro-politics is not satisfied with seeking equity for women within the present military establishment. With the categories of interpersonal agency and engaged individualism we can begin to move beyond issues of women's formal access to military participation and explore the substantive social and symbolic ramifications of sending soldier-mothers and soldier-fathers to perform dangerous military assignments. Political and military leaders are accustomed to casually deploying armies of unquestioning male teenage soldiers in their violent pursuits of national glory. Cyborgean parent-soldiers may be more discretionary combatants, calling for initiatives necessary to promote a more peaceful world order even when these are not politically convenient, and opposing campaigns that do not directly advance the ends of peace.[26]

iii.   When Anita Hill Went to Washington: Passions Are Political

While the issue of women in combat has serious political implications, 1991 was also a year in which women stormed the citadels of the state head-on. A newly intersectional gendering of national politics began when Anita Hill went to Washington in October of 1991 to accuse her former boss, Clarence Thomas, nominated by President George Bush for a seat on the Supreme Court, of sexual harassment. This inadvertent, unseemly, and very upsetting political affair was seen by many commentators at the time as challenging the basic legitimacy of our government. Yet a year later, we may say that for women these special Senate hearings had an opposite effect, providing timely if unexpected encouragement for a renewed belief that a properly constituted United States government just might be capable of addressing women's concerns.

While Anita Hill's dramatic testimony did not prevent Thomas's Supreme Court confirmation, the several days of Senate hearings investigating Hill's accusations against Thomas were a milestone in the public recognition of women's presence in the workplace. Whatever the tone of the Senate hearings, the fact that they took place, combined with the media coverage of Hill's appearance before the Senate Judiciary Committee, transformed the taboo subject of sexual harassment into a serious political issue. Hill's testimony tapped into an immense lode of everyday female experience and anger over sexual harassment, and empowered women to begin taking action against it. Sexual harassment charges filed with the EEOC in the first half of 1992 increased by over 50 percent from the previous year, and further incidents of sexual harassment, most notably the harassment of at least 26 women at the Tailhook Association's convention of naval aviators, have blossomed into major scandals.[27] Moreover, in the 1992 elections, women gained financial backing, ran for office, and were elected to all levels of political office in unprecedented numbers, tripling their representation in the Senate, which had so cavalierly dealt with Anita Hill in front of millions of people.

One of the most important aspects of the Hill-Thomas hearings was that they provided an occasion for white women in this country to experience their own struggles as embodied in those of a black woman. Many women explicitly cited Anita Hill and the lack of respect shown to her by the Senate Judiciary Committee as their inspiration for running for office or for contributing to the campaigns of women who were running. Carol Mosely Braun became the first black female member of the Senate, her campaign a rallying point for women activists of all colors bent upon defeating the two-term incumbent Illinois Senator Alan J. Dixon, who voted to confirm Thomas's nomination to the Supreme Court. Indeed, Braun's victory is a reminder that the Hill-Thomas Senate drama can only be fully appreciated by recognizing its racial as well as its sexual dimensions, and the complicated interplay between them. In this section and the following one, I will investigate the conflicting political agencies that generated this confrontation, its immediate resolution, and its long-term effects.

We should begin by acknowledging that the gender politics sparked by the Hill-Thomas hearings were an inadvertent product of the racial politics surrounding the nomination of Clarence Thomas to the Supreme Court. It is generally understood that President Bush selected Thomas for this highest of judicial honors due to his proven record as a politically accommodating black conservative within the Washington power culture, and despite his striking lack of judicial experience or legal scholarship. In nominating Thomas to replace the retiring Thurgood Marshall on the Supreme Court, President Bush made a point of denying the relevance of Thomas's skin color, and he was not pressed to admit the part race played in his nomination of Thomas because a Supreme Court nomination is supposed to be based primarily upon intellectual merit. But it was precisely his blackness in combination with his Horatio Alger story of rising from an impoverished birth in Pin Point, Georgia, to the heights of government power that made Thomas appealing to a black constituency which would otherwise have opposed him due to his anti-civil rights record as head of the EEOC in the early 1980s. With impeccably perverse political agency, President Bush's strategy allowed him to be recognized for supporting particular black individuals even as he fulfilled a political agenda hostile to people of color in general.

The Senate Judiciary Committee, charged with reviewing the qualifications of Supreme Court nominees, arguably has a responsibility to reject out of hand a candidate as poorly qualified as Clarence Thomas showed himself to be.[28] But had the Senate rejected him outright for his lack of qualifications, people would have suggested that he was being held to unrealistically high standards because of his race. Although Bush had not been forced to admit the role race played in his nomination of an inferior candidate, they would be vulnerable to claims that race had played a part in their rejection of this candidate if they held him to reasonable, yet intangible intellectual standards. Since members of the judiciary committee did not want to be portrayed as less racially sensitive than President Bush, they soft-pedaled the intellectual issues. At the same time, the staffs of Democratic members of the committee conducted a nationwide search of people who had known Thomas, particularly calling upon members of the black intellectual and professional community, seeking incriminating evidence against him.[29] It seems unlikely that Anita Hill would have decided to voice her accusations against Thomas at this time had she not been contacted by the staff of Democratic members of the Senate Judiciary Committee and encouraged to reflect back on the personal and political details of her relationship with Thomas. Precisely because she too was black, her accusations could not be dismissed on racial grounds — or so the Democratic staff assumed.

Thus several years after her decision to leave the power politics of Washington behind by taking a teaching post at the University of Oklahoma Law School, Anita Hill was tracked down as a racially appropriate critic of Clarence Thomas, and induced to submit an affidavit chronicling his acts of sexual harassment against her in the early 1980s. Presented with Hill's written statement, however, the Senate Judiciary Committee failed to pursue the harassment charges; presumably some of them were wary of the sexual politics involved. Only when her affidavit was leaked to the press did Hill's allegations against Thomas become the basis for a major political confrontation. Even after the leak, race continued to be a factor in constructing the political event. Toni Morrison bitterly suggests that had the nominee and his accuser been a white man and a white woman, the nominee would have simply been asked to withdraw at this point, to avoid precisely the unseemly public spectacle that ensued.[30] But because this was a case of a black woman criticizing a black man, the Bush administration did not consider itself implicated in whatever transpired, and duly scheduled hearings from whose gladiatorial aspects it would distance itself.

At the moment on October 7, 1991, when Anita Hill held her first televised news conference explaining the sexual harassment charges she had made against Clarence Thomas, sexual politics became a newly explosive presence in the public sphere. No one, including the many feminist lawyers who provided Hill with legal support during the ensuing special hearings, could have predicted the social resonances of her testimony, nor did anyone assess them adequately during the course of the event. All that was immediately evident was that the public discussion of gender issues rapidly scaled unimagined heights of intensity and confusion. While images of female soldiers evoke strong responses from many people, their exploits remain distant from our everyday lives. Not so with the issue of sexual harassment in the workplace. The sexual harassment situation strikes uncomfortably close to home for any working woman or man.

A majority of men who are now adults were raised in a time when sexualized power relationships with women were taken for granted, and one of the consequences of the social enfranchisement of women has been to extend the opportunity for sexualized power relationships to the workplace. A great many, if not most, normal men have cause to worry that they have engaged in some degree of what is now called sexual harassment at some point in their working lives. Women's testimony to their experiences of harassment now spills forth spontaneously in any small-group discussion of the issue in our post–Anita Hill era, among students who have been in the workforce for only a few years, and among women who have spent decades silently suffering harassment. Prior to the Hill-Thomas hearings, sexual overtures toward subordinates were presumed by many men to be an understood perquisite of power and status, while women had been taught to feel embarrassed and vaguely responsible for incidents of harassment. Few people were aware that there were new laws that made men criminally liable for engaging in sexual harassment, and even fewer had considered how such laws might affect their own lives. Prior to Anita Hill's graphic testimony of the sorts of things Clarence Thomas said to her during the years she worked for him, sexual harassment was not a subject people felt safe discussing openly or even reflecting upon privately. It only began to become a part of a shared fabric of political, economic, and personal narratives as millions of people listened to Anita Hill's unsettling story.

Sexual harassment is a radically new legal concept as well. Only after the 1964 Civil Rights Act made it illegal to discriminate against women in the workplace was there a juridical structure within which to identify hostile or coercive sexual behavior as an unfair labor practice. While sexualized power relationships have surely existed for as long as women have worked in the midst of men, they could be rationalized as natural and inevitable until a universal standard of equal treatment of men and women in the workplace was mandated by the Civil Rights Act. It was not until 1976, twelve years later, that the legal thinker Catharine MacKinnon first proposed the concept of sexual harassment, defining it as "the unwanted imposition of sexual requirements in the context of a relationship of unequal power."[31] In September of 1980, the Equal Employment Opportunity Commission, the federal agency charged with enforcing the anti-discrimination laws, issued employment guidelines defining sexual harassment as "an unwanted and unwelcome sexual advance, request for sexual favors, or any other verbal or physical conduct of a sexual nature that occurs on the job." The guidelines stated that sexual harassment is an illegal act under three conditions: "when submission is made a condition of employment," or "when it unreasonably interferes with one's work performance," or "when it creates an intimidating, hostile or offensive working environment."[32]

It was not until 1986, however, in *Meritor Savings Bank v. Vinson*, that the Supreme Court finally ruled that sexual harassment in the workplace was a form of sex discrimination covered under Title VII of the 1964 Civil Rights Act. Even in *Meritor*, the court left basic issues of employer liability and standards of consent unresolved.[33] It thus took twenty-two years after the Civil Rights Act had been enacted to achieve a legal framework for proscribing sexual coerciveness in the workplace. Since women have been taught to deny or accommodate themselves to such male behavior, it took another five years before the public testimony of Anita Hill made sexual harassment into a subject that women could confront and begin to deal with in their own daily interactions with men.

When Anita Hill began to testify on October 11, the complex subtext of race and gender issues was not yet decipherable. Despite the thrilling sense of empowerment many women felt upon hearing Hill's calmly and bravely transgressive accusations against Thomas on Friday, feminist viewing pleasure ended Saturday morning with Thomas's startling claims that he was a victim of a "high-tech lynching." From that point onward, any play-by-play of the remainder of these hearings encourages the sense that they were a set-up for gender politics. Anita Hill's act of publicly articulating the verbal sexual overtures Clarence Thomas had made to her rendered almost every listener uncomfortable and confused. The Democratic senators who were responsible for her presence before the Judiciary Committee were hardly more supportive of her than were those with partisan political reasons for opposing her. The silence of Teddy Kennedy, the ebulliently effective opponent of the Bush Administration who spearheaded the defeat of Robert Bork's Supreme Court nomination, was indicative of a general male squeamishness, if not moral cowardice, in the face of the topic of sexual harassment. The Bush forces won the round of hearings, as well as the Senate vote on confirmation a few days later, handily, bolstered by a powerful and unspoken interracial, cross-class consensus in fear. The memory of Anita Hill's implacable and conscientious recitation of the sexual politics of the workplace as she had experienced them had to be denied.

Thomas was confirmed by the Senate and is now a Justice of the Supreme Court. It was the sheer staginess of his Saturday-morning declaration of being the victim of "a high-tech lynching" that made it so effective in displacing the prior testimony of Hill. People were terrified of the implications of Hill's testimony for everyday workplace sexual politics. Thomas's melodramatic appeal to the historical victimization of black men in this country was not so scary because it was clearly inappropriate in this particular context. People knew they were not guilty of lynching this black Supreme Court nominee, but Thomas's outrageous speech offered them a splendid means of evading the sexual harassment issue while at the same time cheaply assuaging nebulous feelings of historical racial guilt. White America could disingenuously "admit" their racial guilt toward the Horatio Alger figure of Clarence Thomas, a black man whose successful career could readily be presented as evidence of the lack of racial bias in our system. They could do penance for their pseudo lynching of Thomas by saying they believed his word over Hill's, thereby enabling his confirmation to the Supreme Court and distancing themselves from the more immediately worrisome phenomenon of sexual harassment. Thomas won the round on Capitol Hill, and the best hope for his potentially long Supreme Court tenure is that his skill at political accommodation will enable him to adapt to the liberal agenda of Clinton appointees as readily as he did to that of the Reagan/Bush conservatives.

Yet a year later, what is most notable about the Hill-Thomas hearings is the degree to which *Anita Hill was heard*. She was heard as no woman complaining of sexual harassment has been heard before. Her words were

spoken in the Senate of the United States, and her statement was broadcast
to millions of viewers over the electronic media. Her words are indelibly
inscribed in the proceedings of the Senate Hearings, and her dignified vis-
age is etched into the memories of all those who watched the proceedings
or glanced at the front page of newspapers during the days of the hearings.
Invited to speak within the august chambers of the Senate, Hill's words
become a part of the political discourse of our time, no matter how incon-
gruous they may initially seem, no matter how politically undigestible
they appear to some. Extensively covered by the media as a major actor
in a major political event, Anita Hill became a political subject of a white
male media gaze that has rarely been called upon to recognize the political
agency of black female bodies. Anita Hill represented a startling new
mode of micro-political agency and her testimony created waves of un-
familiar political dynamics that are sure to become more common in our
multicultural age.

Consider the significance of her voice from the perspective of American history. Here was a black woman calmly talking sex on the floor of
the Senate, forcing white senators to engage in a dialogue with her about
the margins of acceptable male sexuality in front of millions of their con-
stituents. How discomfiting for these men to have the shadowy private
boundaries of normal male sexual initiative publicly dissected by this
woman. Moreover, while the sexual exploitation of black female slaves by
white masters was never alluded to, Anita Hill's cool discursive litany of
sexual intimidation by a male employer resonated with the horrific sexual
history of white male owner/employers of black women in this country.[34]
She thus forced the male senators of the Judiciary Committee, and by extension, the predominantly white male Bush Administration, to participate in a deeply embarrassing public exploration of male sexual practices
and identities.

Her testimony also revealed the undeniable presence of highly personal
needs and transactions within a supposedly impersonal workplace. When
we admit that sexual desires are part of the contemporary workplace, we
indirectly acknowledge that professional relationships are likely to be permeated with personal deeds and misdeeds. We thereby open a floodgate
of questions about the proper standards for professional relationships, and
the bearing of inappropriate interpersonal behavior upon our judgments
of professional competence. Until very recently, it was assumed that a
man's sexual behavior had no relevance in assessing his intellectual or
professional capabilities. As media images have come to dominate political
campaigns, however, candidates have become increasingly vulnerable to
judgments of personal "character," opening the door for public concern

with psychotherapy and drug use as well as sex. Political candidates have become subject to de facto political disqualification in the face of evidence of mental instability, drug use, or sexual alliances.[35] But in suggesting that an abusive sexualization of power and authority, long hidden within an otherwise unremarkable work relationship, was grounds for questioning a man's nomination to the Supreme Court, Anita Hill was venturing onto new and threatening feminist territory.

In the immediate moment, Anita Hill's testimony upset many people, her willingness to repeat the graphic sexual phrases of her harasser sullying the genteel traditions of Congressional discourse, and burning the ears of men and women across the nation who had never before admitted to each other that they were familiar with such terms. People were angry with Anita Hill precisely because they heard her words so clearly, and were forced to begin groping to understand their significance. If some women felt empowered, many more felt violated by this sudden articulation of their years of private suffering, and men were furious at being robbed of their previous happy innocence toward their own sexually coercive behavior at work. It is perhaps not surprising that a majority of men and women at the time preferred to tell pollsters that they believed the words of Clarence Thomas over those of Anita Hill. It was a simple "hear no evil, see no evil" response.[36]

A year later, however, sexual harassment has ceased to be a taboo subject and people are more capable of confronting the issues raised at the hearings. In fact, recent polls have discovered that a greater proportion of people are now willing to say they believed Anita Hill than at the time of the hearings. This is a case of *postmodern political agency in a time-release mode.* It was the fact that Hill's voice rang out so boldly, casting sudden glaring illumination on the experiences of so many diverse women in so many different workplaces, that initially made her statement so frightening, and that also made the power of her words grow dramatically over the subsequent months. Sexual harassment is now a site of micro-political ferment in many institutional contexts. Consider only a few of the most prominent cases in 1992: Senators Bob Packwood of Oregon and Daniel K. Inouye of Hawaii currently face multiple charges of sexual harassment, while Senator Brock Adams of Washington decided not to run for reelection due to harassment charges. Randy Daniels, chosen by Mayor Dinkins to become a deputy mayor of New York City, withdrew on the eve of his appointment in response to charges of sexual harassment. The Secretary of the Navy, H. Lawrence Garrett, was forced to resign in response to the Tailhook scandal, indicating that the sexually retrograde behavioral codes of the military are finally being exposed if not yet fully reformed. In the context of gendered micro-politics, Anita Hill scored resoundingly in her performance on Capitol Hill.

iv.   The Micro-Politics of Sexual Harassment

Sexual harassment is a rather complicated site of gendered conflict, however. Properly understood, it can provide an occasion for women to insist upon renegotiating power relations and standards of recognition and reward in the workplace quite generally. Yet we need to be wary of the titillating quality of all references to sexual behavior, and not allow the concern with sexual harassment to be narrowly defined as a campaign against sex. There is a tendency to think of sexual harassment simply as a matter of inappropriate sexual conduct in the workplace. It is that. But its significance lies in the fact that it exists on a continuum with other gendered modes of interaction that interfere with the professional recognition of women, while intersecting with a continuum of nongendered workplace forms of exploitation. My analysis emphasizes the links between sexual harassment and other nonsexual problems of interaction and recognition faced by women in professional contexts. We have all heard of the woman stockbroker or CEO who is repeatedly mistaken for a secretary, the lawyer whose firm will not assign high-profile clients to women, or the successful surgeon who is yet treated in subtly cavalier ways by male colleagues.[37] The failure to recognize women as full participants within professional situations is endemic. As I argued in chapter 2, professional women all too frequently encounter the disconcerting lack of recognition from colleagues that Jacques Lacan was so surprised to experience from a sardine fisherman in a boat off the coast of Brittany.

Women are now partially recognized as participants within most public institutions and discourses, but at various points the patriarchal gaze asserts its presence, and women are subject to oppressive forms of nonrecognition (as opposed to run-of-the-mill Lacanian misrecognition). This nonrecognition takes many forms. At its limit, patriarchal nonrecognition involves a lack of respect for the bodily autonomy of women as liberal public agents. When a woman does not reciprocate a male employer's sexual interest in her, his failure to recognize her recently conferred bodily freedom and equality may lead him to confuse his institutional authority with traditional patriarchal forms of sexual power.

We all operate today within a conjuncture of disparate discourses, and the new legal category of sexual harassment serves as a reminder to women and men alike of the sorts of qualitative changes occurring within gendered relationships. In chapter 2, I argued that the contradictory quality of contemporary discourses constituted women, in particular, as socially critical agents. In the context of sexual harassment, we can begin to see why men as well will be forced to become critical of the discourses within which they have previously recognized themselves and others.

The debates over pornography a decade ago provide an important historical and theoretical background for current struggles around sexual harassment. From the perspective of postmodern agency politics, it is helpful to compare the sexual gaze within pornography and that within sexual harassment. In each case, the basic concern of women is with inappropriate and oppressive forms of sexual recognition directed at them by men. In each case, we can trace the currently offensive forms of sexual recognition to a long patriarchal history of sexual and social recognition relationships between men and women. In the case of pornography, however, the sexual gaze has taken refuge in a constitutionally protected sphere of social behavior. As printed matter, the interactive component of the sexual gaze is formally deemphasized and the sexual gaze is rendered an autonomous act of individual expression. As in the case of the sudden, unwanted sexual leer women frequently encounter on the street, it is impossible to assert standards for an appropriate form of interaction, insofar as no interaction has formally taken place. A woman's best strategy may be to refuse to be engaged by such oppressive gazes.

The workplace, on the other hand, is structured in terms of functionally appropriate and efficient interactions between co-workers. Once there is a general awareness of the potential for sexual forms of recognition to impede the operations of the workplace, there is an institutional interest in defining and enforcing standards of appropriate recognition and reward within professional relationships. Prior to the Hill-Thomas hearings the problem of sexual harassment had not been generally acknowledged. So long as women were primarily employed as secretaries and low-level administrators the sexual gaze was not perceived as endangering corporate productivity or stability, and could remain a perquisite of male economic and political status. In the aftermath of Anita Hill's testimony, however, sexual harassment is out in the open as an illegal abuse of workplace power relationships which may embarrass men who have reached the highest levels of authority, along with their sponsors and associates. We may expect to see male behavior toward women change perceptibly as institutions better delineate the boundaries of appropriate professional interaction.

As a symptom of various less overt forms of patriarchal nonrecognition, sexual harassment may be easier to outlaw than to replace with the sorts of professional recognition women desire and deserve, of course. An underlying trauma of sexual harassment for women lies in the fear that in refusing the patriarchal sexual gaze one becomes invisible altogether. Indeed, in her statement at a conference on sexual harassment at Georgetown University a year after the hearings, Anita Hill emphasized her sense of invisibility as an accuser of Clarence Thomas.[38] Yet as has become apparent since, it was important for the American public to see the blindness of the Senate Judiciary Committee; Anita Hill's Senate testimony gave visibility to an important field of struggle for working women which had been profoundly invisible before the Hill-Thomas hearings.

Anita Hill spoke alone, without the supporting voices of other women. Since that time, sexual harassment proceedings have proliferated, often receiving major media coverage. From the media's perspective these are primarily stories of the downfall of powerful men, but they are typically generated by the voices of large numbers of women finally speaking out in a collective effort to expose the sexual harassment patterns of a powerful man. In this stage of the sexual harassment conflict, groups of individually indistinct, quite ordinary women are suggesting the need for significant alterations in our images of highly visible men. The fact that the women who are jointly bringing harassment charges do not appear at all unusual allows other women to readily identify with them, and to consider whether such conflicts are present in their own workplaces. In a later stage of economic micro-politics, women may become more individually visible in their suggestions for alternative modes of organizing workplaces and recognizing and rewarding those who labor in them.[39]

We need to make every effort to denaturalize and demystify the various social problems associated with the sexual gaze. Sexual harassment has a quite definite social etiology. On the one hand, it is a workplace-specific enactment of the sexual gaze, a permutation of patriarchal recognition relations predictably generated by the participation of women within economic hierarchies. In fact, the interactive, asymmetrical quality of traditional sexual forms of agency is curiously echoed within many workplace relationships, where a cooperative effort may be the product of a unilateral decision by the supervising worker, carried out by a subordinate worker whose job depends upon pleasing the superior. Sexual harassment has much in common with various nongendered forms of employer-employee coercion and intimidation, and these may become recognized and better regulated as a consequence of the debate over sexual harassment.

On the other hand, with the large-scale entry of women into the workplace, we also see the migration of a unique nexus of gendered kinship patterns of behavior into the workplace. Both men and women are accustomed to interacting with each other in terms of familial roles and hierarchies, and these relational habits are not easily shed even within the relatively impersonal context of a business situation.[40] Moreover, the current phase of familial unmooring can only intensify this phenomenon. With the unmooring of women, men, and psychic forms of neediness from the incorporated family, there will be a greater tendency for everyone to bring psychic as well as material motivations into workplace transactions.

I initially formulated the concept of interpersonal agency in chapter 3 in order to make sense of new procreative responsibilities and choices of women. In my analysis of the unmooring of psychic relational neediness from the family in chapter 4, I was predisposed to see men and women as creatively reaching out to connect with others in a wide variety of private and public modalities, responding constructively, if sometimes awkwardly, to the increasingly urgent felt need for individuated forms of interpersonal connection. Insofar as people's responses to the unmooring of material forms of neediness provide a model for understanding responses to the unmooring of psychic forms of neediness, however, the current social prognosis is not totally sanguine. We know that individuals often react violently and destructively when they lack the resources to satisfy material needs. While an individual's response to psychological impoverishment will not necessarily be violent and destructive, it will not always be constructive, controlled, or even particularly self-conscious. Thomas Hobbes's account of the violent war of man against man that ensued whenever material forms of neediness became unmoored from prescribed community relationships is perhaps an apt rendering of the intensity with which individuals may experience and react to unmoored psychic forms of neediness as well.

The structural environment of the workplace makes it a propitious site, however, upon which to renegotiate gendered issues of power, fundamentally distinguishing between professional and sexual gazes. Because of the hierarchical nature of the workplace (typically if not necessarily male), psychic neediness is readily translated into a coercive sexual gaze directed at a (typically, but not necessarily female) subordinate. Because of the coercive quality of capitalist economic relationships, an employee will frequently submit to this intimidating sexual gaze, insofar as it appears a condition of keeping a desirable job. Yet because the hierarchies of the workplace are specified functionally, it is possible to define wrongful behavior at any level of the hierarchy in terms of behavior that makes the workplace less productive or stable. So long as sexual forms of coercive behavior remain a generic form of workplace power, they may not be perceived as an institutional problem. Once an intimidating sexual gaze is defined as a form of sexual discrimination and made illegal, however,

it becomes an economically costly form of behavior, and is subject to corporate sanctions. It is ironic that precisely because personal autonomy and
democratic processes are not part of the workplace, patriarchal forms of
oppressive behavior are more susceptible to institutional regulation there
than elsewhere.

At this point, however, it becomes imperative to define sexual harassment in terms that distinguish it from acceptable forms of sexual interaction, and that explicitly connect it to other issues of gendered professional
recognition. Women enter the workplace seeking institutionally defined
and sanctioned forms of recognition and reward, as do men. The new legal
category of sexual harassment might seem to constitute a criticism of all
sexual recognition between individuals in the workplace, insofar as the
workplace is not an appropriate site for sexual interactions. I will maintain, however, that sexual recognition in the workplace is not per se bad.
There are many instances when sexual forms of recognition develop in a
mutual fashion at work, and the two individuals pursue their personal
relationship elsewhere. So long as neither party experiences the relationship as having a coercive component derived from institutional sources of
personal authority, there is nothing wrong with such an association. It is
only a particular form of one-sided, power-laden sexual recognition that
is wrongful. Sexual harassment situations arise when men (or women) go
beyond silent or respectful forms of sexual recognition of another individual to demand interactive sexual recognition and rewards from that
person. When a man is capable of inducing a particular woman to voluntarily interact with him, harassment is not present, even if improper workplace behavior is. It is only when individuals use their institutional power
to force another individual to recognize or reward them sexually that
harassment occurs.

In response to recent harassment charges against Senator Bob Packwood, it has been suggested that it is unfair that older, less physically appealing men are accused of sexual harassment while younger, more seductive men may engage in highly promiscuous behavior while remaining
uncensured. "Since men in both situations may be seeking extramarital
sex, what is the moral difference?" some have asked. This is precisely the
point at which it should become evident that sexual harassment is not
about enforcing particular sexual norms. It is about political and ethical
norms of individual respect. Mutual sexuality does not violate norms of
interpersonal respect. A sexual relationship may be deemed unwise or immoral on other grounds. But it is only the mutuality of a sexual relationship that is necessary to situate it within public-sphere values of respect
and equality.

Given this analytic framework, it is easy to comprehend the behavior of both Clarence Thomas and Anita Hill as falling within the standard schema of sexual harassment. As a harasser, Thomas occupied a position of direct, personal authority over Anita Hill, who was employed as his aide at both the Department of Education and at the EEOC. Thomas also seems to have had a previous history of failing to properly recognize and respect the actions and the persons of black women. Angela Wright, another former employee of Thomas, was willing to testify to having been harassed by him during the time when she worked for him. In addition, Thomas is said to have opportunistically portrayed his own sister, Emma Mae Martin, as a deadbeat on welfare, saying "She gets mad when the mailman is late with her welfare check. That's how dependent she is." In fact, this sister raised and supported three children on her own, often by holding down two minimum-wage jobs at once. She was only on welfare briefly while caring for an aunt who had suffered a stroke.[41] If Thomas could publicly represent his own sister so heartlessly and misleadingly, we can certainly imagine him as capable of responding with cruel and vindictive verbal sallies to a black female employee who refused to go out with him. In addition, Thomas was going through a divorce during the period in the early 1980s when Anita Hill says that he harassed her. The heightened sense of psychic neediness commonly experienced at such a time does not explain or exonerate harassment. It is, however, a relevant factor in an emerging profile of those who are likely to abuse their professional authority through engaging in sexual harassment.[42]

There was an immediate effort to undermine the force of Hill's testimony by discrediting her identity, attempting to cast her as a spurned woman, a frustrated spinster, or a hostile lesbian. As Hill herself recently pointed out, the Judiciary Committee attempted to pin all sorts of insulting and unwarranted narratives on her rather than attempting to understand who she actually was.[43] Certainly, as a black, female, unmarried, childless, politically conservative law professor from Oklahoma accusing her former boss, Clarence Thomas, of sexual harassment, Anita Hill did not conform to *any* available social narratives. Kimberlé Crenshaw emphasizes the degree to which the immediate popular failure to identify with Anita Hill was a function of the intersectional disempowerment of African-American women in our society.[44] While there is now a stereotype of a white, neoconservative careerist female lawyer, no such popular image exists for a black woman within either black or white culture. In addition, I would add that Hill suffered from the cultural invisibility of any woman today who accuses a powerful man of sexual misdeeds.

A recent case in point is that in which Joy Silverman, a major Republican fundraiser, brought charges of sexual harassment, extortion, black-mail, and kidnapping threats against Sol Wachtler, the Chief Judge of the New York State Court of Appeals. Joy Silverman was an influential and relatively visible woman in political circles, capable of convincing her friend William Sessions, head of the FBI, to investigate the actions of Judge Wachtler, whom she suspected of vindictive behavior after she broke off a long relationship with him. After Judge Wachtler had been ar-rested and indicted for a months-long criminal campaign against his former lover, however, there was an immediate outpouring of public sympathy — not for Joy Silverman and her daughter who remained in hid-ing in response to his kidnapping threats, but for Judge Wachtler's "tragic" fall from grace. With *New York Times* headlines sympathetically alluding to "Wachtler's Reversal of Fortune" it was as if, in the words of Diane McWhorter, Wachtler's actions involved "a fatal but victimless error."[45] The equalizing of power within personal relationships between men and women is a new phenomenon, and we apparently lack the narrative resources for publicly recognizing and condemning the retributive acts of a powerful man spurned by a powerful woman. So we avert our eyes from the evidence against Clarence Thomas, and when the evidence cannot be impeached, as in Judge Wachtler's case, we make every effort to explain the behavior in terms of an external cause. In Wachtler's case, a mysterious medical condition was suggested as a possible ameliorating factor. The case of Joy Silverman shows that no matter how well-connected and white a woman is, we find it extremely difficult to extend appropriate sympathy to her if she has actively asserted her own interests and thereby evoked a powerful man's angry reprisals.

The micro-politics of postmodern agency will rarely involve conven-tional heroic figures or narrative structures. For the moment it must be enough that we can understand and respect the actions of an Anita Hill or a Joy Silverman in terms of the various and sometimes conflicting agency positions they occupy. When we watch a football or tennis player it is their performance on the playing field that counts, and we only be-come interested in the rest of their story in relation to their athletic prow-ess. The problem with gendered struggles today is that the playing fields are typically still under construction, and the rules of postfeminist, inter-sectional micro-politics are not clearly defined. The lives of contemporary women, as multiply-engaged individuals attempting to integrate diverse and conflicting forms of agency, do not fit within available social narra-tives. We can without too much difficulty explain Anita Hill's two-year stint with Clarence Thomas as an employer, her "friendly" professional relationship with Thomas since the incidents almost a decade ago, as well as her recent decision to publicly denounce Thomas, according to the sexual harassment framework articulated above. Yet insofar as her testimony appears to have been a pivotal moment in her own personal development, any effort to come to a definitive understanding of Anita Hill herself would seem premature.

In the first place, Anita Hill's willingness to continue to work for Clarence Thomas between 1981 and 1983, despite the fact that he was sexually harassing her, is not surprising, particularly given recent studies showing how pervasive sexual harassment is in the workplace.[46] The "hostile work environment" created by sexual harassment is something many working women have felt they must endure as a cost of pursuing a desirable career. Moreover, we can appreciate the reasoning behind Hill's decision to accompany Thomas when he was promoted from being in charge of the Office of Civil Rights in the Department of Education and became the head of the EEOC, without resorting to Cornel West's harsh description of Hill as "an exemplary careerist addicted to job promotion."[47] With Clarence Thomas's appointment as head of the EEOC, the job of being his assistant would surely present an exciting challenge to any highly motivated young law school graduate, sufficiently exciting to explain Hill's resolve to endure further sexual harassment, if necessary. Given cultural assumptions that men will sometimes neglect their health, their families, and even break the law in pursuit of professional achievements or acclaim, a woman's decision to endure a sexually hostile workplace should hardly seem remarkable.[48] Of course, Hill was eventually hospitalized for stomach problems, an ailment now recognized as part of a pattern of medical problems arising from the psychic strain of sexual harassment.[49] This exemplary careerist decided to leave the fast-track of a Washington legal career behind altogether when offered a job teaching law at Oral Roberts University in 1983. While Hill had the sense to remain on good terms with Thomas professionally, it looks as if Hill's career goals may have been, at least in part, derailed by her encounter with sexual harassment. Presumably because we do not readily attribute such elevated professional ambitions to black women, the question of whether sexual harassment may have led Hill to abandon hers was not raised at the time.

It is extremely ironic, of course, that Anita Hill encountered sexual harassment when working for the chairman of the EEOC, the federal agency responsible for writing and enforcing the guidelines that first made sexual harassment illegal. However, Thomas became chairman of the EEOC in 1981, only a year after the first guidelines ever to exist against sexual harassment had been issued. Despite his formal authority in administering these historic regulations, it is interesting to speculate how

conscious he actually was at that time of the potential illegality of his behavior toward his aide, Anita Hill. Moreover, given her traditional and religious family background and her conservative political sympathies at the
time, it is quite likely that Hill had a well-conditioned female capability
to deny or suffer silently Thomas's hostile sexual overtures. Of course,
regardless of her awareness of the legal implications of his words, Anita
Hill could not have expected, in her wildest dreams, to bring a successful
case of sexual harassment against her boss in the early 1980s. Who was
there with authority to take her word seriously against that of the EEOC
chairman? Even ten years later, in October of 1991, senators on the Judiciary Committee were able to ridicule the possibility that Thomas would
engage in such behavior.

I want to insist upon the symbolic significance of the sequence of public
developments discussed here. In 1981 Clarence Thomas was head of the
EEOC and the public official in charge of insuring compliance with the
new guidelines defining sexual harassment as a form of illegal workplace
discrimination. Yet he himself was able to engage with impunity in what
we now judge to be blatant practices of sexual harassment. No single fact
could better illustrate the illusory quality of liberal (feminist) ideals of simple workplace equity for women. A full decade after the first guidelines
against sexual harassment had been promulgated, and almost a decade after she had been harassed by Clarence Thomas, Anita Hill was finally in
a position to speak out against his behavior, and indeed seized upon a
highly effective public moment to do so. (Actually another woman,
Angela Wright, was also willing to testify as to Thomas's history as a
harasser during the hearings.)[50] The immediate public response to the testimony of sexual harassment was inchoate and disappointing. Yet gradually, over the ensuing months, Anita Hill's exemplary act began to be appreciated by working women everywhere, and a year later she has become
the standard-bearer of a postfeminist micro-politics. Women of all races,
classes, and ages have begun recoding their own workplace experiences,
those of today as well as those of many years ago, in terms of the narrative
of sexual harassment so powerfully figured by Anita Hill. It is an archeo-
logical moment, as well as a micro-political movement, as women look
back upon their previous workplace relationships and decipher the once
unspeakable moments of sexual harassment.[51]

With the social enfranchisement of women, patriarchy migrated readily
into the protected workplace environment, where the aggressive, one-
sided sexual overture could parasitically embed itself in economic power
relationships.[52] Once this parasitic relationship has been exposed, however, sexual harassment becomes an embarrassing sexual flag calling

attention to a whole spectrum of power-laden, potentially corrupt work-place relationships. From the perspective of an intersectional micro-politics, this is a moment during which workplace recognition-and-respect relationships have become momentarily fluid. With the newly shared awareness and critique of sexual harassment, there is a possibility for constructively discussing the bases for professional interaction more generally. Gendered recognition relations will never return to the patriar-chal innocence and brutality of the early years after women's social enfran-chisement. While it has hardly become obvious how to replace invidiously gendered forms of nonrecognition with appropriate and satisfying forms of recognition, the current battles against sexual harassment mark a poten-tially significant new stage of negotiations.

v. On Trial: The Patriarchal Grammar of Sexual Desire

At the very end of the year, two highly publicized cases of what has been labeled "date rape" (or, alternatively, "acquaintance rape") arose. These two date rape trials present us with a final dramatic arena of gendered conflict in 1991. In each of the cases, a woman accused a man of engaging in sexual intercourse with her against her will, but within the context of a personal or intimate interaction that had been mutually agreed upon. With this charge of date rape, the traditional asymmetries of the sexual gaze are pursued to their logical point of origin, as women protest the pa-triarchal grammar of sexual desire itself. In sexual harassment cases, women are designating boundaries between professional and sexual rela-tionships and asserting that a sexual relationship may not even begin un-less both parties are willing participants. In date rape cases, women are as-serting the relevance of a woman's particular desires *within* any personal encounter. They are declaring the responsibility of a man to recognize the presence or absence of a woman's sexual desires, and his responsibility to act upon his own sexual desires only when he is quite certain of the pres-ence of affirmative female desires. While patriarchy expected men and women to proceed in accordance with male desires for ejaculation within any sexual encounter, women are now insisting instead that sexual en-counters be shaped and determined at each moment by the sexual desires of both partners. I will label this a dynamic of "sexual civility."

The two celebrated cases of 1991 are fascinating when analyzed in rela-tion to each other. While they share one important feature — in each case the man accused of date rape was someone of great media interest — they are most interesting for their differences. Because race and class were both variables in these cases, the intersectional political dynamics existing within as well as between the two trials are complex and absorbing. Were we to look merely at the resolutions of the cases we might be tempted by a cynically reductive social analysis. William Kennedy Smith, a young, undistinguished scion of the Kennedy family, was readily acquitted of raping Patricia Bowman on a late-night walk on the beach in front of the Kennedy family compound in Palm Beach. Mike Tyson, the former world heavyweight boxing champion, was promptly convicted of raping Desiree Washington in the bedroom of his hotel suite in Indianapolis at 2 A.M. a few months later. Race and social class did play a significant role in the acquittal of Willie Smith as well as in the conviction of Mike Tyson. Yet from the perspective of a postfeminist symbolic politics, a lot more was going on in these trials.

Consider first the historical context of current accusations of date rape. As with sexual harassment, charges of date rape are a response of contemporary women to a very old modality of aggressive male sexual agency which has recently been denaturalized and rendered subject to political critique. As discussed in chapter 2, gendered notions of sexual agency were defined in terms of an asymmetrical conception of heterosexual relationships for hundreds of years under patriarchy. Men were historically presumed to have implicit rights of sexual usage upon socially and physically available female bodies which there could be no pretense of justifying according to liberal standards of bodily autonomy. Within the patriarchal family of liberalism, norms of equality and consent were not seen as pertinent to either domestic or sexual relationships between men and women. Moreover, liberal notions of individual bodily autonomy were not applied to the persons of women even when they ventured alone into the public sphere.

Women and men were both taught to believe that men were subject to natural and often uncontrollable sexual urges which could lead a man to initiate sexual intercourse with a woman whenever he found himself in a position to do so. Women were responsible for recognizing this fact and behaving accordingly. A woman was generally assumed to be complicit when sexual intercourse occurred, and was even blamed for its occurrence insofar as her body was the occasion for the act. Should a woman find herself sexually accosted by a man during a private encounter in which she had voluntarily participated, and should she dare to complain about it, her complaints would typically be dismissed. She was, and frequently still is, presumed "to be asking for it" in such situations, regardless of any verbal or physical gestures she may have made to the contrary. Even walking unaccompanied on a public thoroughfare after a certain hour can still be grounds for labeling a woman a sexual seductress, and thereby finding her responsible for the physical assault of a strange man, so long as the assault has a sexual component.[53]

To put this in terms of gendered notions of agency, when a man was within physical proximity of a woman, traditional Western notions of male sexual agency placed a great priority upon what were taken to be a man's natural phallic designs upon the body of a woman. The sexual gaze in all its contemporary forms is an artifact of this patriarchal emphasis upon male sexual desire. By contrast, traditional notions of female sexual agency emphasized a woman's responsibility to avoid all activities that might provide the occasion for nonsanctioned sexual contact. It was a woman's duty to recognize the male sexual gaze and respond by protecting her person against it, insofar as it emanated from any man not her husband. In the case of her husband, her responsibility was wholly reversed. A woman was expected to willingly accede to her husband's desires for intercourse, without concern for her own state of desire.

Men frequently earned social recognition and respect for sexual conquests of women who were not their wives, while a sexually active woman earned only social contempt. Should a woman be so unwise or unlucky as to become pregnant in the course of sexual activities outside of marriage she was subject to harsh forms of social stigmatization. The binaries of normative sexual identity were thus rigidly articulated in terms of "the good nonsexual woman who says 'No' outside of marriage, and remains silent in the marriage bed" and "the naturally potent man whose penis always says 'Yes' regardless of the social context." While these identities did not presume to delimit the diversity of homosexual and heterosexual behaviors of individuals, they rigidly delineated the normative boundaries of women's social and sexual agency.

Second-wave feminists began to critically examine patriarchal notions of sexuality, particularly in the context of the so-called sexual revolution in the late 1960s and early 1970s. Associated with the radicalism and social upheavals of the peace movement and the women's movement as well as gay liberation, the sexual revolution had a confusing relationship with feminism. The ideology of sexual liberation was that contraception, along with a rejection of oppressive bourgeois social mores, would free women and men from previous biological and social constraints upon their sexuality. Yet women who attempted to embrace the ideology of sexual liberation found themselves confronted with men who continued to take patriarchal notions of sexual agency for granted. In this context, the lowest common denominator of sexual liberation was that women's bodies became more readily accessible to male desires. Accordingly, feminists began to explore the ways in which the dynamics of sexual relationships were bound up with other oppressive forms of male social power.

In seminal works like Kathleen Barry's *Female Sexual Slavery* and Adrienne Rich's "Compulsory Heterosexuality and Lesbian Existence," feminists began to question the patriarchal coding of all aspects of heterosexual relationships. Labeling heterosexuality an oppressive political institution, Rich repudiated previous notions of a natural "male sex-right to women" as well as the mythical "penis-with-a-life-of-its-own."[54] Because of the one-sidedness of the male initiative assumed within patriarchal sexual encounters and the lack of concern for women's active consent, not to mention for their affirmative sexual desires, some feminists suggested that heterosexual intercourse in general looked a lot like rape.[55] Yet many women resisted such an interpretation. Despite the fact that the institution of patriarchy shows little concern for the existence of women's sexual desires, individual women experienced desire and even satisfaction in many instances of intercourse under patriarchy. The feminist critique does not show that sexual intercourse necessarily takes place without a woman's knowing consent, or even without her desire, under patriarchy. What this analysis does demonstrate is that sexual intercourse occurs in a hierarchical context that typically makes a woman's desire or consent irrelevant to a man's decision to have intercourse.

From the perspective of a gendered micro-politics, the problem today is one of recoding heterosexual interactions so that female desires become as important in directing the chain of sexual events as male desires.[56] Once this change occurs, men will attempt to read the desires of women as the necessary complement to their own sexual desires, just as women have traditionally been solicitous to the desires of men in whom they had an interest. Sexual civility requires that each person understand the desires of their partner as a necessary component of any relationship in which they hope to satisfy their own desires. Since patriarchal sexual encounters did not emphasize mutual respect, this is a rather confusing new sexual mandate for women as well as men. Patriarchal sexual dynamics emphasize the desires of the male partner in everything from the initiation of sexual behavior to the trajectory of the sexual encounter, typically leading towards and ending with male ejaculation. Sexual civility implies changes at every stage of the sexual encounter; respect for female desires will imply female initiation of sexual interactions, as well as trajectories of sexual interaction which may or may not end with intercourse. Women will, no doubt, express and act upon desires they have never before articulated, while men will become accustomed to responding to female desires as women have responded to theirs. The emphasis upon civility and mutual respect will make for substantive differences in the practices and discourses of sexuality.

One of the most basic requirements of civility involves the right of either party to refuse to proceed further with the (sexual) interaction. Men who initiate intercourse in many of the conventional ways fail to comply with a standard of mutual respect insofar as tradition did not require them to obtain agreement from a female sexual partner before proceeding to intercourse.[57] Women are beginning to insist, however, that sexual civility requires men to accept responsibility for ascertaining and acting in accordance with negative as well as positive desires of a sexual partner. A man who proceeds from intimate sexual foreplay to intercourse without having sufficient concern for whether or not the woman wishes to do so is likely to incur a woman's anger. A woman may feel morally wronged if her willing participation in kissing or embracing activities leads a man to assume his right to proceed to engage her in sexual intercourse that she does not desire.

Women who charge date rape today are claiming their right to refuse to proceed from other forms of sexual intimacy to intercourse. The men they accuse of raping them typically claim to have acted in accordance with the women's apparent desires for intercourse. Minimally, there has been a problem of communication in such situations. Given the fact that until very recently men have been taught that women want intercourse even when they say "no," and the additional fact that women were taught that it was ladylike to say "no" even when one wanted intercourse, women who say "no" today are set up to be misread as actually consenting.[58]

In addition to a problem of communication, however, the disagreement over whether women have actually consented to intercourse is also a function of changing notions of sexual entitlement. Insofar as men were taught they had the natural right to proceed from other sexual behavior to a culmination in intercourse, they did not need to listen to female requests to stop short of intercourse. Women who charge date rape are denying the legitimacy of this traditional notion of male sexual entitlement, and demanding the right to say "yes" and to say "no" at discrete junctures within a sexual encounter. It is interesting that accusations of date rape are being made by women like Patricia Bowman and Desiree Washington, who are no more devotees of recent feminist theory than the men they accuse. They rather seem to have been affected by a general cultural ambience in which new lip service, at least, is paid to the equal rights of women in all walks of life. These "untutored" charges of date rape reflect how egregiously traditional sexual practices ignore the rights of women.

Presuming that we agree that traditional notions of male sexual entitlement were oppressive and unfair to women, we are yet likely to feel uncertain about the actual points at which it is reasonable or unreasonable
for one person to call a stop to a sexual interaction, as well as about the
ways in which such consent and refusal might be communicated, whether
verbally or by physical gestures alone. For example, suppose we agree that
the mere physical presence of a woman in a man's room or on a man's private beach, even late at night, does not necessarily indicate her consent to
sexual intercourse. If we reject the standard of mere physical presence, the
question then becomes one of determining what words or physical
gestures should count as consent in such a situation. Is consent implied
when a woman kisses a man, or when she lies down next to a man on his
beach while kissing and embracing him? Is consent implied when a
woman removes some of her clothing in such a situation, or even all of
it? According to standards twenty years ago, any woman who allowed
herself to be alone with a man late at night was a likely seductress, and any
complicit sexual behavior at all would have been deemed enough to indicate full sexual consent. But no longer. Women are questioning the traditional patriarchal assumption that sexual interactions necessarily progress
toward and culminate in male penetration of a woman in intercourse.
Kissing and erotic touching have a different sexual and physical quality
than does intercourse. Charges of date rape are often predicated on
women's assertions that their desire for kissing and embracing was unaccompanied by a further desire for intercourse.

Furthermore, now that traditional notions of female sexual participation have been exposed as brittle shells of male phallic privilege, the whole
notion of sexual consent has been problematized. A recent film—*Love
Crimes*, directed by Lizzie Borden—is about a man who poses as a fashion
photographer, seducing women as they bare themselves in the flattering
intensity of his camera's flashing eye. After the fact, many of the women
feel that they have been sexually abused, and the film suggests that there
may be circumstances in which a woman who has been seduced into consensual sex will later feel she has been wrongfully manipulated. It is not
unreasonable to think that there may be morally legitimate and illegitimate ways of securing another person's consent to proceed within sexual
relationships. Within economic relationships, by analogy, one is pro-
hibited from using various forms of deceit in order to get another party
to sign a contract. And within logic, there is a whole category of persuasive techniques called "fallacies" that are deemed illegitimate ways of convincing someone to accept a particular conclusion. One shows a lack of
respect for the other person by relying upon fallacious forms of reasoning

in order to convince him or her of a particular conclusion, and once the fallacy has been exposed the conclusion is invalidated. In sexual relationships patriarchal power differentials were previously the ultimate basis for female "consent" to intercourse. In contemporary situations where some large power differential provides the dominant context and primary explanation for sexual interaction, we may sometimes conclude that sexual abuse has occurred, regardless of whether formal gestures of consent have been made.[59]

If we consider sexual interactions as a form of interpersonal agency, defining sexual behavior as but one possible response to various sorts of psychic relational neediness, the psychophysical drives of male sexual desire cease to have the exalted status accorded them within psychoanalytic theory. Without ignoring the potential intensity of sexual desires, the moral and legal appropriateness of an act of sexual agency is necessarily a function of all three dimensions of interpersonal agency. We will be concerned with the quality of an individual's sense of responsibility to themselves and the other person, as well as with the quality of their notions of recognition and reward in a sexual situation. We may judge a case of sexual interaction morally or legally wrongful if one or both parties has a deficient sense of their responsibility to the other person in the particular situation. Or we might be critical of the operative notions of self-recognition, or of the recognition of one party by the other.[60]

Several hundred years ago, in the course of articulating the principles of liberal democracy, John Locke declared that a political agent could not consent to his own enslavement, or even to an absolutist and potentially despotic form of government such as that recommended by Thomas Hobbes in the *Leviathan*. In the course of articulating principles of postmodern interpersonal civility, I will argue that a postfeminist sexual agent cannot be understood as consenting to humiliating or self-destructive forms of sexual interaction insofar as this consent appears to be the sole product of preexisting power relationships between.[61]

It is hardly surprising that a great many women have become interested in altering the dynamics of sexual interactions to accord more respect and concern to their own desires and pleasure. Yet the proposed changes deprive men of their previously dominant position in the pursuit of individual sexual pleasure, and it is not obvious that they will participate in such changes with alacrity. Nevertheless, liberal norms of equality and fairness are central commitments within the political discourses of our society, and the universalist pretensions of such liberal recognition factors are helpful in arguing that respect for women must extend beyond the public sphere and into the sphere of personal and sexual relationships. After twenty years of discussion about this issue, a number of men have come to accept the notion that sexual agency should incorporate notions of female as well as male sexual desire. Not only is mutual respect increasingly thought to be a necessary basis for sexual morality, but female consent to intercourse has been taken as relevant within a marriage as well as between people more casually interacting on a date.[62]

As a consequence of developing a heightened concern with the quality of female sexual desires, a sexual-intercourse perquisite of traditional manhood is on its way to becoming a morally unjustifiable act of physical coercion. Because of the intimate nature of sexual interactions, efforts to alter the dynamics of sexual relationships so as to fulfill the new ideals of civility will proceed largely through private forms of negotiation. If women as a group are ever to succeed with the project of remaking the dynamics of sexual relationships, it will be because individual women have taken it upon themselves to critically engage with individual male sexual partners. Women and men are quite capable of practicing greater respect for female sexual desires and male sexual generosity.

Yet such a micro-politics requires macro-political and symbolic forms of reinforcement. It is important that the new ethical considerations within sexual interactions are beginning to be legally enforceable. In a certain number of instances, when men egregiously fail to recognize the expectations of women for civility and respect for their physical personhood within sexual relationships, women need to be able to call upon legal sanctions to emphasize the seriousness of these evolving sexual norms. In the next section, I will discuss whether the new category of "date rape" is the most appropriate vehicle for legally representing our new concerns with sexual civility.

A symbolic media politics may be as important in reinforcing the typically private, individuated struggles within a sexual micro-politics as are legal forms of recognition and enforcement. The professional capabilities of women soldiers became visible in the media coverage of the Persian Gulf War; Anita Hill's Senate testimony in front of millions of viewers made sexual harassment a socially articulable and thereby unavoidable problem; and the two televised date rape trials at the end of 1991 and in early 1992 began to make issues of sexual civility a concrete micro-political concern within intimate spaces across the land.

vi. Becoming Civil about Sex

This is the micro-political framework for the cases of Patricia Bowman against William Kennedy Smith, and of Desiree Washington against Mike

Tyson. The Bowman-Smith incident occurred on Easter weekend of 1991 in Palm Beach, Florida, when Patricia Bowman met William Kennedy Smith, a nephew of Senator Ted Kennedy, at Au Bar, a trendy local hangout. After agreeing to drive him home to the Kennedy compound when the bar closed, Bowman accepted Smith's invitation to tour the house and take a walk on the beach in front of the Kennedy home. Bowman says she was tackled and raped by Smith after she had declined his invitation to go for a swim and climbed the stairs from the beach and begun walking back to her car. The Washington-Tyson incident occurred in July of 1992 when 18-year-old Desiree Washington went to Indianapolis to participate in the Miss Black America beauty pageant and met Mike Tyson, who was participating in one of the beauty pageant events. Tyson called Desiree Washington from his limousine at 2 A.M. on July 19, inviting her to come down from her hotel room and join him in driving around to some of the celebrity-filled parties that were going on that night as part of a cultural festival, Indiana Black Expo, of which the beauty pageant was a part. After she joined him, Tyson made an excuse to go up to his hotel room before going on to the parties, and once there, Washington says, he attacked and raped her.

Bowman and Washington each claimed to have been raped, while Smith and Tyson asserted that Bowman and Washington consented to have intercourse with them. As plaintiffs in a criminal trial, Bowman and Washington had the burden of proof, and indeed each had to convince a jury "beyond a reasonable doubt" that they had not consented to intercourse. Two distinct features of any date rape scenario today make it very difficult to prove such a charge. First, and most obviously, the private quality of a typical date rape situation makes it highly unlikely that anyone other than the two parties will have been present to testify to what occurred. In order for a jury to be convinced "beyond a reasonable doubt" that a woman did not consent to intercourse, there must be powerful circumstantial indications supporting her charges. The sexual and social history of both plaintiff and defendant becomes extremely important in establishing the relative likelihood of male coercion or assault or, alternatively, of female consent.

In the Washington-Tyson case, the extreme contrast between the pure and virginal social profile of Desiree Washington and the violent profile of Tyson was dramatic. Washington testified that she was a Sunday school teacher and a Big Sister to a little girl in foster care, and school records showed her to be an exemplary college freshman, a former high school cheerleader and National Honor Society member. Her mother tearfully testified to the damaging effects of the incident on her young and innocent daughter: "When I saw her she didn't seem like the same daughter that I sent down here."[63] Our legal system assumes that defendants are innocent until proven guilty and so does not allow testimony as to prior transgressions of defendants, yet Mike Tyson's popular persona was that of heavyweight boxing celebrity who had been publicly accused of sexually abusive behavior by several women, including his former wife, Robin Givens.

By comparison, in the Bowman-Smith case, neither plaintiff nor defendant fell into stereotypes of virginity or male brutality. Patricia Bowman was a single mother who lived on a trust fund, and admitted to having seven male lovers in the past five years. William Kennedy Smith was a medical student with an inoffensive appearance and ingratiating persona. (In fact, three women were willing to testify that he had attempted to sexually assault them in the past, but none of them had gone public with these charges before, and rules against evidence pertaining to a defendant's prior behavior kept their testimony from the record.) The additional factor in this case was the social status and wealth of William Kennedy Smith. While many men continue to assume coercive male intercourse rights in the marriage bed or on a hot date, men of wealth and social status have always had phallic rights of larger proportions than other men. Their wealth and power led many women to voluntarily submit to and even encourage their urges for intercourse, while those women who dared to spurn their advances could be bribed or intimidated into remaining silent about anything that transpired. A properly intersectional analysis recognizes when sexual politics are thus complicated by a subtext of repressed class politics.

In the second place, even if there was a videotape of what occurred, a male defendant might continue to claim his accuser had consented even as the female plaintiff insisted she had been raped. Given longstanding assumptions that women who placed themselves in a position to be date raped were "asking for it," regardless of their immediate gestures or words to the contrary, members of the jury might find themselves uncertain or conflicted about whether or not consent could or should have been inferred by the man from the woman's actions. In order to convince a jury "beyond a reasonable doubt" that date rape has occurred, a woman has to persuade the members of the jury not simply of her authentic desire not to have intercourse but also that a man should not have interpreted her behavior as consenting to intercourse. It is precisely standards of sexual consent that are at issue in date rape trials, however, so reasonable doubts on the part of the judge and jury would seem endemic to such cases.

Yet in the Washington-Tyson trial the circumstances pointed to an actual physical assault by a violence-prone heavyweight boxer upon the relatively unsuspecting and innocent body of a young girl. Even the medical evidence of vaginal abrasions supported the notion that this had been a violent act of penetration. It was relatively easy for a jury to conclude not merely that Washington had not wanted intercourse but also that her behavior had not given Tyson grounds for inferring her consent to intercourse. In the Bowman-Smith case, there was a great deal more ambiguity, both about what had actually happened after they arrived at the Kennedy compound and about the appropriate interpretation of the interactive behavior of Patricia Bowman and William Kennedy Smith that night. There was no medical or forensic evidence that Bowman had been violently subjected to intercourse, although she claimed that Smith had tackled her from behind. The narrative of the several hours they spent together prior to the moment of sexual conflict portrays a series of jointly taken actions, each extending the relationship a bit further. While the sexual quality of the interaction is not clear, Bowman admits to kissing Smith at several different points in the evening, so despite her claims on the witness stand that she was not sexually interested in Smith there was an evident sexual component to the interaction. For the jury, the question was not merely whether Bowman truly said "No" but also when and how she said "No," and whether Smith could have reasonably interpreted her behavior as consenting to intercourse. One can be convinced of Bowman's experience of sexual violation that night while fully appreciating the jury's inability to convict Smith of date rape.

In terms of the symbolic politics of gender, the conviction of Mike Tyson for date rape was significant. The finding in this case offers clear legal support for the principle that a woman does not, by her mere presence in a man's room late at night, indicate her consent to sexual intercourse.[64] Moreover, it is also significant that once again, as in the case of Anita Hill, a black woman has become the standard-bearer for all women on this postfeminist site of gendered conflict. As bell hooks first pointed out more than a decade ago, and as a chorus of black feminists now intones with increasing impatience, black women ever since slavery have been culturally portrayed as embodying the "dark" sexually wanton side of the female persona, and feminism has done very little to address this intersectional intensification of black women's oppression.[65] To now have the images of two black women personifying postfeminist struggles for professional and sexual respect for all women is an important development within intersectional politics.

Yet Desiree Washington's victory will not necessarily enter our symbolic memory as a signal event within an intersectional micro-politics of gender. Kimberlé Crenshaw points out that the social and cultural devalu-

ation of black women has been such that within the black community
women and men alike failed to recognize or support the claims of Desiree
Washington. "Leaders ranging from Benjamin Hooks to Louis Farrakhan
expressed their concern and support for Tyson, yet no established Black
leader voiced any concern for Washington."[66] Insofar as white "lynch
mob" accusations of rape against black men are painfully recent paradigms
of racial injustice within our society, the intraracial specificity of Desiree
Washington's claims was ignored within the black community.

Within the multiracial national community as well, the gendered
micro-politics of Tyson's conviction were problematic. While Washington's victory signaled a possible shift toward more just standards of sexual
consent, Mike Tyson served all too conveniently as an aberrant sexual
scapegoat. Coming immediately after the acquittal of William Kennedy
Smith, Tyson's conviction provided a symbolic vehicle for registering
sympathy for women's evolving sense of sexual entitlement without unduly encouraging women to interrogate their everyday relationships. In
Mike Tyson, a black boxer with an already extensive public record of violent personal and professional behavior, the Indiana court found a man
whose conviction served to suggest the racial and socioeconomic specificity, and corresponding rarity, of date rape. Men without such a fearsome
profile—most men—were allowed to distance themselves from the issue.
A year later, the subtle issues of gendered sexual initiative and power
raised within these date rape trials have receded from the public consciousness, as news reports of blatant sexual abuse and harassment
proliferate.

In the aftermath of these two trials, I think we should consider whether
the criminal charge of date rape provides the best means for legally reinforcing ongoing processes of intimate sexual renegotiation. In purely
practical terms, these cases make clear how difficult it is to win a date rape
conviction. The exceptional, almost exaggerated clarity of Washington's
case against Tyson contrasted dramatically with the more typical am-
biguities riddling Bowman's case against Smith. Unlike Desiree Washington, and like Patricia Bowman, most women are going to have histories
of sexual participation that will cast at least a shadow of doubt upon their
denial of sexual participation in the instance where they claim to have been
raped.[67] Unlike Mike Tyson, and like Willie Smith, most men will not
have public histories of violent behavior against women, as well as against
men in the course of their professional activities. While his Kennedy family ties gave William Kennedy Smith an unusual degree of social and economic clout relative to his accuser, the men women accuse of date rape
will quite typically possess greater wealth and status than their accusers,

given the gendered distribution of these advantages today. Furthermore, as in the case of Bowman and Smith, most charges of date rape will occur in the context of some extended period of mutual interaction prior to the alleged rape, rather than with the brutal spontaneity of Tyson's attack on Washington. The question of female consent to intercourse will typically be submerged in a muddy pool of social preconceptions and immediate transactional issues involving relative degrees of desire, recognition, and power. Insofar as we are sympathetic with the efforts of a woman like Patricia Bowman to have her specific sexual desires respected more fully, we need to acknowledge that we are not going to be able to provide her with much support in the context of a date rape trial.

One alternative is for women like Bowman to file a civil lawsuit instead of pressing criminal charges. While date rape is usually presumed to be a subset of the traditional criminal category of rape (often referred to recently as "stranger rape" to distinguish it from date rape), it may also be considered an "intentional tort," which is a civil offense.[68] According to the common law, an intentional tort occurs whenever one person commits assault, battery, false imprisonment, or intentionally inflicts emotional distress upon another person. Indeed, Catharine MacKinnon points out that "sexual touching that women do not want has historically been considered tortious," and she discusses tort claims at length as a possible (though not in her opinion optimal) legal response to sexual harassment.[69] In purely pragmatic terms, the advantage of filing a civil lawsuit is that the standard of proof is much easier for a victim of sexual coercion or assault to meet. As Burt Neuborne, a professor at New York University Law School, said in commenting upon the Bowman-Smith case, the standard of proof "beyond a reasonable doubt" demanded of the prosecution in order to obtain a criminal conviction makes an acquittal in date rape cases almost a foregone conclusion.[70] By contrast, in a civil lawsuit the standard of proof is much lower, requiring a tort victim to demonstrate either by a "preponderance of the evidence," or with "clear and convincing evidence" that a wrong has been committed. In addition, as Eileen N. Wagner reports, "a criminal charge of rape usually requires proof of genital penetration, while the tort of battery requires only proof of 'offensive touching.'"[71]

In a civil lawsuit, of course, the person who has been harmed sues the person who has committed the offense in order to recover monetary damages for the injuries they have incurred. To many people, however, the idea that a woman who has been the victim of date rape could accept monetary damages as appropriate recompense for such an offense profanes deeply held notions of sexuality. It seems to violate traditional as-

sumptions about the spiritual and psychic significance of sexual encounters for a woman to respond to an instance of sexual assault or coercion
with such an impersonal, even crass sense of material redress. The very
idea of vindicating an act of sexual dishonor with monetary damages horrifies many women. Yet I think that such a response reflects the coy and
constrained way women have been taught to value their sexuality rather
than the actual implications of a civil lawsuit. Like it or not, in our society
money is the primary vehicle for representing value, and also for revaluing
resources and relationships when these are publicly contested. In nonsexual contexts, it is well understood that in suing for monetary damages one
may be suing to vindicate personal or professional honor, or to punish and
deter actions of various immoral sorts.

    Consider a recent civil rights suit: a nineteen-year-old black man was
slain in 1986 in Coney Island by four bat- and knife-wielding white men
who were subsequently convicted of murder and lesser charges. In 1987
the parents of the slain man decided to file a separate federal civil suit, alleging that this had been a case of racial bias. They were recently awarded
$1 million in damages by a jury that decided Samuel Spencer's civil rights
had indeed been violated. Despite the fact that the money would never be
collected "unless someone hit the lottery," the response of those in the
courtroom to the decision was very emotional. Michael Winerip speculates that "perhaps because only an idea was at stake everyone in court was
moved."[72] In awarding monetary damages, a jury symbolically recognizes
the seriousness of the civil offenses committed by one party against another. Given a developing awareness of the civil offensiveness of racist
acts and sexist acts, monetary damages are a primary token of fungible
power relations within noncriminal legal discourses. Insofar as women
seek juridical support for their efforts to reconfigure gendered sexual relationships, they may need to develop a strategic sense of what often seems
like a very personal struggle, and accept the political significance of an
award of monetary damages in civil suits charging men with sexual
assault.

    In fact, there are clear historical and ideological explanations for why
this issue has initially been framed in terms of "rape," and compelling ideological grounds for advocating that women pursue civil lawsuits in future
cases. Rape has been perceived as a criminal act for the several millennia
during which it has been defined in the context of traditional notions of
male and female sexual and social agency. In the Anglo-American tradition it has primarily been understood as a crime against a man's property;
the rapist commits the crime of devaluing another man's daughter or wife.
The seriousness of the crime of rape reflected the seriousness with which

men took their right to exclusive sexual possession of daughters and wives. As a result of the patriarchal focus of rape laws, only certain forms of sexual assault or coercion have been illegal. As Deborah Rhode explains, "One form of abuse—intercourse achieved through physical force against a chaste woman by a stranger—has been treated as the archetypal antisocial crime. By contrast, coercive sex that has departed from this paradigm frequently has been denied or discounted."[73] By means of the legal category of date rape, women are currently attempting to broaden the juridical perception of actionable sexual forms of assault or coercion.[74] The problem is that the rape paradigm is geared to enforce certain sorts of patriarchal (and racist) relationships, and proves an obstacle to rethinking gendered as well as racial patterns of sexual initiative and desire.

According to the rape narrative of "chaste victim–violent stranger" there can be no affirmative conception of a woman's own sexual desires that does not render her deserving of the act of rape. A woman's legitimate sexual agency is only fulfilled through efforts to remain virginal until marriage and thereafter chaste. In case of sexual assault by a stranger a woman must prove chastity through physical resistance. Insofar as black women were considered promiscuous by nature, they were incapable of proving chastity, and so, as Angela Harris explains, "the rape of a black woman by any man, white or black, was simply not a crime."[75] The bittersweet quality of Desiree Washington's victory is due to the fact that finally a black woman has been socially positioned to represent traditional norms of female sexual purity—ironically just at that cultural moment when women are beginning to throw off the mantle of chastity and claim their rights to affirmative forms of sexual desire.

The classical rape paradigm also gives a skewed picture of the man who engages in sexual assault. He must reveal himself as a lowly criminal who does not respect another man's sexual property rather than as simply a man who does not respect a woman's desires. He must be a violent stranger because a chaste woman is responsible for avoiding the inappropriate advances of men she is familiar with. Insofar as black men have been perceived as violent, sexual "strangers" within a racist Southern culture, black feminists emphasize that this rape paradigm has been the occasion for a systemic, enduring pattern of terrorism against black men. The discourse of rape in this country is a racist one, historically, and no matter how legally justifiable Mike Tyson's conviction was, it was tainted by inevitable echoes of past racial injustices.

The rape paradigm is an unwieldy anachronism which misrepresents the quality of women's anger and expectations when sexual coercion or assault occurs within the context of a personal relationship. On the one hand, rape laws exist to punish abnormal forms of sexual behavior per-petrated by "criminals." But women make charges of date rape against men they have chosen to have intimate contact with. Does it make narra-tive sense to think that such a man suddenly becomes a criminal, or reveals himself to have been a monstrous individual all along when he coercively proceeds to intercourse? Does he change from being a person a woman wants to share intimate moments with to being a criminal assaulting her when he becomes obnoxiously forward with his penis? The sorts of coer-cive and assaultive sexual behavior women are presently demanding an end to are all too normal in our society, and the men who commit coercive or even assaultive sexual acts within the context of intimate relationships are rarely perceived as criminals, even by the women whom they have mistreated. The struggles of women to have their sexual desires recog-nized and respected by men are a very basic component of heterosexual life today, as are the various phenomena of male resistance to any diminishment of their patriarchal sexual perquisites. It is in the interests of women to normalize the critique of coercive and assaultive male sexual behavior, precisely in order to make the critique more inclusive and rele-vant to everyday issues of sexual initiative and choice.

On the other hand, the rape laws seek to reward chaste female victims who have been socially devalued by the experience of rape. Yet those who complain of sexual coercion and assault today are frequently sexually ex-perienced women who feel morally and politically wronged, but not so-cially devalued, by particular forms of sexual experience. Women today turn to the law not as passive victims but in the dual capacity of injured citizens and micro-political agents seeking social recognition and vindica-tion of the sexual injustices that a particular man has committed. Women want redress for specific harms done to their individual psyches. A woman might claim that her sense of sexual confidence — or more generally, her sense of personal autonomy — was damaged by this encounter. She might claim to suffer from lasting psychological effects, nightmares, or fears of sexual intimacy with other men as a result of sexual coercion at the hands of a particular man. Such women reasonably seek the sorts of monetary damages individuals obtain in a variety of circumstances in which they feel injured by the behavior of another person. Yet women are also concerned with micro-political goals of education and deterrence. They need a chance to go back over the patriarchal sexual game plan, so that they may point out exactly where a man has stepped out of bounds according to the new rules of civility. Only thus can they hope to ensure that a man who has mistreated them does not go on to treat other women similarly.[76]

In claiming that a man has committed an intentional sexual tort against them women enter the legal system as wronged but formally equal citizens, rather than as female victims of rape. Rather than submitting herself to the criminal justice system, a woman maintains important procedural elements of control when pursuing a civil lawsuit, deciding if the case will go to trial as well as when it will be settled. Furthermore, substantive analysis of the harm of sexual coercion is more likely to occur in a tort proceeding than in a criminal trial. As Catharine MacKinnon points out, "The examination of tort shows that the law is quite accustomed to treating cloudy issues of motive and intent, the meaning of ambiguous acts, the effect of words on liability for acts, and the role of excessive sensitivity in determining liability and damages, all in a sexual context. These issues have arisen before. They have not been thought so subtle as to preclude a judicial resolution once a real injury was perceived to exist."[77] If our micro-political goal is to rethink the sexual practices of normal men and women, renegotiating sexual transactions so as to embody notions of equality and respect for the sexual desires of each party, then civil lawsuits would seem to offer a better source of juridical support for this project than criminal lawsuits.

vii.   An Ultra-Social Agency

Martin Heidegger notoriously envied the Greeks for having had what he judged to be the first crack at naming things in the Western philosophical tradition. "Language, by naming beings for the first time, first brings beings to word and to appearance." Heidegger's great respect for language was grounded in his metaphysical assumption that "Being speaks through every language," and his belief that philosophy should seek authentic ways of revealing the uniqueness of Being.[78] Jacques Derrida's critique of Heidegger's "onto-theological" project, and, indeed, of Western philosophy's historical search for the metaphysical origins of language, has, we may say with a touch of irony, become a foundational moment of postmodern theory. Derrida's antimetaphysical solution to the question of what language is about, is to say that it is about itself: "Only the text signifies."[79] In Derrida's fervent efforts to demonstrate that there can be no metaphysical authority *behind* language, he loses a sense of language's social embeddedness, its active engagement with our lives.

As a postfeminist, I have a social project that leads me beyond a purely intertextual interest in language. I am as dissatisfied as Heidegger was, for example, with modern conceptions of "man," and I too believe in the power and responsibility of thinkers to address such issues through language. Yet my aims are unabashedly and irreducibly social rather than metaphysical. What particularly excites me about the present historical moment is the conceptual strangeness of various social situations and relationships, and the sense that they can only be adequately comprehended through reworking our systems of signification to better articulate basic social categories. Inspired by a postmodern social theorist's commitment to acting within conjunctural discourses, I have spent a great deal of time in this chapter analyzing conflictual contemporary events, hoping to rearticulate them and contribute to the emergence of postpatriarchal institutions and discourses.

As an *ultra-social* philosopher, I seek to extend the understanding of individual agency to enable individuals to more constructively participate within current social conflicts and relationships. By focusing on the situation of soldier–mothers and fathers, I have demonstrated the trajectory of a breakdown in gendered dichotomies of individual responsibility. In analyzing the Hill–Thomas hearings and the groundswell of concern with sexual harassment in the workplace, I have sought to demystify current conflicts surrounding sexed and gendered forms of recognition, and to render them more amenable to negotiated solutions.

While a postmodern philosopher can attempt to clear a path for new modes of social recognition to occur, she can no more create new forms of recognition than can a traditional philosopher create new beings. In the case of the date rape trials, the quality and distribution of sexual desires and responsibilities is at issue. With the unmooring of individuals from the family, sexual desires take on new shapes, as do other forms of psychic neediness no longer satisfied within well-defined kinship relationships. Individuals may construct interpersonal relationships in highly diverse modes. The boundaries of sexual and nonsexual forms of desire shift, as individuals begin to perceive the possibilities of interpersonal agency differently and engage with each other creatively. We may find it helpful to think in terms of Derrida's playful image of the "incalculable choreographies" which "can carry, divide, multiply the body of each 'individual,' whether he be classified as 'man' or as 'woman' according to the criteria of usage." Yet the unself-conscious male pronoun alerts us to the embodied quality of even deconstructive proposals. A postfeminist micropolitics never forgets the gendered configurations of power that are at stake in remaking relationships.[80]

Socrates' thinking was a result of placing himself in the "draft of Being," according to Heidegger's metaphysical imagery.[81] Because so many gendered relationships and significant actions of women have remained outside of written discourses until recently, when one writes about gendered issues today, one often experiences, quite spontaneously and unexpectedly, a sense of being brushed by a "draft of social becoming." While hardly affording a sense of metaphysical authorization, this is simply an experience of the social con-text of one's writing. This context is not a subtext and not a pretext. It is the fabric of one's motivations, responsibilities, and expectations of recognition and reward as a thinker. The social context of postfeminist writing encourages a constructive theoretical orientation often lacking in other postmodern writing. One knowingly walks a fine line between an ultra-social postfeminist analysis and various micro-political distractions. It's a fertile site of risk, however, and I can only hope to cultivate it further.

Epilogue: Engaging on a Postfeminist Frontier

Postmodernism and postfeminism are both frontier discourses. They bring us to the edge of what we know, and encourage us to go beyond. But what sort of frontier is it? While we associate a geographical frontier like the nineteenth-century American West with an abandonment of the cultural trappings of "civilization," medical frontiers today are reached by traversing the most sophisticated technologies. We reach the limits of knowledge and experience by many routes. Postfeminism is a cultural frontier resulting from the breakdown of previous social organizing structures that continue to exist only in various states of disarray. We have been propelled onto this frontier by the social enfranchisement of women and the unmooring of women, men, and children from the patriarchal family.

As on other frontiers, there is a sense of lawlessness resulting from having partially left behind hoary patriarchal institutions and norms, without yet having developed new sources of legitimate authority. There is also a heightened sense of violence, as much because some very old kinship-based forms of interpersonal abuse have become newly visible as due to new forms of violent behavior. At the same time, a sense of freedom and new possibilities for action is subtly pervasive, because the disaggregation of our familial, gendered, racial, sexual, economic, and political identities leaves us with no choice but to remake our lives on a daily basis. The physical and emotional harshness of life on past frontiers has been ameliorated by women's painstaking efforts to recreate versions of "civilized" domesticity within a home to which men could periodically return to escape frontier rigors. The current frontier is different insofar as it results from women's embrace of public forms of agency; the contemporary home is as much a frontier as anywhere. Social hierarchies are at stake on all frontiers and the leading social roles belong to those who are challenging the old hierarchies. Many of the challengers on this frontier are women.[1]

In June of 1991, a film entitled *Thelma and Louise* suddenly appeared and blazed into controversial public space for a month or more. Then it disappeared as rapidly as it had arrived, having provoked a remarkable level of open hostility from many men and some women. For many other women, it provided electric moments of identification. Not often a passionate film viewer, I loved this film for its frontier vision. I want to conclude this investigation of gendered micro-politics by analyzing the brief saga of Thelma and Louise as a postfeminist frontier parable.

The story takes place in the contemporary Southwest of the United States, and unfolds quite simply. Thelma (Geena Davis) is a naive young housewife, conventionally married to her high school sweetheart Daryl, a late-patriarchal nitwit. Louise (Susan Sarandon) is her older and wiser friend who works as a waitress at a local diner. Louise invites Thelma to go away for the weekend to a friend's house in the mountains and they leave in Louise's old convertible, Thelma having decided not to tell Daryl for fear that he would not allow her to go. An inexperienced packer, Thelma brings the contents of her bureau drawers, including a pearl-handled pistol Daryl has given her to protect herself on all the nights he is out until four in the morning "working." They drive until evening comes on, and Thelma begs to stop at a roadhouse, where they have a drink, and Thelma dances with a friendly cowboy. When she becomes sick from the unaccustomed drinking, the cowboy leads her out to the parking lot and tries to rape her. Louise comes along just in time to save Thelma, handily pointing the pearl-handled pistol at the cowboy and commanding him to return his penis to his pants. After he does so, and Louise is leading the sobbing Thelma away, the cowboy continues to yell sexual insults after them. Louise turns around, and points the pistol at him again, reminding him of the authority relations that prevail when one person is pointing a gun at another person. She tells him to apologize or shut up. He continues to make obscene noises and gestures. As he sneeringly says "Suck my cock," Louise fires one shot, silencing him and killing him.[2]

Shocked at their own actions, and convinced that the law will have little sympathy for Louise's murder of the cowboy, Thelma and Louise take flight. Heading for Mexico, hundreds of miles away, their behavior becomes more and more transgressive as they seek to escape the FBI search that ensues after the cowboy's body is discovered. Losing all their money to a young and amiable thief who has provided Thelma with her first experience of sexual pleasure, they readily adapt to the demands of an outlaw existence. The sweet young thief has obligingly explained the techniques of his craft to Thelma, and she proceeds to successfully rob a convenience store. When a state policeman pulls them over for speeding, they conclude they must interrupt his radio call back to headquarters, and having done so, they decide it prudent to lock him in the trunk of his car. Finally they confront a trucker who has repeatedly greeted them with obscene gestures as they have passed each other on the road, and who has even adorned his truck with graphic sexual images. As he approaches them at a truck stop with the leering suggestiveness that seems to be his only mode of interacting with women, Thelma and Louse decide to enlighten him about the nonsexual agency of contemporary women in terms he will understand. They respond to his boorish friendliness by casually shooting out the tires of his tanker, finally emphasizing their point by aiming at the oil tanks themselves, dramatically igniting them.

All the while the law is closing in on Thelma and Louise. They make several desperate escapes from oncoming law enforcement vehicles, which manage to crash into each other in disastrous ways. But finally they are surrounded by hundreds of police cars and FBI agents in helicopters, all training their eyes and their guns on the two female fugitives. Their decision is easy to make, and not particularly disheartening. They have no desire to return to the lives they led before, even if that were possible, and it is not. Thelma says that the only thing she regrets is that she was not the one to have shot the cowboy. They accept the situation they are in as a meaningful culmination of their actions in the past several days. The Grand Canyon lies in front of them. They embrace each other briefly and start up their car one more time and sail over the canyon's rim. Hundreds of law enforcement officials look on, unable to apprehend these female outlaws. It is a strangely exhilarating moment. A sympathetic FBI agent races futilely after them; he will ensure that their tale is recounted in such a way as to lend some degree of dignity to their murder of the rapist and their flight from the law.

As I watched *Thelma and Louise*, I became aware for the first time of the attractions of the buddy movie, the road movie, the western, male film genres with which I personally have felt little sympathy in the past. In the developing camaraderie of Thelma and Louise, in their rather undermotivated movements across a vast expanse of Western landscape, in their violent interactions with various humorously caricatured male characters, I suddenly saw metaphors of freedom and justice, of individual rights, and of personal honor which I had rarely noticed in more typical western buddy movies. As Louise shot the man who had attempted to rape her friend and who then unwisely sneered at her, I saw good opposing evil at the boundaries of socially sanctioned behavior. I suppose it is this sort of metaphorical projection that explains why so many people enjoy traditional "shoot'em ups," as my grandfather fondly referred to westerns. Surprisingly, however, sophisticated reviewers who usually accept the brutality and anarchy of contemporary films as unobjectionable cultural and political tropes found it difficult to respond to the narrative of *Thelma and Louise* metaphorically. Instead, an anxious and hostile torrent of literal readings of the film developed. Reviewers were particularly distressed by the excessive violence of the heroines and vehemently protested the broad caricatures of male figures of social authority. It was left to a few astute film critics, most notably Janet Maslin of the *New York Times*, to explain that the power of the movie was based on a reversal of gender roles, and to suggest that male reviewers "lighten up" and accept the discomfort of being on the wrong side of normative gender stereotypes for a change.[3]

Of course, the film is about more than a reversal of roles; it is about the devolution of patriarchal forms of agency, and about women's budding sense of their own possibilities for action. It might be a classic road movie, but for the fact that when women go on a journey of self-discovery today there are threatening ramifications for men, whose sense of sexual and so-cial agency has been built upon relationships to women who could not act on their own behalf. As women seize the postfeminist moment, claiming new desires and insisting that they themselves, as well as their desires, be recognized by men, male agency is undermined insofar as it adheres to traditional forms. While patriarchal structures of power still tend to deter-mine the final outcome in the micro-politics of everyday life, male agency has become increasingly embattled and uncertain as women's sense of agency has begun to develop.[4]

Consider *Thelma and Louise* in this light. As often in parables, its narra-tive presents the issues with exaggerated clarity. Even before they leave home, the domineering yet ridiculous figure of Thelma's husband Daryl suggests the empty quality of patriarchal authority today. As the two women set off across the desert in Louise's big blue convertible, we are vaguely prepared for yet another film of adventure to gradually unfold be-fore our eyes. The pivotal interaction at the roadhouse occurs with startling haste. No sooner do Thelma and Louise begin to loosen up and enjoy them-selves in this rare escape from their everyday lives than does traditional male desire enter the picture in the form of the cowboy. Realizing the dangers, Louise is wary, but Thelma innocently follows her own immedi-ate desires and throws herself into the seemingly safe sexuality of dancing. When male sexual desire takes its traditional course and the cowboy is about to rape Thelma, however, Louise appears and orders the cowboy to return his penis to his pants. Classic male phallic desire is thus partially enacted, but thwarted at the moment of its satisfaction. Not able to com-prehend the alteration in gendered power relationships signaled by Louise's opportune appearance, the cowboy crassly verbalizes his unre-lenting sense of sexual entitlement, demanding of Louise, "Suck my cock." When Louise responds by shooting him dead, she goes beyond patriarchal motifs of the castrating woman. She does not focus on his sexual parts; she does not act out her rage in a countersexual feminine mode. This is not a sexual game. She expects her nonsexual agency as the wielder of a gun to be properly respected, and the cowboy refuses her this quite basic form of interpersonal frontier regard. She kills him for his blind resistance to her (female) authority, for his nonrecognition of her immediate social and political agency. In the dramatic manner of parables, her shot signals that male unwillingness to recognize the social and political agency of women will increasingly prove fatal to men, to their sexual and nonsexual desires alike.[5]

With the placement of this incident at the very beginning of this female road movie, we are put on notice that a tale of female adventure cannot even get started without confronting and overcoming conventionally oppressive forms of male desire. Thelma's ecstatic sexual interlude with the cute young thief signals that male desire can still be acceptable when it comes in unconventional packages; yet when he runs off with all of their money, the implication is that any form of male desire is likely to be dangerous to women's efforts to realize themselves. The older and wiser Louise explains to her loyal but uncomprehending boyfriend that she has come to a juncture in her life when she must leave him behind. The FBI agent who shows sympathy for Thelma and Louise's plight is quite an implausible character in this film, and Louise is only momentarily tempted by his desires to aid them. But he shows the future possibility for male desire to alter its qualities such that it will no longer be threatening to women's ventures, and may even be capable of participating in them.[6]

As the film develops, Thelma and Louise are increasingly aware of the breadth of their own capacities for desire and social recognition, as well as the potential destructiveness of their newfound sense of agency in relation to the world they have left behind. When they finally arrive at the edge of the Grand Canyon, there is no question of returning to that world. It simply would not make sense. The men in their lives are portrayed in such a way that it is clear that there is no one really at home waiting for either of them. As they drive over the rim of the Grand Canyon, it is a moment charged with desire, erotic in its immensity and in its impossibility of fulfillment.

Thelma and Louise are postfeminist heroines in their resourceful and courageous response to the unexpected turn their lives have taken. Accepting a gendered struggle on the terms by which it arose, they have seized the micro-political moment and made the most of it, as one must do on frontiers. If all the male law enforcement officers gathered to watch the final arc of Thelma and Louise cannot yet comprehend their journey, they may possibly recognize the surplus of social desires which carries these women beyond their juridical grasp.

Notes

Introductory Reflections

1. The issue of how narrowly or broadly to construe one's feminist project has recently become a site of controversy, with bourgeois feminist universalism a particular focus of wrath, much of it deserved. As a white, heterosexual philosopher in New York City, I can hardly expect to speak to, and certainly not for, women the world over. Yet I would hope that my ideas will have relevance even for some who do not share my immediate demographic points of reference. Linda Alcoff has articulated a notion of feminist "positionality" that I find helpful: "The concept of woman is a relational term identifiable only within a (constantly moving) context; but . . . the position that women find themselves in can be actively utilized (rather than transcended) as a location for the construction of meaning." See Alcoff, "Cultural Feminism versus Post-Structuralism: The Identity Crisis in Feminist Theory," *Signs* 13, 3 (1988), p. 434. As a feminist social theorist, I am seeking to alter hegemonic patriarchal discourses, attempting to construct alternative ways of understanding a number of significant social relationships that look rather different according to my gendered micropolitical account. I offer this set of alternative meanings to anyone who can make use of them.

2. See Bernard Williams, *Ethics and the Limits of Philosophy* (Cambridge, Mass.: Harvard University Press, 1985); and Alasdair MacIntyre, *After Virtue* (Notre Dame: University of Notre Dame Press, 1981).

3. There has been some bitter wrangling inspired by the term "postfeminism." Many feminist thinkers associate it with a current "backlash" against feminism, and a celebration of the end of a socially critical feminist politics. See Suzanna Danuta Walters, "Premature Postmortems: 'Postfeminism' and Popular Culture," *New Politics*, 3, 2 (Winter 1991) for a chronicle of the angry reaction of feminists to the term. My point is that regardless of how various commentators have used the term, feminists should appropriate it to announce the advent of a significantly different stage of gendered social conflicts and changes. Gender is no longer a narrow ideological set of issues in a postfeminist age; rather, it is a prominent site of change in everyone's life.

4. Judith Butler, *Gender Trouble* (New York: Routledge, 1990), pp. 139–49.

5. Simone de Beauvoir, *The Second Sex* (Vintage: New York, 1952), p. xxii.

6. Notice that I am not denying the relevance of either identity or consciousness in an analysis of social and political activity. I am suggesting that the theoretical focus of social analysis shift slightly, moving away from the historically dominant emphasis upon either states of consciousness or the physical and social causes of those states. I advocate, instead, that we highlight decisions to act, constructing an analytical framework out of categories that enable us to evaluate variable social and individual components of decisions to act. Poststructuralist theorists who would leave individual consciousness behind altogether, to discuss individual performances as merely the effects of signifying practices, go too far. In their zealous pursuit of a decentered subject they lose subjects altogether, thereby losing the ability to say anything interesting about contemporary social actions or relationships.

7. See Linda Gordon, *Woman's Body, Woman's Right* (New York: Penguin, 1974), p. 52; See my chapter 3. See Catharine MacKinnon, *The Sexual Harassment of Working Women* (New Haven: Yale University Press, 1979), for the first definition of this as a legal issue. See my chapter 5.

8. This appears to be a case in which the political context of liberalism makes a very significant difference in the possibility for gendered social changes. In African societies such as exist in Kenya, for example, women have long had sources of independent income, and in some cases women are the dominant economic agents within a society. Yet patriarchy persists insofar as women's identities are subsumed within that of a male head of the family. Rose Arungu-Olende, a lawyer with the Kenya Mission in New York City, maintains that patriarchal structures are beginning to break down in Kenya as well, but not in precisely the same ways as within Western societies.

9. Aristotle, *Nichomachean Ethics*, in *The Basic Works of Aristotle*, ed. Richard McKeon (New York: Random House, 1941), Book 5.

10. Donald Davidson, *Actions and Events* (Oxford: Clarendon Press, 1980), p. 41.

11. Michel Foucault utilized his genealogical techniques most effectively in historical investigations. He showed how knowledge and power were articulated together, producing subjects of particular sorts of knowledge and power in the context of historically evolving institutions and discourses of mental illness, prisons, and sexuality. See Michel Foucault, *The Birth of the Clinic*, trans. Alan Sheridan (New York: Vintage/Random House, 1975); *Discipline and Punish*, trans. Alan Sheridan (New York: Vintage, 1979); *The History of Sexuality: Volume I*, trans. Robert Hurley (New York: Vintage, 1980). Contemporary thinkers who attempt to appropriate Foucault's historical genealogical approach and use it as the basis for their theories of social relations achieve disappointing results, producing rigorous technologies of behavior but not social theories.

My work is certainly informed by a Foucauldian awareness of the relationships between individuals and the social discourses they/we are immersed in. The problem is how to properly assimilate such an awareness into a project of contemporary theorizing. The theory of agency presented in this book is my current answer to this question.

12. See Michel Foucault, *Discipline and Punish*, pp. 191–94, 201–9, 252, for his theory of "the gaze" as an explicit disciplinary tactic in the context of nineteenth-century prisons. See his *History of Sexuality* for his explanation of how forms of sexual subjectivity are discursively constructed.

13. See particularly Jacques Lacan, "God and the Jouissance of the Woman. A Love Letter," in *Feminine Sexuality*, ed. Juliet Mitchell and Jacqueline Rose (New York: Norton, 1982), where he states, "Once the 'the' of 'the' woman is formulated . . . there can be no 'the' here other than crossed through" (p. 151).

14. See Donald Davidson, *Actions and Events* (Oxford: Clarendon Press, 1980), for an exemplary analytic treatment of agency. Harry Frankfurt has gone so far as to define personhood normatively in terms of the possession of what he calls "second-order desires." "First-order desires" are simply desires to do something, and second-order desires and volitions are desires to have particular first-order desires. See "Freedom of the Will and the Concept of a Person," *The Journal of Philosophy* 68, 1 (January 1971), pp. 5–20.

15. It is this metaphysical approach to agency that led many philosophers and psychologists to wrongly interpret Carol Gilligan's provocative theory of an alternative form of ethical agency in an essentialist way. Gilligan was quite explicit in her book *In A Different Voice* (Cambridge, Mass.: Harvard University Press, 1981) that while she discovered the possibility for a different way of thinking about ethical decisions in studies of women, a caring form of ethical agency was neither exclusive to women nor always found in women. But without a social conception of agency, her argument was falsely read as an essentialist metaphysical claim about male and female forms of ethical thinking.

16. See Mary Wollstonecraft, *A Vindication of the Rights of Women*, ed. Carol H. Poston (New York: W. W. Norton, 1975); Simone de Beauvoir, *The Second Sex* (New York: Vin-

tage, 1974); Catharine Beecher, *A Treatise on Domestic Economy* (New York: Schocken, 1977); Sara Ruddick, *Maternal Thinking* (New York: Ballantine, 1989).

17. See Alexandre Koyre, *From the Closed World to the Infinite Universe* (Baltimore: Johns Hopkins University Press, 1957); and E. A. Burt, *The Metaphysical Foundations of Modern Science* (New York: Doubleday, 1952).

18. Even procreative agency need not be seen as an inherently gendered form of agency, as science draws ever closer to achieving the technological ability to bring about gestation outside a woman's womb. Yet the degree of social responsibility women now bear for the physical gestation of the fetus, as well as for children's care subsequent to birth, justifies the feminist insistence on women's ultimate procreative authority today in relation to abortion and other basic reproductive decisions.

19. See Linda Alcoff, "Feminist Politics and Foucault: The Limits of a Collaboration," Society for Women in Philosophy conference, SUNY Stonybrook, Spring 1989. She argues that Foucault's rejection of notions of reflective and potentially critical subjectivity leave him without a basis for any meaningful conception of political agency and resistance. Her critique is compelling, but I think we must articulate postmodern agency in ways that place more emphasis upon a dynamic context of action and less upon an individual political consciousness.

20. See Jacques Derrida, *Of Grammatology* (Baltimore: Johns Hopkins University Press, 1974); Richard Rorty, *Contingency, Irony, Solidarity* (New York: Cambridge University Press, 1989); Jürgen Habermas, *The Legitimation Crisis* (Boston: Beacon, 1975); Bernard Williams, *Ethics and the Limits of Philosophy* (Cambridge, Mass.: Harvard University Press, 1985); Alasdair MacIntyre, *After Virtue*; Jean-François Lyotard, *The Postmodern Condition* (Minneapolis: University of Minnesota Press, 1979); Gilles Deleuze and Felix Guattari, *Anti-Oedipus* (Minneapolis: University of Minnesota Press, 1983).

21. Alasdair MacIntyre, *Whose Justice? Which Rationality?* (Notre Dame: University of Notre Dame Press, 1988), p. 362. Of course, MacIntyre does not suggest that our modern liberal tradition will soon be surpassed by a postmodern one. He focuses his attention on the relationships between the four different traditions which have so far defined the Western philosophical trajectory.

22. Susan Faludi's *Backlash: The Undeclared War Against American Women* (New York: Crown, 1991), has capitalized on this sense of frustration, explaining it in simplistic terms and scapegoating the media.

23. Jürgen Habermas has characterized relationships within the family as "normatively secured," distinguishing them from public-sphere relationships in which consensus must be "communicatively achieved." His terminology is helpful for delineating the radical quality of the transformations now occurring within the family as a result of the social enfranchisement of women. Habermas, while duly classifying the current women's movement as one of several "new social movements" with emancipatory goals, is hardly prepared to recognize its radical implications for society or for his theory of how society is organized. See his *The Theory of Communicative Action: Lifeworld and System*, vol. 2, trans. Thomas McCarthy (Boston: Beacon, 1987).

24. I refer to "neediness forms" rather than to needs intentionally. What we take for granted as our "needs" are functions of particular social ways in which we have learned to satisfy our various material and psychic forms of neediness. Georg Lukács made the classic critique of the "reified" quality of our basic needs under capitalism. See *History and Class Consciousness* (Cambridge, Mass.: MIT Press, 1971). Herbert Marcuse extended this analysis of the oppressive creation and satisfaction of false needs by capitalism. See *One-Dimensional Man* (Boston: Beacon Press, 1964). I argue that the quality of our perceived needs has also been a function of patriarchy, and that we will be forced to perceive our needs differently as familial unmooring progresses and we begin to construct new ways of satisfying material and psychic forms of neediness.

25. It is interesting that in one of his last interviews, Michel Foucault was concerned with

precisely the sorts of issues I have identified in terms of a notion of interpersonal agency. See *The Final Foucault*, ed. James Bernauer and David Rasmussen (Cambridge, Mass.: MIT Press, 1988), p. 20. According to Foucault, "we can imagine that there are societies in which the way one determines the behavior of others is so well determined in advance, that there is nothing left to do. On the other hand, in a society like ours—it is very evident in family relationships, for example, in sexual and affective relations—the games can be extremely numerous and thus the temptation to determine the conduct of others is that much greater. However, the more that people are free in respect to each other, the greater the temptation on both sides to determine the conduct of others." [January 20, 1984, interview].

26. Richard Rorty, *Contingency, Irony, Solidarity*, pp. 9, 37.

27. See Susan Bordo, *The Flight to Objectivity* (Albany: SUNY Press, 1987), for an influential example of this genre.

28. See Kimberlé Crenshaw, "Mapping the Margins: Identity Politics, Intersectionality, and Violence Against Women," *Stanford Law Review* 43 (July 1991). Crenshaw analyzes the way in which women of color are typically left out of the political perspectives of both male black nationalists and white feminists. She offers the term "intersectionality" to refer to the political problems arising when multiple forms of domination affect women of color, given the inability of most political theories to deal with more than one dimension of oppression at a time. I have constructed a micro-political analysis with the aim of more adequately treating such situations, which I take as the norm rather than the exception today.

29. Sexual harassment charges brought against Senator Bob Packwood of Oregon and former Senator Brock Adams of Washington (who decided not to run for reelection in the face of the charges), and the possibility of charges against Senator Daniel Inouye of Hawaii in the wake of the Hill-Thomas hearings have at least alerted Congressional men to a new standard of behavior, and provide encouragement for women in other employment contexts to consider bringing charges against powerful men.

30. See Sarah Lyall, "2 Admit They Harassed Assemblywoman," *New York Times*, January 14, 1993.

31. See Deborah Rhode, *Justice and Gender* (Cambridge, Mass.: Harvard University Press, 1989).

32. National news coverage of an interview Desiree Washington gave on an Indianapolis television station, January 26, 1993. In the same interview, Washington went on to say, "Now my whole life is destroyed. It was taken away in one night." See "Tyson Mildly (65 Cents a Day) Does His Time in Indiana," *New York Times*, February 7, 1993.

33. Contemporary challenges to the continuing exclusion of women from combat roles in the military constitute a last frontier, in this regard. See "Female P.O.W. Is Abused, Kindling Debate," by Elaine Sciolino, *New York Times*, June 29, 1992, for the most recent riff on the old military argument that women are not fit for combat roles.

34. The Secretary of the Navy, H. Lawrence Garrett, was forced to resign on June 26, 1992, as a result of the Tailhook controversy. See Larry Rohter, "Naval Training Changes to Curb Sex Harassment," *New York Times*, June 22, 1992.

35. Anthony Lewis, "The Issue is Bigotry," *New York Times*, January 29, 1993. Lewis points out that "if sexual conduct were the real concern of the critics, they would focus on the clear and present problem. You don't have to be a genius to know what that is: assaults on women in the armed forces." Those arguing against openly allowing gays in the military frequently make an analogy between our presumption against housing men and women together and their fears of housing gay and straight men together. The immediate answer is that gay and straight men have long shared sleeping space and showers, so the analogy is false. The longer answer is that were men and women not socialized to assume heterosexual male predatoriness, there would be no reason for men and women not to share sleeping quarters or showers. In fact, college dormitories were sexually integrated in the 1970s, and at Yale University the undergraduates even shared bathrooms and showers in many college residences.

36. The self-conscious use of "mass rape as a strategy of war" in Bosnia and Herzegovina (where it is estimated that 20,000 Muslim women have been raped since fighting began in April of 1992) shows a new and increasingly global capacity for cynicism about the predatory quality of male sexual desires. See Tamar Lewin, "The Balkans Rapes: a Legal Test for the Outraged," *New York Times*, January 15, 1993. "While rape by soldiers is as old as war itself, lawyers say, it has rarely been treated as a war crime or a human rights offense. But they say this conflict, in which Bosnian Serb soldiers are reportedly being ordered to rape Muslim women as a part of a pattern of abuse aimed at driving them from their homes, may signal a change in attitudes toward wartime rape."

37. Eric Schmitt, "The Top Soldier Is Torn Between 2 Loyalties," *New York Times*, February 6, 1993. Schmitt reports that "friends and associates say he [Powell] is equally driven by an emotional, almost mystical, commitment to the 1.8 million–member armed forces, and to a military culture that has defined his 35-year career."

38. Michael R. Gordon, "Panel Is Against Letting Women Fly in Combat," *New York Times*, November 4, 1992. "The head of the Presidential commission, Robert T. Herres, a retired Air Force general and the former vice chairman of the Joint Chiefs of Staff, told the panel that he knew of no compelling reason to ban women from flying combat planes. And General Draude, the director of Marine Corps public affairs, added his voice to those who advocate letting women fly combat missions, noting in an emotional address that his daughter was training to be a Navy pilot."

1. Love and Injustice in Families

1. My primary frame of reference is the situation of women and men in the United States today; my historical references are, for the most part, limited to the Western philosophical tradition. Moreover, my analysis does not apply equally to every cultural group even in this country. Yet I offer this analysis as *potentially relevant* in various contemporary societies and cultures. A social theorist must walk a fine line between hubris and false modesty today. We must generalize beyond our immediate experiences in order to offer insights to others whose shoes we are not in, yet we must accept the fact that in each act of generalization there is a potential act of false generalization. The traditional white male philosopher in the Western tradition who believed in universal truths was typically in a position to impose his faulty generalizations on people who had no social or theoretical standing to protest their falsity. There is reason to think that the power relations between theorist and reader have shifted *somewhat* today, insofar as we are more aware of the fallibility of theory. As a theorist who accepts her inability to recognize the particular boundedness of her notions, I leave it to the reader to generalize beyond the immediate cultural frame of reference.

2. While contemporary women's issues increasingly impinge on the most basic moral and political problems of philosophy, analytic philosophers typically relegate discussions of gender and other social themes to specific areas of applied philosophy such as medical ethics. Feminist philosophy is gaining deserved institutional recognition recently, but as a disciplinary specialization with its own themes and participants. See a vicious exchange of letters between the feminist philosophers Sandra Lee Bartky, Marilyn Friedman, Alison M. Jaggar et al., and Christina Hoff Sommers, a self-appointed scourge of those she calls "gender feminists," in the American Philosophical Association's *Proceedings and Addresses* 65, 7 (June 1992) for a painful lesson in the still-embattled status of feminism within philosophy.

3. See Arlie Hochschild, with Anne Machung, *The Second Shift* (New York: Viking, 1989), for a sociologist's report on how little has changed in the domestic division of labor. See also Marian Burros, "Women: Out of the House But Not Out of the Kitchen," *New York Times*, February 24, 1988.

4. See Alasdair MacIntyre, *After Virtue* (Notre Dame: University of Notre Dame Press, 1981), p. 175, for an explanation of the family as a last remaining form of what he calls "a traditional moral practice."

5. David Heyd, *Supererogation: Its Status in Ethical Theory* (New York: Cambridge University Press, 1982), p. 134. Marcia Baron, in her "Kantian Ethics and Supererogation," *Journal of Philosophy* 84 (1987), p. 253, cites Heyd. Baron is pointing to a typical unwillingness to consider traditional female behavior in moral terms even of supererogation. My aim is to criticize our inability to see traditional female activities as embodying rationally purposive behavior of any sort.

6. John Rawls, *A Theory of Justice* (Cambridge, Mass.: Harvard University Press, 1971). See Susan Moller Okin, *Justice, Gender, and the Family* (New York: Basic Books, 1989), for a powerful feminist critique of Rawls's failure to recognize the family as a major site of injustice. Okin argues that Rawls could have addressed injustices within the family by explicitly including women in the "Original Position." This is the imaginary political moment in which individuals in Rawls's theory come together to impartially decide upon the basic principles of participation and distribution in a just society. Their impartiality is guaranteed by not knowing their future position in society, according to Rawls. But their concern for fairness is unduly circumscribed by not sufficiently recognizing potential differences such as gender, as Okin points out.

7. Alasdair MacIntyre, *After Virtue*, pp. 175, 217, 222, 226, 233. While MacIntyre seems to consider the family the last remaining example of a traditional moral practice, and also to recognize its decline, he never discusses the new status of women as a factor in this decline!

8. G. W. F. Hegel, *Philosophy of Right*, trans. T. M. Knox (London: Oxford University Press, 1967), p. 110.

9. See "Rate of Marriage Continues Decline," by Felicity Barringer, *New York Times*, July 17, 1992. "The median age at first marriage has also been increasing. It now stands at 26.3 years for men and 24.1 years for women, higher than at any time in the last century, and continuing long-established trends." Robert F. Willis, director of economic research for the University of Chicago's National Opinion Research Center, is quoted as saying that for women "there are two activities that are extremely time-intensive: bearing and raising children, and establishing yourself in a career. A lot of people are trying different ways of sequencing them. . . . It seems to me until people have found a right way to travel through this, it'll be very difficult to predict how these statistics are going to change." Notice that the problem for women is evident, but the solution is not articulated in terms of a redistribution of men's and women's familial duties.

10. Roberto Mangabeira Unger, *Social Theory: Its Situation and Its Task* (New York: Cambridge University Press, 1987), p. 1.

11. See Roberto Mangabeira Unger, *False Necessity* (New York: Cambridge University Press, 1987), pp. 102–5. See Susan Moller Okin, *Justice, Gender, and the Family* (New York: Basic Books, 1989), pp. 117–24, for a feminist critique of Unger's views, and even more for his *lack of views*, on the family.

12. In the nineteenth century, Mary Wollstonecraft made the case for applying the supposedly universal norms of liberalism to women. But the presumption of a natural sexual division of labor placed great obstacles in the path of any serious application of standards of equality and mutual respect between men and women. While J. S. Mill denounced the despotism of husbands within the family and insisted that women should be protected against male personal tyranny by being granted full political rights, his words were not heeded. It was John Ruskin's theory of "the separate spheres" of men and women, emphasizing the complementary nature of men's and women's roles and glossing over their inequality, which served the needs of nineteenth-century liberalism. See J. S. Mill, *The Subjection of Women*, in Alice S. Rossi, ed., *Essays on Sex Equality* (Chicago: University of Chicago Press, 1970). See John Ruskin, "Of Queen's Gardens," in *Sesame and Lilies* (London: A. L. Burt, 1871).

13. I use the notion of "liberalism" to refer very broadly to the social and political discourses that have developed in the context of capitalist, democratic institutions in Western Europe and North America since the seventeenth century. Marx and subsequent theorists

contrasted liberalism, as a doctrine of individual rights, with socialism, as a theory of collective rights and interests. By contrast, when the media uses the term "liberalism" today, they are typically referring to (Keynesian-derived) macroeconomic policies of redistribution and state planning, as distinct from classical (but also liberal in my terminology) microeconomic doctrines privileging "free" market forces.

14. Jean Bethke Elshtain, "Antigone's Daughters: Reflections on Female Identity and the State," in *Families, Politics, and Public Policy*, ed. Irene Diamond (New York: Longman, 1983), p. 301.

15. A. I. Melden, *Rights and Persons* (Berkeley: University of California Press, 1977), pp. 76, 78. Presumably, as a latter-day Kantian, Melden would not object to homosexual families. The gendered patterns of family injustice we are concerned with could arise, after all, as a consequence of *gendered role-playing* on the part of two men, or two women.

16. Ibid., pp. 176, 78.

17. Ibid., pp. 104, 137.

18. Ibid., p. 134.

19. John Hardwig, "Should Women Think in Terms of Rights?," *Ethics* 94 (April, 1984), pp. 441–55. See also Virginia Held, "Non-contractual Society: A Feminist View," in *Science, Morality and Feminist Theory*, ed. Marsha Hanen and Kai Nielsen (Calgary: University of Calgary Press, 1987).

20. A similar problem may undermine recent efforts to articulate an expanded conception of rights in the public sphere. Alan Gewirth's theory that rights to well-being are a precondition for social agency is both conceptually plausible and politically impotent. Our notions of economic agency make only provision for oneself and one's immediate dependents a matter of rational obligation, in an important sense. See Gewirth's *Reason and Morality* (Chicago: University of Chicago Press, 1978). See also Andrew Hacker, "Getting Rough on the Poor," *New York Review of Books*, October 13, 1988.

21. Friedrich Engels, *The Origins of the Family, Private Property and the State*, ed. Eleanor Burke Leacock (New York: International Publishers, 1972).

22. Heidi Hartmann, "The Unhappy Marriage of Marxism and Feminism," in *Women and Revolution*, ed. Lydia Sargent (Boston: South End Press, 1981), p. 15.

23. See Ann Ferguson, *Blood at the Root: Motherhood, Sexuality and Male Dominance* (London: Pandora, 1989); Margaret Benston, "The Political Economy of Women's Liberation," in *From Feminism to Liberation*, ed. Edith Hoshino Altbach (Cambridge, Mass.: Schenkman, 1980).

24. Mary O'Brien, *The Politics of Reproduction* (Boston: Routledge and Kegan Paul, 1983).

25. See Carol Brown, "Mothers, Fathers and Children: From Private to Public Patriarchy," in *Women and Revolution*. Her notion of "public patriarchy" is helpful in capturing the shift from individual male power over individual women to a more generalized power of male-dominated economic and political structures over the lives of women.

26. Orlando Patterson, *Slavery and Social Death* (Cambridge, Mass.: Harvard University Press, 1982), p. 342. See his recent two-volume work, *Freedom* (New York: Basic Books, 1991), where Patterson has pursued his critique in interesting directions.

27. Ibid., p. 55.

28. Aristotle, *Politics*, in *The Basic Works of Aristotle*, ed. Richard McKeon (New York: Random House, 1941), 1254b, 1260a.

29. Patterson, *Slavery*, pp. 294–330.

30. Patterson argues that wage laborers were radicalized by the presence of slavery, seeing their own degradation in being forced to work for others dramatized by the more extreme degradation of the slaves. *Slavery*, p. 34.

31. See Adrienne Rich, *Of Woman Born* (New York: Norton, 1976). See also Sara Ruddick, "Maternal Thinking," in *Mothering*, ed. Joyce Trebilcot (Totowa, N.J.: Rowman and Allanheld, 1984).

32. See Patricia S. Mann, "Socialism Under the Influence," *Social Text* 19/20 (1988), pp.

223–36. I argue that when one thus interrogates the liberal notion of freedom, as Patterson suggests, one comes to see the ability to act in one's own name as a "social birth" condition necessary before one can even consider applying the category of freedom or Patterson's concept of "social death." See chapter 2 for further elaboration of how the relationship of social recognition has contributed to patriarchal forms of oppression.

33. Women first demonstrated their capacity for public personhood as wage-earners during World War II, but with the return of men from the war, they were unceremoniously banished from the workplace and forced to return to traditional wifely relationships of patriarchal dependency and servitude. Having witnessed women's capacities for social independence, however, a number of male social commentators in the 1950s had malevolent visions of the quality of women's domestic powers over men and children. The extreme woman-hating vitriol of Philip Wylie in his book *A Generation of Vipers*, found amid piles of cast-off books in the family basement during adolescence, is etched in my memory. See Barbara Ehrenreich, *The Hearts of Men* (New York: Anchor Press, 1984), pp. 36–37, for a more complete listing of hostile, confused male responses to the gradual recognition of women's capacities for full personhood in the 1950s and 1960s.

34. Feminism has, of course, been accused of devaluing the role of the housewife. This is a case of blaming the messenger for the message. Feminists have made the lowly status of traditionally female domestic activities an issue, and have been on the forefront of those arguing for a revaluation of traditional female activities. See Sara Ruddick, *Maternal Thinking* (New York: Ballantine, 1989).

35. See Alasdair MacIntyre, *After Virtue*. It was Freud's great inspiration to conflate male forms of psychic neediness with a longstanding notion of instinctive sexual desire. As sexual desire, male psychic neediness could be camouflaged as yet another variation on self-interested agency. Alan Gewirth's notion of "the right to well-being" is a more politicized expression of the contemporary concern with the limits of the ideal of autonomy. See his *Reason and Morality*.

36. Teaching provides painfully clear evidence of the significance of the distinction between activities associated with tangible, material forms of individual achievement and those associated with services to others, even in the public sphere of wage labor. It is a profession with very low wages and social prestige relative to others requiring a comparable amount of intellectual preparation. Moreover, the product-versus-service distinction operates even within a profession such as college "teaching." It is the production of articles and books rather than teaching / serving the needs of students that counts most when we evaluate a professor's abilities and achievements. And we tend to count the number of books and articles more readily than their quality, or other intangible professorial acts of social significance.

37. John Rawls's assertion that non-tuism, or mutual disinterest, rather than egoism was the appropriate assumption to make about persons in the original position has set the tone for much of recent theory. See *A Theory of Justice* (Cambridge, Mass.: Harvard University Press, 1971), p. 13. Thomas Nagel, in *The Possibility of Altruism* (Oxford: Oxford University Press, 1970), and Lawrence Blum, in *Friendship, Altruism, and Morality* (London: Routledge and Kegan Paul, 1980), have argued for various other-directed orientations. While these works seek to make sense of the existence of altruistic behavior, they do not presume to critique the self-other dichotomy underlying our theories of rational motivation. And they make no effort to assert grounds upon which we might choose other-directed activities, in competition with self-directed activities.

38. David Gauthier, *Morals By Agreement* (Oxford: Clarendon Press, 1986). See chapters 10 and 11 particularly.

39. Gauthier, pp. 350, 327.

40. Aristotle, *Nichomachean Ethics*, in *The Basic Works of Aristotle*, ed. Richard McKeon (New York: Random House, 1941), 1158b, 1159a, 1169b.

41. Ibid., 1162b, 1163b.

42. Ibid., 1168a.

43. Bernard Williams bravely explores the ethical issues that arise when men no longer see their families as extensions of themselves. He identifies a potential conflict between the personal integrity of individual men and women and the potentially very great demands of their families. See his "Moral Luck," in *Moral Luck* (Cambridge: Cambridge University Press, 1985) for an interesting analysis of the personal/familial/artistic conflicts experienced by an artist he calls Gauguin and a woman he calls Anna Karenina. While he is quite right that neither Kantian nor consequentialist ethical theories adequately explain familial commitments, his alternate notion of personal integrity needs to be carefully articulated as an ethical category. Williams's case of the unemployed scientist he calls George, whose political commitments are part of his personal integrity, and whose responsibilities to his family are, by contrast, theorized as impositions of impersonal morality that compromise his personal integrity (!) illustrates the dangers of an impoverished notion of contemporary selfhood in the wake of women's social enfranchisement. See Bernard Williams and J. J. C. Smart, *Utilitarianism: For and Against* (New York: Cambridge University Press, 1973), pp.82–117. See also Lynne McFall, "Integrity," *Ethics* 98 (October 1987), pp. 5–20, for a subtle analysis of possible variables in our notions of personal integrity.

44. Second-wave feminism has elaborated upon Marxism's theory of the ideological forms of knowledge generated by those in positions of social power. Patriarchy, like capitalism, produces and is maintained by fundamentally biased structures of belief. See Sandra Lee Bartky, "Towards a Phenomenology of Feminist Consciousness," in *Feminism and Philosophy*, ed. Mary Vetterling Braggin, Frederick Elliston, and Jane English (Totowa, N.J.: Littlefield Adams, 1981), for a good description of the experience of developing a feminist worldview within a society still dominated by a patriarchal worldview.

45. Donald Davidson, *Actions and Events* (Oxford: Clarendon Press, 1980), p. 21.

46. Ibid., p. 30.

47. Ibid., pp. 41–42.

48. Ibid., pp. 221–22.

49. While an analytic philosopher such as Davidson will rarely admit that his reasoning derives from particular social conditions, Davidson does remark in a footnote that he has found no previous case in which a philosopher recognizes that incontinence is not simply a problem of morality! See footnote 14 on p. 30 of Davidson's essay.

50. Derek Parfit, *Reasons and Persons* (Oxford: Oxford University Press, 1986), pp. 210, 215- 217.

51. Ibid., pp. 254–73.

52. Ibid., pp. 199–202.

53. Ibid., p. 281.

2. Glancing at Pornography: Recognizing Men

1. See Deborah Rhode, *Justice and Gender* (Cambridge, Mass.: Harvard University Press, 1989), p. 266.

2. See *American Booksellers Association v. Hudnut*, 771 F. 2d 323 (7th Cir. 1985), aff'd sub nom. *Hudnut v. American Booksellers Association*, 106 S. Ct. 1172, rehearing denied 106 S. Ct. 1664 (1986).

3. Rhode, *Justice*, p. 271. Rhode reports that "according to public-opinion surveys in the mid-1980s, some two-thirds of Americans favored prohibitions on sexual violence in magazines and movies." See Varda Burstyn, ed., *Women Against Censorship* (Vancouver: Douglas and McIntyre, 1985).

4. See Andrea Dworkin, *Pornography: Men Possessing Women* (New York: Perigee, 1979); Catharine MacKinnon, *Feminism Unmodified* (Cambridge, Mass.: Harvard University Press, 1987).

5. Linda Lovelace's account of her experiences while filming *Deep Throat* is cited as one

of the primary examples of such coercion. See Linda Lovelace and Michael McGrady, *Ordeal* (1981).

6. See MacKinnon, *Feminism*, p. 171, where she states that "pornography sexualizes rape, battery, sexual harassment, prostitution, and child sexual abuse; it thereby celebrates, promotes, authorizes, and legitimizes them."

7. Ibid., p. 195.

8. Ibid., pp. 155, 196.

9. There is an interesting comparison to be made between nineteenth-century "social purity" movements in which women focused their ire upon common male practices concerning alcohol and prostitution, and the twentieth-century antipornography movement, which directed its anger at male sexual objectification of women. The social purity movements displaced their underlying criticism of customary male behavior with their focus on an abuse of alcohol or consorting with "bad women." Individual men thus had grounds for exempting themselves from the criticism and proclaiming their own personal virtue. The twentieth-century antipornography movement homed in on a more elemental level of conflict between men and women, potentially indicting all men for their sexualized visions of women. The frequent decision of religious fundamentalists and right-wing conservatives to make alliances with the antipornography struggles of radical feminists betrays a failure to recognize the much more radical social ramifications of the twentieth-century antipornography movement.

See Judith Walkowitz, "Male Vice and Female Virtue: Feminism and the Politics of Prostitution in Nineteenth-Century Britain," in *Powers of Desire*, ed. Ann Snitow, Christine Stansell, and Sharon Thompson (New York: Monthly Review Press, 1983), on the dangers of a radical feminist analysis slipping back into a nineteenth-century politics of sexual repression.

10. Varda Burstyn, "Political Precedents and Moral Crusades: Women, Sex, and the State," in *Women Against Censorship*, ed. Varda Burstyn, p. 24.

11. See Kate Ellis, "I'm Black and Blue from the Rolling Stones and I'm Not Sure How I Feel about It: Pornography and the Feminist Imagination," *Socialist Review*, nos. 75, 76 (vol. 14, nos. 3, 4), May–August 1984, for a flamboyant statement of this position. Several male members of the (then) New York Collective of *Socialist Review* were highly offended by Kate's blithe discussion of the potential value of fantasies of violence, and opposed publication of her piece on these grounds — thus exemplifying just how close to home the forces of censorship may reside.

12. See Lisa Duggan, Nan Hunter, and Carole S. Vance, "False Promises: Feminist Antipornography Legislation in the U.S.," in Burstyn, ed., *Women Against Censorship*, p. 151. See *Coming To Power: Writings and Graphics on Lesbian S/M*, ed. SAMOIS (Boston: Alyson Publications, 1982), for a good example of the sort of feminist text likely to become an object of conservative censorship efforts.

13. John Stuart Mill, *On Liberty* (New York: Penguin, 1984), pp. 61, 68, 141.

14. See *American Booksellers Inc. v. Hudnut*, 598 F. Supp. 1326 (S.D. Ind. 1984). See also Rae Langton, "Whose Right? Ronald Dworkin, Women, and Pornographers," *Philosophy and Public Affairs* 19, 4 (Fall 1990), p. 336.

15. Rae Langton maintains that Ronald Dworkin's much esteemed account of a liberal democratic government's responsibility to "treat those whom it governs with equal concern and respect" has straightforward implications for the pornography issue. She challenges Dworkin's analysis of pornography in "Do We Have A Right to Pornography?" in *A Matter of Principle* (Cambridge, Mass.: Harvard University Press, 1985), confronting Dworkin's pornography analysis with the theory of rights he articulated earlier in *Taking Rights Seriously* (Cambridge, Mass.: Harvard University Press, 1977). See Langton's "Whose Right? Ronald Dworkin, Women, and Pornographers," *Philosophy and Public Affairs* 19, 4 (Fall 1990).

16. Owen Fiss, "Freedom and Feminism," a talk presented to the New York University Colloquium in Law, Philosophy, and Political Theory, November 14, 1991.

17. David Dyzenhaus, "John Stuart Mill and the Harm of Pornography," *Ethics* 102 (April, 1992).

18. See Norman Bryson, *Vision and Painting: The Logic of the Gaze* (New Haven: Yale University Press, 1983), p. xii, for an explanation of this distinction in relation to the interpretation of paintings.

19. See Donna Haraway, " 'Gender' for a Marxist Dictionary: The Sexual Politics of a Word," in *Simians, Cyborgs, and Women* (New York: Routledge, 1991), for a clear critique of both tendencies.

20. I am quite aware of the historical and anthropological limitations of any such account of "traditional" forms of sexual or social agency. Compare my analysis, which begins with the gendered aspects of social agency, with Claude Lévi-Strauss's account in *The Elementary Structures of Kinship* (Boston: Beacon Press, 1969). Lévi-Strauss posits that a universal principle of exchange(!) is the basis for all systems of kinship.

21. It is interesting that such sexualized power relationships exist between men today in prisons. See Wilbert Rideau and Ron Wikberg, *Life Sentences: Rage and Survival Behind Bars* (New York: Random House, 1992). Rideau and Wikberg are award-winning journalists who are also prisoners, and they write that "while homosexual rape in prison is initially a macho/power thing, slaves are created because a need exists for slaves—to serve as women—substitutes, for the expression and reinforcement of one's masculinity, for a sexual outlet, for income and/or service." They quote one fellow prisoner, Dunn, as explaining that "During my first week here, I saw 14 guys rape one youngster 'cause he refused to submit. . . . Man, I didn't want none of that kind of action, and my only protection was in sticking with my old man, the guy who raped me."

22. Notice how common this vicarious sense of participation in worldly events has become in contemporary society. We all derive much of our sense of political participation through identifying with the actions of those we view on the various screens of the electronic media. See my "Representing the Viewer," *Social Text* 27 (Spring, 1991).

23. See Orlando Patterson, *Slavery and Social Death* (Cambridge, Mass.: Harvard University Press, 1982), p. 4.

24. I borrow this felicitous phrase from Louis Althusser. See Louis Althusser and Etienne Balibar, *Reading Capital* (London: New Left Books, 1970).

25. Mary O'Brien, *The Politics of Reproduction* (Boston: Routledge and Kegan Paul, 1981).

26. See Alison Bass, "Domestic Violence: The Roots Go Deep," *Boston Globe*, June 5, 1992. According to the New York State Office for the Prevention of Domestic Violence, domestic violence was responsible for the deaths of three out of four women killed in the United States in 1991. See Diana Jean Schemo, "Amid the Gentility of the East End, A Town Confronts Domestic Abuse," *New York Times*, August 13, 1992.

27. Judith Kegan Gardiner, "Psychoanalysis and Feminism: An American Humanist's View," *Signs* (Winter 1992), pp. 438–39.

28. See Juliet Mitchell's *Psychoanalysis and Feminism* (New York: Vintage, 1975).

29. Laura Mulvey, "Visual Pleasure and Narrative Cinema," *Screen* 16, 3 (Autumn 1975).

30. See Ellie Ragland-Sullivan, *Jacques Lacan and the Philosophy of Psychoanalysis* (Urbana: University of Illinois Press, 1986). As Ragland-Sullivan says, "The sexual identity of both boys and girls is established in relation to the mother's attitudes toward the Phallus" (p. 294). It would thus seem that even if the worldly mother remains the primary early nurturer of the child, her new status in relationship to men and to society will impact directly upon her child's understanding of sexual identity.

31. Laura Mulvey, "Visual Pleasure and Narrative Cinema," *Screen* 16, 3 (Autumn 1975), p. 13.

32. Ibid., p. 14.

33. See Ann Barr Snitow, "Mass Market Romance: Pornography for Women Is Different," in *Powers of Desire*.

34. See the Milan Women's Bookstore Collective's *Sexual Difference: A Theory of Social-*

Symbolic Practice (Bloomington: Indiana University Press, 1991), for a compelling argument for developing relations of recognition between women. Disillusioned after two decades of conventional feminist political struggle, these theorists argue for an anti-institutional political project that puts an "entrustment" relationship of symbolic exchange between women, and an articulation of female difference at its center.

35. Jacques Lacan, *Écrits*, trans. Alan Sheridan (New York: Norton, 1977), pp. 4, 11, 21. See also Ellie Ragland-Sullivan, *Jacques Lacan and the Philosophy of Psychoanalysis* (Urbana: University of Illinois Press, 1986), pp. 19–34, 40–41.

36. See Ellie Ragland-Sullivan, *Jacques Lacan*, p. 282. "Although there is no intrinsic gender meaning to this structural drama, it first becomes confused at a secondary, substantive level with gender, and later with sexual organs." See Lacan, *Seminaire XX*, p. 69. See also p. 292, where she cites Lacan as maintaining that sexual desire becomes part of the larger drama of Desire (*Seminaire XX*, p. 14).

37. See Jacques Lacan, "The Mirror Stage," in *Ecrits*, trans. Alan Sheridan (New York: Norton, 1977), pp. 1–7.

38. See Ragland-Sullivan, *Jacques Lacan*, p. 55.

39. Lacan, *Ecrits*, p. 198.

40. Ragland-Sullivan, *Jacques Lacan*, pp. 298, 282. See Lacan, *Seminaire XX*, p. 69.

41. Jacques Lacan, "The Subject and the Other: Alienation," in *Four Fundamental Concepts of Psycho-Analysis*, trans. Alan Sheridan (New York: Norton, 1981), p. 207.

42. Jacques Lacan, "A Love Letter," in *Feminine Sexuality*, ed. Juliet Mitchell and Jacqueline Rose (New York: Norton, 1985), pp. 151–52.

43. Jacques Lacan, "The Line and Light," in *The Four Fundamental Concepts*, pp. 95–96.

44. Lacan, *The Four Fundamental Concepts*, pp. 109, 92, 99–101.

45. Norman Bryson, *Vision and Painting: The Logic of the Gaze* (New Haven: Yale University Press, 1983), p. 156.

46. Bryson, *Vision and Painting*, p. 89.

47. We might be tempted by a notion of a feminist anticipatory gaze modeled on the anticipatory gazes of women within traditional sexual recognition relationships. Yet the wifely gaze creatively anticipating the social accomplishments of husbands operated under the sanction of the patriarchal sexual gaze. Having accepted patriarchal social orderings, women participated through recognizing husbands and sons in ways that empowered them to act on behalf of women as well as men. This anticipatory gaze of women was socially effective precisely insofar as it was subsumed under the patriarchal gaze. A feminist anticipatory gaze is a utopian idea so long as patriarchal social institutions prevail.

48. One possible response to this potentially tragic dimension of the feminist project is to accept the inability of patriarchal signifying systems to capture the experiences of women. There is a recent tradition of French feminists (*"écriture feminine"*) who have insisted that instead of seeking to participate in masculine traditions of law and language, women must affirm feminine sexual difference, and attempt to write a new language of the feminine body. See Luce Irigaray, *This Sex Which Is Not One*, trans. Catherine Porter (Ithaca: Cornell University Press, 1985). See also Drucilla Cornell, *Beyond Accommodation* (New York: Routledge, 1991), for an attempt to meld a feminism of sexual difference with Jacques Derrida.

The sexual metaphysics of such theorists are unpersuasive to me. The language I write in is a patriarchal language insofar as it assumes and perpetuates gendered oppositions and hierarchies—as does the society I live in. But it is nonetheless my language and my society, for all that. My relationship to language and society is different from that of men whom it privileges, yet it is not necessarily less serious than theirs. In fact, my engagement with language and society may be more intense than that of the men it privileges, insofar as I am impelled to attempt to alter it.

The Milan Women's Bookstore Collective offers a more socially grounded and thereby more poignant version of the French feminist advocacy of a woman's language. Weary after several decades of activism, and persuaded that women today continue to enter society as "a losing sex," they propose "relationships of entrustment" between women, in which women articulate their respect and gratitude for other women. See their *Sexual Difference* (Bloomington: Indiana University Press, 1991).

Surely such relationships are an important basis of psychic support for women in a patriarchal society. But they hardly take the place of what I deem to be the necessarily critical and constructive engagements of women today within the late-patriarchal discourses of theory and daily life.

3. Cyborgean Motherhood and Abortion

1. Surely Simone de Beauvoir's analysis of maternity was dominated by the emphasis existentialism placed upon human choice. The involuntariness of the maternal role horrified de Beauvoir, and she described women as being "in bondage to the species," and as experiencing "maternal servitude" because of the *social status* of motherhood as a life project/process that women could not choose but must submit to. See *The Second Sex* (New York: Vintage, 1974), pp. 25, 29, 39, 41. She has been strenuously criticized by many second-wave feminist theorists for her failure to appreciate the human meaningfulness of maternal activities. But feminist celebrations of maternity today never fail to emphasize that it must be a voluntary activity! De Beauvoir wrote *The Second Sex* in 1948, at a time when a naturalistic identification of women with motherhood still existed. It is impossible to project ourselves back into such a different historical time, but it is presumptuous to assume that we would have been any less focused on the involuntariness of maternity than de Beauvoir was in 1948.

2. Virginia Held argues that human birth and mothering have always been intrinsically "human" practices, and she is dismissive of thinkers such as Hannah Arendt and Simone de Beauvoir who accepted the patriarchal view of them as natural processes. If we think in terms of the different dimensions of agency, we can sympathize with Held's defense of the human meaningfulness of maternal activities historically, while understanding why social theorists such as Arendt and de Beauvoir would designate maternity as a natural activity so long as it remained an involuntary practice required of those human beings born with the biological capacity to give birth, not deemed worthy of the sorts of recognition and reward attached to the social activities of men. See Virginia Held, "Birth and Death," *Ethics* 99 (January 1989), p. 385.

3. See Jane Roland Martin, *Reclaiming a Conversation* (New Haven: Yale University Press, 1985), for a probing analysis of the ideas of important thinkers such as Mary Wollstonecraft, Catharine Beecher (*A Treatise on Domestic Economy*), and Charlotte Perkins Gilman on the role of women in the home.

4. Aristotle, *Politics*, Book 7, Chapter 16, 1335b20, in *The Basic Works of Aristotle*, ed. Richard McKeon (New York: Random House, 1941).

5. According to Linda Gordon, in *Woman's Body, Woman's Right* (New York: Penguin, 1976), pp. 35, 52–53, "Almost all preindustrial societies accepted abortion," particularly prior to quickening, which was designated by Aristotle as 40 days after conception for males and 90 days after conception for females. Fathers of the Catholic church such as Thomas Aquinas also accepted abortions done within this period, identifying it as the period prior to ensoulment of the fetus.

6. See Steven W. Sinding and Sheldon J. Segal, "Birth Rate News," Op-Ed in *The New York Times*, December 19, 1991, reporting that "Third world women are averaging 3.9 children, and more than 50 percent of the women use some form of contraception, according to U.N. estimates. This is a stunning change from the 8 percent who used contraception in 1965 when they were averaging more than 6 children."

7. Simone de Beauvoir, *The Second Sex* (New York: Vintage, 1952), pp. 76–77.

8. Gayatri Chakravorty Spivak, "Subaltern Studies: Deconstructing Historiography," in *In Other Worlds* (New York: Routledge, 1988), p. 197.

9. See Beverly Wildung Harrison, *Our Right to Choose* (Boston: Beacon, 1983) for a strong feminist analysis of the theological debate on the question of abortion.

10. Kristin Luker, *Abortion and the Politics of Motherhood* (Berkeley: University of California Press, 1984).

11. Mary Ann Lamanna, "Social Science and Ethical Issues: The Policy Implications of Poll Data on Abortion," *Abortion: Understanding Differences*, ed. Sidney and Daniel Callahan (New York: Plenum, 1984), pp.1–23; see also Donald Granberg and Beth Wellman Granberg, "Abortion Attitudes, 1965–1980: Trends and Determinants," *Family Planning Perspectives* 12 (September/October 1980), pp. 251–52; see also Frederick Jaffe, Barbara L. Lindheim, and Philip R. Lee, *Abortion Politics: Private Morality and Public Policy* (New York: McGraw-Hill, 1981), p. 101.

12. Lawrence Tribe, *Abortion: The Clash of Absolutes* (New York: Norton, 1990).

13. Denise Riley, *Am I That Name* (Minneapolis: University of Minnesota Press, 1988).

14. Tribe, *Abortion*, p. 240.

15. See Michael Tooley, "Abortion and Infanticide," *Philosophy and Public Affairs* 2, 1 (Fall 1972); and his *Abortion and Infanticide* (Oxford: Clarendon Press, 1983), and Mary Anne Warren, "On the Moral and Legal Status of Abortion," *Monist* 57 (January 1973), for heroic efforts to formulate criteria according to which the fetus is not at any stage of pregnancy a person. Tooley argues that personhood is the relevant category for deciding duties to persons. He is thereby led to conclude that infanticide may be a legitimate moral choice insofar as infants are not yet fully persons. Roger Wertheimer, "Understanding the Abortion Argument," *Philosophy and Public Affairs* 1, 1 (Fall 1971), after considering various criteria and concluding none can finally make the case for or against fetal personhood, arrives at what has become the standard liberal compromise: "[This argument] does not show that abortions are morally okay; at best it shows that legal prohibitions are not."

16. Bernard Williams, *Ethics and the Limits of Philosophy* (Cambridge, Mass.: Harvard University Press, 1985), pp. 112–17, 170.

17. Rosalind Petchesky, *Abortion and Woman's Choice* (New York: Longman, 1984), pp. 132, 365, and chapters 9 and 10, generally.

18. Teresa de Lauretis, "Upping the Anti (Sic) In Feminist Theory," in *Conflicts in Feminism*, ed. Marianne Hirsch and Evelyn Fox Keller (New York: Routledge, 1990), p. 265.

19. There has been some bitter wrangling inspired by the term "postfeminism." Many feminist thinkers associate it with a current "backlash" against feminism, and a celebration of the end of a socially critical feminist politics. See Suzanna Danuta Walters, "Premature Postmortems: 'Postfeminism' and Popular Culture," *New Politics* 3, 2 (Winter 1991) for a chronicle of the angry reaction of feminists to the term. My point is that regardless of how various commentators have used the term, feminists should appropriate it to announce the fact that feminist concerns have entered the mainstream.

20. See *Roe v. Wade* (1973); and *Webster v. Reproductive Health Services* (1989). The convoluted logic of the majority opinion in the recent Supreme Court holding of *Rust v. Sullivan* (1991), whereby medical doctors working in clinics receiving public funding are denied the right to mention abortion as an option to their pregnant patients, is also made possible by this confusion.

21. Ronald Green, *Population Growth and Justice: An Examination of Moral Issues Raised By Population Growth* (Missoula, Mont.: Scholars Press, 1976), has offered a Rawlsian argument that if men and women were both present in the original position, abortion would be justified. Such a contractualist justification of abortion is also a formal one, rather than a substantive moral one.

22. Ronald Dworkin, the legal philosopher who formulated this notion of strong rights that "trump" lesser rights, applies it to cases of explicitly mandated Constitutional rights such as that of free speech. See Ronald Dworkin, *Taking Rights Seriously* (Cambridge, Mass.: Harvard University Press, 1977). Beverly Wildung Harrison develops a powerful theory of the primacy of a woman's moral right to bodily integrity, arguing that such a right is fun-

damental to the human dignity and the well-being of women. See Harrison, *Our Right to Choose* (Boston: Beacon, 1983), chapter 7.

23. Judith Jarvis Thomson, "A Defense of Abortion," *Philosophy and Public Affairs* 1, 1 (Fall 1971).

24. Thomson, "A Defense of Abortion," as reprinted in *The Rights and Wrongs of Abortion*, ed. Marshall Cohen, Thomas Nagel, and Thomas Scanlon (Princeton: Princeton University Press, 1974), p. 17. See Oliver Wendell Holmes, Jr., dissenting in *United States v. Schwimmer*, 1929.

25. See Daniel Callahan: *Abortion: Law, Choice and Morality* (New York: Macmillan, 1970), pp. 473–75.

26. This is one basis for Lawrence Tribe's argument in *Abortion: The Clash of Absolutes*. In philosophy today, abortion might be deemed to exemplify the problems that can arise when a so-called "impartial" moral methodology such as utilitarianism seems to prescribe an act that an individual agent finds morally wrong. See *Consequentialism and Its Critics*, ed. Samuel Scheffler (New York: Oxford University Press, 1988). Yet such a construction oversimplifies the problem; for abortion is a case where many people find their own basic personal values in conflict.

27. Calling himself a "51 percent prochoice advocate," Daniel Callahan takes this approach in "The Abortion Debate," in *Abortion: Understanding Differences*, ed. Sidney and Daniel Callahan (New York: Plenum, 1984), p. 321.

28. Carol Gilligan, *In A Different Voice* (Cambridge, Mass.: Harvard University Press, 1982), pp. 64–127.

29. Ibid., pp. 73–74.

30. Ibid., pp. 103, 166, 174.

31. Many feminist thinkers, of course, have read her in a more nuanced way, as is evident from the papers delivered at a March 1985 conference at SUNY Stony Brook on Gilligan's work, published in *Women and Moral Theory*, ed. Eva Feder Kittay and Diana T. Meyers (Totowa, N.J.: Rowman & Littlefield, 1989). The political usefulness of Gilligan's theory for feminism, however, seems to have lured many people to a celebratory female essentialism beyond the careful limits of Gilligan's own analysis, creating the conditions for a strong reaction against it within feminist social science. See Martha T. Mednick, "On the Politics of Psychological Constructs: Stop the Bandwagon, I Want to Get Off," *American Psychologist* 44, 8 (August 1989), for the critique from within feminist social psychology. See Nancy Fraser and Linda Nicholson, "Social Criticism Without Philosophy: An Encounter Between Feminism and Postmodernism," in *Feminism/Postmodernism*, ed. Linda Nicholson (New York: Routledge, 1990), for a relatively evenhanded poststructuralist critique of Gilligan.

Such critiques overlook the choke-hold that essentialist paradigms of human nature still have within disciplines such as psychology and philosophy, and the rigid disciplinary enforcement of a pseudo-naturalism in any "serious" contribution in these fields. I am suggesting that in order to make a theoretical intervention in the empiricist milieu of psychology Gilligan almost had to offer her own theoretical construct as a "better" model of what remained an essentialist theory of moral development. In disregarding the disciplinary context of her contribution, recent feminist critiques may themselves be accused of failing to recognize what is theoretically at stake.

32. David Wong, in his "Coping With Moral Conflict and Ambiguity," a talk delivered at the "Pluralism and Responsibility" conference at University of Massachusetts, Boston, on April 10, 1991, is a welcome recent exception, linking Gilligan's work with that of the Confucian tradition, which also encourages people "to maintain or develop relationships." Sandra Harding has also drawn parallels between Gilligan's theory and African cultural assumptions in "The Curious Coincidence of Feminine and African Moralities: Challenges for Feminist Theory," in *Women and Moral Theory*, ed. Eva Feder Kittay and Diana T. Meyers.

33. Nel Noddings, *Caring: A Feminine Approach to Ethics and Moral Education* (Berkeley: University of California Press, 1984).

34. Bernard Williams has criticized traditional utilitarian and rights-based moral theories for similarly discounting the moral agent's own concerns. Yet with his insistence upon the relevance of what he has termed personal "integrity" he fails to call into question the self-other binary as Gilligan begins to do by taking "care" as a basic category of individual motivation. See Bernard Williams, "A Critique of Utilitarianism," in J. J. Smart and Bernard Williams, *Utilitarianism: For and Against* (New York: Cambridge University Press, 1973).

35. Donna Haraway, "A Cyborg Manifesto: Science, Technology, and Socialist-Feminism in the Late Twentieth Century," in *Simians, Cyborgs, and Women* (New York: Routledge, 1991), p. 149.

36. See Mary O'Brien, *The Politics of Reproduction* (Boston: Routledge, 1983). Her arguments for the "world-historical significance of the Contraceptive Revolution" have played a seminal role in my own thinking. But while she emphasizes the revolutionary implications of women's new control over the social relations of reproduction, O'Brien hopes that women will lead the way in seeking a human reintegration with nature (pp. 63–64, 201–10). A cyborgean vision might well enable such a reintegration; but it was not a conceivable route a decade ago when O'Brien wrote her powerful book.

37. Haraway, *Simians, Cyborgs, and Women*, p.150; also p. 162.

38. Notice that a cyborgean conception of personhood and procreation does not require us to deny the existence of God, any more than did Newtonian mechanics, Galileo's telescope, or the other theories associated with the Copernican Revolution. But, as in the case of seventeenth-century scientific theories of material causality and the lawlike relationships governing the movements of the cosmos, a theory of the cyborgean reproductive agency of individual women and men provides an explanation of important phenomena that makes references to the intervention of God relatively superfluous. See Alexandre Koyre, *From the Closed World to the Infinite Universe* (Baltimore: Johns Hopkins University Press, 1957); and E. A. Burt, *The Metaphysical Foundations of Modern Science* (New York: Doubleday, 1952).

39. Shulamith Firestone, *The Dialectic of Sex* (New York: Bantam, 1970), p. 199.

40. Even Mary O'Brien, who has an unusually strong sense of the historical and material grounds upon which social relationships have developed, is unwilling to imagine a cyborgean future in which women do not still necessarily value their bodily capacity to bear children. She finally dismisses Shulamith Firestone, asserting, "In the last analysis, Firestone wants women to become men." See *The Politics of Reproduction*, p. 82.

41. Adrienne Rich, *Of Woman Born* (New York: W. W. Norton, 1976), pp. 40, 280, 285.

42. See Barbara Katz Rothman, *Recreating Motherhood* (New York: W. W. Norton, 1989).

43. Sara Ruddick, *Maternal Thinking* (New York: Ballantine, 1989), pp. 40–44. I may be overly pessimistic about the response of such feminists to this postmodern theory of procreation. In her nuanced reflections on motherhood Ruddick has already moved part of the way toward a theory of social offspring. In *Maternal Thinking*, she maintains that insofar as a person must consciously commit themselves to "protecting, nurturing, and training" a particular child in order to be regarded as its parent once it has been born, "all mothers are adoptive" (pp. 49–51). Ruddick thereby manages to give mothers a social and voluntary status without questioning the natural origins of children in the labor of pregnant women. In some respects, Ruddick has found a pragmatic way of addressing the fact that even if women experience pregnancy as a natural process over which they have little control, our society demands that women exert a great deal of individual control over their circumstances as parents. The advantage of a cyborgean account is that it provides women with a moral basis for exerting personal control much earlier, by denying that pregnancy and offspring are at any point natural phenomena.

In a more recent paper, "Thinking Mothers / Conceiving Birth," delivered at the New York Institute of Humanities, December 13, 1991, Ruddick attempts to formulate a conception of "natal thinking" to complement her prior analysis of "maternal thinking." Her difficulty in achieving an integrated understanding of procreative practices before and after the birth of the child, however, is a consequence of her emphasis upon "reason" as the feature of mothering that legitimates it as a form of human activity to be compared with the activities of men in the public world. By focusing on the multidimensional *agency* of women engaging in procreative practices, I shift the focus away from distracting mind/body and human/natural binaries.

44. Jane Roland Martin has compellingly argued that feminist thinkers should be as wary of the disabling effects of eschewing such general categories of thought as they are of the dangers of false generalization. See Martin's "Methodological Essentialism and Other Dangerous Traps," a paper presented at the Eastern Division meeting of the American Philosophical Association, December 1991, where Jane Martin was being honored as the Woman Philosopher of the Year. Martin suggests that we think of our use of general categories such as "women" as expressing what Ludwig Wittgenstein called "family resemblances," relevant similarities rather than necessary commonalities. See Judith Butler, *Gender Trouble* (New York: Routledge, 1990), for the definitive poststructuralist critique of feminist identity politics.

45. See Ellen Chesler, *Woman of Valor: Margaret Sanger and the Birth Control Movement in America* (New York: Simon and Schuster, 1992), for a powerful portrait of this early-twentieth-century birth-control crusader, and of the social conditions that subverted Sanger's goal of enabling women to control their reproductive lives. Of course, the fight goes on today. The drug companies who profit from sales of birth-control pills oppose the development and distribution of simpler, potentially more economical methods such as the recent Norplant insert, which lasts for five years. At the same time, judges have shown interest in punitively prescribing the insertion of Norplant as a means of forestalling the pregnancies of women they deem socially irresponsible.

46. Ann Snitow, "What Feminism Has Said About Motherhood," *Feminist Review* (Fall 1991).

47. Haraway, p. 149. Mine is an admittedly weak form of cyborgeanism. But what interests me is a micropolitical theory of interactions between individuals, and how these change in the context of our intimate couplings with machines. Whereas mine is a resolutely social vision, Haraway's view shares more with both the scientist and the science-fictionist. Technology potentially goes all the way up; the computer technology that enhances our ability to write is connected with information systems that might ultimately control and reconfigure us.

4. A Genealogy of Individualism

1. John Dewey, *Theory of the Moral Life* (New York: Holt, Rinehart and Winston, 1932), pp. 7, 29.

2. Friedrich Nietzsche, *On the Genealogy of Morals*, ed. Walter Kaufmann (New York: Vintage, 1969), p. 20.

3. Karl Marx, *Grundrisse* (New York: Vintage, 1973), p. 85. Marx excoriates socialist thinkers such as John Gray and M. Proudhon as fiercely as neoclassical economists such as Frederic Bastiat, Henry Charles Carey, and Jean-Baptiste Say. See also *The Poverty of Philosophy* (Peking: Foreign Language Press, 1978), for an extended analysis of Proudhon. It was not that such thinkers denied historical change entirely. But they had the metaphysical gall to believe that "the institutions of feudalism are artificial institutions, [and] those of the bourgeoisie are natural institutions" (p. 115).

4. Marx, *Poverty of Philosophy*.

5. See Francis Fukuyama, "The End of History?" in *The National Interest* 16 (Summer 1989), for a controversial attempt to claim that the recent decline of communist hopes in China and the former Soviet Union signals the end of history. Other intellectuals, mostly conservative, respond to his ideas in this same issue of *The National Interest*.

6. Alasdair MacIntyre, *After Virtue* (Notre Dame: University of Notre Dame Press, 1981).

7. While Alasdair MacIntyre is the most frequently cited conservative today, Michael Sandel, *Liberalism and the Limits of Justice* (Cambridge: Cambridge University Press, 1982), is the thinker typically taken as representative of radical communitarian views. See Amy Gutmann, "Communitarian Critics of Liberalism," *Philosophy and Public Affairs* 14 (1985), pp. 308–22, for a discussion of the contemporary communitarian perspective.

8. See Annette Baier, "Trust and Antitrust," *Ethics* 96 (1986), pp. 231–60; and Virginia Held, "Non-contractual Society," in *Science, Morality, and Feminist Theory*, ed. Marsha Hanen and Kai Nielson, *Canadian Journal of Philosophy* 13, Suppl. (1987), pp. 111–38.

9. See Jean Grimshaw, "Autonomy and Identity in Feminist Thinking," in *Feminist Perspectives in Philosophy*, ed. Morwenna Griffiths and Margaret Whitford (Bloomington: Indiana University Press, 1988), for a thoughtful assessment of the concept of autonomy in feminist theory and practice.

10. See Marilyn Friedman, "Feminism and Modern Friendship: Dislocating the Community," *Ethics* 99 (January 1989), pp. 275–90, for a discussion of such problems with the communitarian viewpoint.

11. Iris Young, *Justice and the Politics of Difference* (Princeton: Princeton University Press, 1990), chapter 8. See chapter 5 for Young's insightful analysis of racism today.

12. Ibid. Young discusses various "virtues" of her ideal of city life in terms of the affirmation of group differences. But when she mentions "eroticism" as one of the virtues of urban difference, it is clear that she recognizes that many of the relationships affirmed within such a society will have an individuated character (p. 239). Yet when Young explicitly refers to individual forms of agency, it seems that she understands it on a model of liberal individualism stripped as far as possible of its politically negative aspects (pp. 250–51).

13. See Michel Foucault, *Madness and Civilization: A History of Insanity in the Age of Reason*, trans. Richard Howard (New York: Vintage, 1973); and *The History of Sexuality. Volume I: An Introduction*, trans. Robert Hurley (New York: Vintage, 1980).

14. See Karl Marx, *The German Ideology* (Moscow: Progress Publishers, 1976), pp. 77, 40.

15. See Philippe Aries, *Centuries of Childhood: A Social History of Family Life*, trans. Robert Baldick (New York: Knopf, 1962); Peter Laslett, *The World We Have Lost* (New York: Scribner's, 1965); Lawrence Stone, *The Family, Sex, and Marriage in England, 1500–1800* (New York: Harper and Row, 1979), for discussions of changing family life in this period generally. See Joan Kelly, *Women, History and Theory* (Chicago: University of Chicago Press, 1984), for a feminist perspective on this history.

16. See Alice Kessler-Harris, "*Equal Employment Opportunity Commission vs. Sears, Roebuck and Company*: A Personal Account," *Radical History Review* 35, 1986, for an account of one of the most wrenching public battles waged in terms of the equality-versus-difference approaches.

17. Felicity Barringer, "Changes in U.S. Households: Single Parents Amid Solitude," *New York Times*, June 7, 1991.

18. In one of his last interviews, Michel Foucault referred to an increasingly problematic dynamic of control within interpersonal relationships in contemporary society. See *The Final Foucault*, ed. James Bernauer and David Rasmussen (Cambridge, Mass.: MIT Press, 1988), p. 20. According to Foucault, "We can imagine that there are societies in which the way one determines the behavior of others is so well determined in advance, that there is nothing left to do. On the other hand, in a society like ours—it is very evident in family relationships, for example, in sexual and affective relations—the games can be extremely numerous and thus the temptation to determine the conduct of others is that much greater. However, the more that people are free in respect to each other, the greater the temptation on both sides to determine the conduct of others" (January 20, 1984, interview).

19. Plato, *Republic*, in *The Collected Dialogues of Plato*, ed. Edith Hamilton and Huntington Cairns (Princeton: Princeton University Press, 1961); Aristotle, *Politics*, in *The Basic Works of Aristotle*, ed. Richard McKeon (New York: Random House, 1941).

20. See John Ruskin, "Of Queens' Gardens," in *Sesame and Lilies* (London: A. L. Burt, 1871).

21. When Carol Gilligan attempted to criticize the self-interested/altruistic binary, her work was rapidly reinterpreted and appropriated as if it too took this binary for granted. Many feminists took her work as supporting normative claims about the importance of women's maternal and caring practices and values, which it did. But the immediate presumption was that support for these practices implied a rejection of a traditional male-identified set of justice concerns. Gilligan explicitly rejected the demand to choose between the two, and repeatedly attempted to explain the significance of both in male and female lives alike. But, as I explained in chapter 3, our present conceptual structures render us unable to make sense of the operation of both. Her own reference to Wittgenstein's duck/rabbit perceptual puzzle is all too relevant. See Carol Gilligan, "Moral Orientation and Moral Development," in *Women and Moral Theory*, ed. Eva Kittay and Diana Meyers (Totowa, N.J.: Rowman and Littlefield, 1987). See *Beyond Self-Interest*, ed. Jane Mansbridge (Chicago: University of Chicago Press, 1990), for a good selection of recent essays on this theme. Jean Bethke Elshtain, in *Public Man, Private Woman* (Princeton: Princeton University Press, 1981), also provides a helpful historical perspective on the separate spheres analysis.

22. Feminist historians have criticized the very notion of a division of public and private life as ideological, and as a means of making the important economic and political contributions of women invisible. See particularly Joan Kelly's "The Doubled Vision of Feminist Theory," in *Women, History and Theory*, for one of the seminal formulations of this critique. I fully agree with this critique. My interests lie in understanding the way in which this ideology has operated to determine our notions of agency, and in explaining the gendered basis for the decline of this ideology.

23. Thomas Hobbes, *Leviathan*, ed. C. B. MacPherson (New York: Penguin, 1981), pp. 118, 119, 120, 119.

24. Ibid., pp. 183, 184, 185.

25. John Locke, *The Second Treatise of Government* (New York: Liberal Arts Press, 1952), chapter 5.

26. Ibid. Locke acknowledges, with apparent disapproval, the unequal division of land that modern men had consented to. But the most important point for him was the fact that such a division had indeed been consented to, and thus given the democratic sanction (p. 29).

27. Ibid., chapter 2.

28. Adam Smith, *The Wealth of Nations* (New York: Oxford University Press, 1980).

29. Ibid.

30. Seyla Benhabib indignantly quotes Hobbes as saying, "Let us consider men . . . as if but even now sprung out of the earth, and suddenly, like mushrooms, come to full maturity," as exemplary of the willingness of political thinkers to wholly read women out of the picture. See Benhabib's "The Generalized and the Concrete Other," in *Women and Moral Theory*, ed. Eva Feder Kittay and Diana Meyers (Totowa, N.J.: Rowman and Littlefield, 1987), p. 161. Of course defenders of Hobbes will point out that he is quite egalitarian at those points at which he considers women. Indeed, he asserts that each child has "two that are equally parents" and accordingly "dominion over the child should belong equally to both." Nevertheless, he immediately acknowledges that such equal power is impossible, and points out that civil law, erected by Fathers, tends to rule in favor of Fathers. See Thomas Hobbes, *Leviathan* (New York: Penguin, 1983), p. 252. I agree with Benhabib's retort that the issue is not really what Hobbes or any of the other theorists says specifically about women, but rather "that in this universe the experience of the early modern female has no place" (p. 162).

31. Gilles Deleuze, "The Condition of the Question: What Is Philosophy?" *Critical Inquiry* 17, 3 (Spring 1991), p. 471.

32. Of course, there were women who argued that the new political ideals of equality and individual consent should be operative between men and women within the family. See Abigail Adams's famous "Remember the Ladies" letter to her husband John Adams in 1776,

for a forthright assertion of the relevance of the principles of liberal democratic theory to the situation of women. Adams specifically applied the notion that "Law must provide individuals with protection against the Natural Tyranny of Men" to the situation of women in relation to their husbands, and insisted that women must have rights within any new code of laws. But also see the jocular reply of John Adams to Abigail's plea for including women. His shockingly cavalier response is nicely complemented by a quite serious letter to a colleague in which he discusses the necessary limitations on the principle of "consent of the people," and particularly why women must be excluded, along with men without property and children. See *The Feminist Papers*, ed. Alice S. Rossi (Boston: Northeastern University Press, 1973), pp. 7–15. Lawrence Stone, *The Family, Sex and Marriage in England* (New York: Harper and Row, 1979), shows the tensions that developed within the family during this period, as a consequence of the conflict between public doctrines of equality and consent and the continuing patriarchal authority of the man as husband and father.

33. See Linda Nicholson, *Gender and History* (New York: Columbia University Press, 1986), for a historical perspective on gender and family relationships.

34. See John Locke, *The Second Treatise of Government*, chapter 7, p. 44. See Immanuel Kant, *The Philosophy of Law*, trans. W. Hastie (Edinburgh: T. and T. Clark, 1887), p. 110. Kant is quite literal about the nature of the contract, defining marriage as "the union of two persons of different sex for the lifelong reciprocal possession of their sexual faculties."

35. See Carole Pateman, "The Shame of the Marriage Contract," in *Women's Views of the Political World of Men*, ed. Judith Stiehm (Dobbs Ferry, N.Y.: Transnational Publishers, 1984).

36. Actually John Locke was willing to consider it as conditional to a degree. See *The Second Treatise of Government*, chapter 7, p. 46. "The wife has in many cases a liberty to separate from him where natural right or their contract allows it . . . "

37. Despite Kant's theoretical commitment to the Categorical Imperative, abjuring all but human rationality as the grounds for equal moral and political treatment, he assumed quite unself-consciously and explicitly that economic autonomy was a prerequisite for both moral and political personhood. On political personhood, see Immanuel Kant, *The Metaphysical Elements of Justice*, trans. John Ladd (New York: MacMillan, 1985). Kant relies upon a distinction between those who are "independent" and those who exist in "dependence on the Will of others" in order to define political personhood. "To be fit to vote, a person must be independent and not . . . a passive citizen." A passive citizen is "a servant; a minor; all women; and generally anyone who must depend for his support (subsistence and protection), not on his own industry, but on arrangements by others" (p. 79).

On moral personhood, see Immanuel Kant, *Observations on the Feeling of the Beautiful and the Sublime*, trans. John Goldthwait (Berkeley: University of California, 1960), "Her philosophy is not to reason, but to sense. . . . I hardly believe that the fair sex is capable of principles. . . . The principal object is that the man should become more perfect as a man, and the woman as a wife. . . . In matrimonial life the united pair should, as it were, constitute a single moral person, which is animated and governed by the understanding of the man and the taste of the wife" (pp. 76–81).

38. Carole Pateman, *The Sexual Contract* (Stanford: Stanford University Press, 1988), p. ix.

39. Ibid., particularly pp. 219–34.

40. Feminist thinkers, as late as the nineteenth century, tended to write as if they accepted the traditional notion of male and female roles. See Jane Roland Martin, *Reclaiming a Conversation* (New Haven: Yale University Press, 1985), for a discussion of the theoretical conflicts this involved such feminists in.

41. See G. W. F. Hegel, *The Philosophy of Right*, trans. T. M. Knox (London: Oxford University Press, 1967), pp. 58, 110–16, for a powerful repudiation of any contractual understanding of the family. My analysis also corresponds with Alasdair MacIntyre's assessment of the family as the last remaining instance of a traditional community practice in *After Virtue*.

42. Michel Foucault, *Power/Knowledge*, ed. Colin Gordon (New York: Pantheon, 1972). See particularly the essay "Truth and Power."

43. See Joan Kelly, *Women, History, and Theory*.

44. See Kant's analysis of this in footnote 37. John Adams, when writing the American Constitution, explicitly decided to exclude women from citizenship on such an economic basis. See the letters of Abigail and John Adams in *The Feminist Papers*, Alice Rossi, ed., pp. 10–15.

45. The corporate metaphor for the family was quite common in popular culture in the 1950s. David Futrelle, in "The Honeymooners Is Over," *The Nation*, September 28, 1992, reports that "Singer Pat Boone in his best-selling teen advice book of 1959 spoke of his own family as a "Happy Home Corporation," under the guidance of the corporation president (himself), with the cheerful compliance of the 'vice-president in charge of housekeeping' (his wife) and all the little vice presidents" (p. 331).

46. This assumption of a single incorporated male family self is reflected, for example, in rape laws. Husbands were explicitly exempted from liability for coercive intercourse in the late eighteenth century. A woman's obligation to submit to her husband's sexual desires was grounded not only in her promise to love, honor, and obey her husband, but also in the notion that "since common-law notions of marital unity held that husband and wife were one, a married man could not readily be found guilty of raping himself." See Deborah L. Rhode, *Justice and Gender* (Cambridge, Mass.: Harvard University Press, 1989), p. 250.

47. See James Fishkin, *Justice, Equal Opportunity, and the Family* (New Haven: Yale University Press, 1983).

48. There is no question that liberalism's ideology of human equality made the natural subordination associated with women's family identity theoretically open to question. Prior to liberalism, the hierarchical relationship between a husband and wife was a subset of a much broader category of normal hierarchical social relationships between men, whether between kings and subjects, older and younger, or wealthier and poorer men. With liberalism, these other forms of inequality became socially suspect, an abstract equal self presumed to lurk behind unequal appearances. The natural inequality of women became an exceptional case. Mary Wollstonecraft, a preeminent feminist thinker of the eighteenth century, famously denied Edmund Burke's claims of women's natural inferiority, asserting that women possessed the same capacity for rationality as men, and thereby must be included within revolutionary declarations about the abstract equality of individual men. She also incisively critiqued Jean-Jacques Rousseau's insidious arguments for educating little girls so that they might best achieve their "natural" role of dependent and obedient wives and mothers. See Mary Wollstonecraft, *A Vindication of the Rights of Women*, ed. Carol Poston (New York: W.W. Norton, 1975); Jean-Jacques Rousseau, *Emile*, trans. Allan Bloom (New York: Basic Books, 1979).

Friedrich Engels, the cofounder of Marxism, drew explicit theoretical parallels between the oppression of workers by capitalists and the oppression of wives by their husbands. Yet his arguments, as well as those of other socialists such as August Bebel and Clara Zetkin, failed to incite serious challenges to the patriarchal hierarchies and practices in the family. See Engels, *The Origins of the Family, Private Property and the State*, ed. Eleanor Burke Leacock (New York: International Publishers, 1972).

49. It is noteworthy that the social logic of women's subsumed familial agency has continued even where women achieved economic autonomy from men in socialist countries, in the twentieth century! The failure of women to achieve substantive public identities or voices in socialist countries where they have participated fully in the public workforce for fifty years is all too evident today in the former Soviet Union and Eastern Europe as they seek to "Westernize." Former government policies of universal female employment, child-care and abortion-on-demand are now being jettisoned with no concern for the interests of women in retaining them. See Andrew Kopkind, "From Russia With Love," *The Nation*, January 18, 1993. The social enfranchisement of women was short-circuited in socialist soci-

eties which expected women to become industrial workers while ignoring liberal ideals of individual equality and mutual respect as the foundations of public sphere relationships.

50. Recent studies by labor economists show that women are finally beginning to make large gains in traditional liberal recognition factors, registering an economic leap during the decade of the 1980s, going from earning on average 60 percent (a figure that had remained constant for almost a century) to on average 70 percent of what men earn. See Sylvia Nasar, "Women's Progress Stalled? Just Not So," *New York Times*, October 18, 1992. See also Claudia Goldin, *Understanding the Gender Gap: An Economic History of American Women* (New York: Oxford University Press, 1990); Francine Blau and Marianne Ferber, *The Economics of Women, Men and Work* (New York: Prentice-Hall, 1986).

51. See Susan Faludi, *Backlash: The Undeclared War Against American Women* (New York: Anchor/Doubleday, 1991).

52. Ibid. It is hardly coincidental that one of Susan Faludi's most celebrated acts of feminist debunking involves a Harvard study of the marriage possibilities of women as they grow older. The study concluded that because men can more easily marry younger women, single women over forty had almost no chance of finding a man to marry them. Faludi shows that the statistics show no such thing, and concludes that social scientists and the media are out to scare independent women into marrying young and going to great lengths to hold onto any man they do marry. Perhaps they are. But this is also a case in which the changing motivations and desires of women may well have proved beyond the understanding of the Harvard social scientists. If a large portion of divorced or single women over forty are not (re)marrying, one can either conclude that men are not available to marry them, or that these women do not want to marry the available men. Only the former inference makes sense according to traditional models of female agency, and the Harvard social scientists predictably settled on it without ascertaining whether statistics about the numbers of single men confirmed it.

I remember hearing about the Harvard study and immediately questioning it. From my own experience, the second inference, that women did not choose to marry the available men, was all too obvious. I did not feel that either the Harvard scientists or the media that trumpeted their conclusions were out to get me. Rather I felt they were deluded about the values and attitudes of contemporary women. Either one is a problem for women, of course.

53. It can be both frustrating and illuminating to observe analytic philosophers wrestling with moral problems raised by changing family roles. It is clear to some that the "special obligations" of men toward their families no longer hold in the same way. But because there was no conceptualization of the incorporated male family self, it has become difficult even to represent the quality of the former male sense of familial obligation. Bernard Williams struggles to articulate a notion of individual "integrity" to explain a current male sense that family responsibilities must have some limits in relation to individual male desires and interests. See Bernard Williams and J. J. C. Smart, *Utilitarianism: For and Against* (New York: Cambridge University Press, 1973), pp. 82–117.

54. See Leonore J. Weitzman, *The Divorce Revolution: The Unexpected Social and Economic Consequences for Women and Children in America* (New York: The Free Press, 1985).

55. The recent case in which twelve-year-old Gregory Kingsley "divorced" his biological mother in order to be adopted by a foster family is a case in point. It raised issues of parental and child rights and responsibilities which were left unexplored in Judge Thomas S. Kirk's decision to grant Gregory his plea to end the parental rights of his natural mother. The decision demonstrates, however, the degree to which any natural category of families and parenthood is rapidly ceasing to be viable. See Anthony DePalma, "Custody Decision Dividing Experts," *New York Times*, September 27, 1992.

56. In *A Theory of Justice* (Cambridge, Mass.: Harvard University Press, 1971), p. 490, John Rawls maintained that "family institutions are just" within liberalism, and posited that children acquire their basic sense of justice within such families. He never seemed to notice the peculiarity of thinking that children learn liberal notions of equality and fairness

within a supremely hierarchical and unfair institution like the patriarchal family. Susan Okin has taken him to task for this in *Justice, Gender and the Family* (New York: Basic Books, 1989), pp. 97–100. But Okin fails to recognize that as family relationships become more egalitarian, they are likely to encourage distinctly postliberal forms of community relationships. My analysis of the changing qualities and distributions of agency in the context of particular situations allows us to comprehend how various relationships are likely to be transformed.

57. See Jane Roland Martin, *The Schoolhome* (Cambridge, Mass.: Harvard University Press, 1992), for an important discussion of the new role of schools.

58. Derrick Bell, *Faces at the Bottom of the Well* (New York: Basic Books, 1992).

59. See Jacques Derrida, "Women in the Beehive," in *Men in Feminism*, ed. Alice Jardine and Paul Smith (New York: Methuen, 1987); Nancy Fraser, *Unruly Practices* (Minneapolis: University of Minnesota Press, 1989).

60. See Amartya Sen, "Equality of What?" in *Choice, Welfare and Measurement* (Oxford: Blackwell, 1982). See also "Well-Being, Agency and Freedom," The Dewey Lectures 1984, in *The Journal of Philosophy*, 82, 4 (April 1985). Sen offers the example of the person who is eating their lunch and suddenly sees a person drowning. "If . . . given the choice, you would rather have the opportunity of saving the drowning person than eat your sandwich without anxiety . . . there is clearly a net gain in terms of your *agency freedom*. . . . But in terms of your *well-being freedom* there is a net loss (p. 207).

61. As Martha Nussbaum judiciously points out, "Two people who believe that more income and wealth is always better than less are likely to have difficulties about the division of labor at home that people less attached to acquisition may not have; and professions that are based on this principle impose well-known burdens on their aspiring young members, making it very difficult for them to be just to their partners." See Nussbaum, "Justice For Women!" in *The New York Review of Books*, October 8, 1992, p. 47.

62. Juliet Schor, *The Overworked American* (New York: Basic Books, 1992).

63. John Rawls, *A Theory of Justice*, p. 13. David Gauthier, *Morals By Agreement* (New York: Oxford University Press, 1986), pp. 87, 311. Gauthier credits this notion of "non-tuism" to P. H. Wicksteed, *The Common Sense of Political Economy and Selected Papers and Reviews on Economic Theory*, ed. L. Robbins, 2 vols. (London, 1933), vol. 1, p. 180.

64. See Susan Moller Okin, *Justice, Gender, and the Family*, for a critique of the continuing conflation of male individuals and their families within all varieties of contemporary political theory. From conservatives like Robert Nozick to liberals like John Rawls to progressives and communitarians like Roberto Unger, Okin dissects the patriarchal assumptions of an astonishing array of contemporary political theorists. Seyla Benhabib, *Situating the Self: Gender, Community and Postmodernism in Contemporary Ethics* (New York: Routledge, 1992), performs a critical exegesis of Jürgen Habermas's distinction between properly universal concerns of justice and those merely private concerns pertaining to "the good life." Like Okin, Benhabib believes that we can no longer make absolute distinctions between the sorts of relationships appropriate within the family and those called for in more public situations. See particularly chapter 3.

Both these theorists believe that feminists can appropriate important elements of the Rawlsian and Habermasian theories they criticize. Okin argues that Rawls's Original Position is a fine mechanism for theorizing a just society so long as one explicitly includes women along with men in the Original Position. Benhabib believes that Habermas's theory of a communicative ethics will work quite well as a means of resolving issues about the good life as well as about justice.

5. Agency and Politics in a Postfeminist Decade

1. See my criticism of the feminist appropriation of the socialist model of revolution in chapter 1. The most obvious disanalogy for feminists is that while the proletarian revolution

was defined in terms of the goal of destroying the capitalist class, women are much less comfortable with the goal of destroying the men who embody patriarchy. In each case, of course,
the actual goal is one of destroying oppressive relationships rather than particular persons.
Yet even here, the straightforward Marxist goal of destruction is easily criticized in a gendered context. While it has come to be recognized in the case of economic relationships as
well, it is more readily evident in the case of gender relationships that the goal is actually
a more complicated one of transforming and replacing one quality of relationships with another sort.

2. John Rawls, *A Theory of Justice* (Cambridge, Mass.: Harvard University Press, 1971).

3. See Patricia Williams, *The Alchemy of Race and Rights* (Cambridge, Mass.: Harvard
University Press, 1991), p. 121. As Williams puts it, "Blacks and women are the objects of
a constitutional omission that has been incorporated into a theory of neutrality." She remains
hopeful that this omission can be rectified by means of liberal democratic policies such as
affirmative action. "It is thus that affirmative action is an affirmation; the affirmative act of
hiring—or hearing—blacks is a recognition of individuality that includes blacks as a social
presence, that is profoundly linked to the fate of blacks and whites and women and men either as subgroups or as one group."

4. See Rosi Braidotti, *Patterns of Dissonance* (New York: Routledge, 1991), for her perceptive overview of these quite different modalities of "sexual difference" theory. She is also
interesting for her careful avoidance of unsubtle forms of identity politics, and despite that
her final commitment to a theory of sexual difference.

5. See Denise Riley, *Am I That Name* (Minneapolis: University of Minnesota Press,
1988) for a clear statement of this idea with regard to historical feminist concerns. The idea
of multiple subject positions has more recently been used to express the multiply cultured,
raced, and sexed possibilities of individuals within a multicultural, postmodern world.

6. A now notorious *New York Times* Op-Ed article by black Harvard sociologist
Orlando Patterson provides a good illustration of the potential for claims about the multiple
subject positions of women to be used to undercut feminist politics. Patterson defended
Clarence Thomas's sexual remarks to Anita Hill as a "down-home style of courting" familiar
and accepted in the black community. He criticized white feminists for failing to comprehend the ways in which gender issues differ across race and class lines. See Orlando Patterson, "Race, Gender, and Liberal Fallacies," *New York Times*, October 21, 1991. As Kimberlé
Crenshaw says, "The overall strategy of Patterson's defense seems to rest on an assumption
that merely identifying the culturally specific dimensions of some practice or dynamic constitutes a normative shield against any criticism of it" (p. 430). Crenshaw maintains that "one
of the thorniest issues that black women must confront is represented by Patterson's descent
into cultural relativism." See Kimberlé Crenshaw, "Whose Story Is It Anyway? Feminist and
Antiracist Appropriations of Anita Hill," in *Racing Justice, Engendering Power*, ed. Toni Morrison (New York: Pantheon, 1992), p. 424.

7. Kimberlé Crenshaw, "Mapping the Margins: Identity Politics, Intersectionality, and
Violence Against Women," *Stanford Law Review* 43 (July 1991).

8. Chantal Mouffe also calls for "an approach that permits us to understand how the
subject is constructed through different discourses and subject positions." But she articulates
the goal in terms of achieving a notion of citizenship that would guarantee us "democratic
equivalence." See "Feminism and Radical Politics," in *Feminists Theorize the Political*, ed. Judith
Butler and Joan Scott (New York: Routledge, 1992), pp. 382, 376, 379.

9. Christina Hoff Sommers, "Sister Soldiers," *The New Republic*, October 5, 1992.

10. It is no accident that the German philosopher of language Ludwig Wittgenstein chose
the collateral category of "games" to illustrate his theory of "family resemblance," refuting
at once the Platonic theory of ideal types (of games and all other categories), and also refuting
nominalist theories of the singular references of particular (game) terms. Like the category
of games, the category of sports refers to a richly varied "family" of activities which resemble
each other in one or many ways. We tend to know a sport when we see a certain nexus of

physical exertion and/or interaction, focused individual and/or group efforts, rules that define competitive behavior and/or criteria for winning. We know that people may participate in and/or passionately observe others participate in sports. People may participate in one sport or many, for a brief period of time, or throughout their lives. It is in precisely such terms that we may begin to understand the parameters of micropolitical agency today.

11. Tamar Lewin, "Feminists Wonder If It Was Progress to Become 'Victims'," *New York Times*, May 10, 1992.

12. See Derrick Bell, *Faces In The Bottom of the Well* (New York: Basic Books, 1992). Bell argues similarly that racism may never be overcome, but that the struggle against it has great meaning and value.

13. I will admit to a more specific ideological interest in a sports metaphor. In the fifties, I experienced the oppressiveness of feminine difference most painfully and graphically in the context of my own exclusion from sports activities bizarrely reserved for little boys. I still remember the day when my father and I left the ice-skating rink as little boys in hockey gear scrambled onto it, and I innocently asked when I would be old enough to play hockey. Without a moment's hesitation, my father responded that "little girls don't play hockey." I was nonplussed, as four-year-olds frequently are, perhaps. But that is the beginning of my memory of a highly oppositional girlhood which only ended when I was happily swept up by the second wave of feminism in the early 1970s. In the 1990s, as gendered conflicts and dislocations become dispersed across the lands, women still do not participate in the soaring flights of pole vaulting or Presidential races. But the increasing acceptance of women's bodies as athletically and socially viable vehicles of participation requires symbolic narratives of postgendered agency. See Iris Marion Young, "Throwing Like a Girl," in *Throwing Like a Girl and Other Essays In Feminist Philosophy and Social Theory* (Bloomington: Indiana University Press, 1990), for a phenomenological take on the impoverishment of women's physical occupation of their bodies and of the resulting inhibitions placed upon their "free and open engagement with the world."

14. See Natalie Angier, "Two Experts Say Women Who Run May Overtake Men," *New York Times*, January 7, 1992, reporting on the recent publication of the findings of Drs. Brian J. Whipp and Susan A. Ward in the British journal *Nature*.

15. Mainstream economists often sound much more radical than other professional intellectuals precisely because theirs is a study reflecting numerically the raw data of the gendered changes in wage-earning, economic responsibility for children, and so on.

16. See Tanya L. Domi, "Let Women Prove They Can Fight," *New York Times*, November 12, 1992; Jane Gross, "Servicewomen's Families Speak Out on Abuse," *New York Times*, July 26, 1992; and Michael Gordon, "Panel Is Against Letting Women Fly in Combat," *New York Times*, November 4, 1992.

17. See *She Went to War: The Rhonda Cornum Story* (Presidio Press, 1992). Maj. Rhonda Cornum, a flight surgeon and biochemist, believes that her mission in the military is "to go to war." Given this sense of agency, her assessment of her treatment as a P.O.W. in Iraq lacks the sense of female victimization we still expect. She asserts that the sexual assault she experienced in Iraq in 1991 "ranks as unpleasant; that's all it ranks." And she argues that the abuse suffered by male P.O.W.s was much worse than she endured.

18. See "Ended Glory: A Year After the War," *New York Times*, January 16, 1992.

19. See Sara Ruddick, *Maternal Thinking: Toward a Politics of Peace* (New York: Ballantine, 1989). Ruddick, however, argues that men as well as women can undertake the practices of mothering. Presumably she would argue that insofar as men engaged themselves deeply in these practices, they too would have a greater predisposition toward opposing the physical violence of war.

20. Katha Pollit, New York Institute of the Humanities presentation, Spring 1991.

21. This would seem an impressive example of the psychoanalytic operations of displacement and condensation operating on a grand social psychic scale.

22. Adrienne Rich, *Of Woman Born* (New York: Norton, 1986).

23. Of course, superficial readings of the familial status of these black foremothers which ignore the intense forms of patriarchal oppression they suffered under despite their relative economic power within the family are inappropriate. Many black feminists have responded with anger to the infamous "black matriarchy" thesis of Daniel P. Moynihan, wherein he blamed the lack of progress of the black community in the United States on the matriarchal structure of black families. It is self-evidently racism rather than black women who have placed the most "crushing burden on the Negro male," of course; and it is racism that has thus given black women a relative degree of power in their families. See "The Moynihan Report," particularly the chapter entitled "The Tangle of Pathology." This report was issued under the more formal title "The Negro Family: The Case For National Action 29" (1965), produced by the Office of Policy Planning and Research, U.S. Department of Labor, reprinted in Lee Rainwater and William L. Yancey, *The Moynihan Report and the Politics of Controversy* 75 (1967).

Given my theory of the process of familial unmooring we are currently undergoing as a result of the social enfranchisement of women, I see black women as pioneers and foremothers of the contemporary struggles of a great many women of all races today. The "breakdown" of the black family was simply an early forerunner of the more general kinship "breakdown" now experienced by all races and classes in our society.

Unfortunately, policymakers like Moynihan still tend to see pathology and the need for social cures when, in fact, they are looking at irreversible processes of social transformation. Moynihan's latest concern is with the growth of dependency. He argues that "dependency is becoming the defining issue of post-industrial society." See Jason DeParle, "In New Social Era, Moynihan Sees New Social Ills," *New York Times*, December 9, 1991. This is an ironic thesis, to say the least, given the dramatic movement of women out of the home (and dependency upon a husband's wages) and into the workplace. Clearly some forms of dependency are good and others are pathological. Moynihan would do better, theoretically speaking, to attempt to extend his matriarchy thesis to all women today. While it is no more true to say today that women in general have the social power of matriarchs than it was to say 25 years ago that black women possessed the social power of matriarchs, at least it is an argument that reflects gendered changes in familial roles and relative power.

24. See Vicki Schultz, "Women Before the Law," in *Feminists Theorize the Political*, ed. Judith Butler and Joan Scott (New York: Routledge, 1992). Schultz argues that women "disrupt the dominant definition of feminine gender identity by expanding it to encompass aspirations and activities traditionally defined in opposition to it." As an example of this pattern within nontraditional employment, Schultz cites Christine Williams's study of female Marines. Williams found that women in the Marines "value femininity and identify themselves as feminine" through challenging the cultural construction of the military as masculine. See Christine Williams, *Gender Differences at Work: Women and Men in Nontraditional Occupations* (Berkeley: University of California Press, 1989), pp. 72–74.

25. See "Ended Glory: A Year After the War," *New York Times*, January 18, 1992.

26. See Anthony Lewis, "Changing the Rules," *New York Times*, December 12, 1992, for a discussion of the need for articulating new ground rules for military intervention abroad, given the decision of George Bush to send American troops to Somalia under United Nations auspices. Lewis argues that peacemaking rather than national security will increasingly need to be the rationale for military intervention.

27. See Jane Gross, "Suffering in Silence No More," *New York Times*, July 13, 1992, where Ann F. Lewis, a Democratic political consultant, is quoted as saying, "It will never be a joke again. Both the seriousness of sexual harassment and its force as a political issue have been established."

28. See Manning Marable, "Clarence Thomas and the Crisis of Black Political Culture," in *Racing Justice, Engendering Power*, ed. Toni Morrison (New York: Pantheon, 1992), p. 64.

29. My philosophic colleague Leonard Harris, currently Chair of the African-American

Studies Program at Purdue University, informed me that every member of this community was contacted by Democratic staff over a several-month period.

30. Toni Morrison, "Introduction: Friday on the Potomac," in *Racing Justice, Engendering Power*. Morrison maintains that "an accusation of such weight as sexual misconduct would probably have disqualified a white candidate on its face . . . it seems blazingly clear that with this unprecedented opportunity to hover over and to cluck at . . . the excesses of black bodies . . . there would be no recommendation of withdrawal. . . . No. The participants were black, so what could it matter?" (p. xvii). In fact, only now, a year after Hill's testimony, are accusations of sexual misconduct against major white political figures such as Senator Brock Adams and Senator Bob Packwood coming to light. Prior to the Anita Hill case, it was the accusations of women that were disqualified out of hand. Peculiarly enough, it may have been the racism of "They are black, so what could it matter" thinking that allowed sexual harassment claims to begin to matter legally and politically.

31. Catharine MacKinnon, *Sexual Harassment of Working Women* (New Haven: Yale University Press, 1979), p. 1.

32. See Paula S. Rothenberg, *Racism and Sexism: An Integrated Study* (New York: St. Martin's Press, 1988), pp. 140–41.

33. Susan Ehrlich Martin, "Sexual Harassment: The Link Joining Gender Stratification, Sexuality, and Women's Economic Status," in Jo Freeman, ed. *Women: A Feminist Perspective* (Mayfield, Calif.: Mayfield Press, 1989), p. 69.

34. See David Brion Davis, "Life and Death in Slavery," *New York Review of Books*, January 30, 1992; reviewing Melton A. McLaurin's *Celia: A Slave* (Athens: University of Georgia Press, 1991). McLaurin investigates a nineteenth-century murder trial in which the defense argued that a Missouri law allowing women to use force to defend their sexual honor should be extended to apply to Celia, a young slave. This defense was not accepted, and as Davis states, McLaurin "conveys the raw horror and psychic costs of a legal and thoroughly American institution that condoned the rape, sexual abuse, and hanging of a girl known only as Celia."

35. The antiwar vice-presidential candidate Thomas Eagleton was derailed by accusations of earlier mental problems; the Supreme Court nominee Douglas Ginsburg was rejected for having indulged in marijuana; Gary Hart is the most notorious example of a leading presidential candidate derailed by the sexual issue.

36. See "Men Say Worry About Harassment Leads Them to Tone Down Conduct," by Peter Kilborn, in the *New York Times*, November 7, 1991, for a report on the degree to which men feel they must now change their workplace behavior. A *New York Times*/CBS News poll at the time of the hearings found that four out of ten women have experienced "unwanted sexual advances or remarks from men they work for"; while five out of ten men admitted to having "said or done something that could have been construed by a female colleague as harassment." See "Sexual Harassment at Work Is Pervasive, Survey Suggests," by Elizabeth Kolbert, *New York Times*, October 11, 1991. Given such mass testimony to the experience of sexual harassment, it was difficult to understand the polls reporting that "twice as many of those who were polled" [on October 13, after three days of the hearings] said they believed Clarence Thomas's account more than that of Anita Hill. Moreover, the poll recorded "little difference in response between men and women, or between blacks and whites." The political quality of the hearings may have been best reflected in the finding that "Republicans were more inclined to believe Judge Thomas than were Democrats." See "Most in National Survey Say Judge Is the More Believable," by Elizabeth Kolbert, *New York Times*, October 15, 1991. The fact that the same *New York Times*/CBS News poll that found that four out of ten women have experienced sexual harassment also found that only one out of ten women who had experienced sexual harassment had also reported it may also indicate the likelihood of a strong popular desire to deny the ugly normality of Thomas's behavior as recounted by Hill.

37. Dr. Francis K. Conley, a (full) professor of neurosurgery at Stanford Medical School,

quit in the spring of 1992 to protest sexism in academic medicine, and to finally protest harassment by some of her own colleagues which she had endured silently for several decades. She agreed to return in the hopes of bringing about reform. See Jane Gross, "Suffering in Silence No More: Fighting Sexual Harassment," *New York Times*, July 13, 1992.

38. See Anita Hill, "Marriage and Patronage in the Empowerment and Disempowerment of African-American Women," a paper delivered at "Race, Gender and Power in America," a Georgetown University Law School conference, October 1992, a year after her Senate testimony.

39. See Barbara Presley Noble, "Economics as if Women Mattered," *New York Times*, December 13, 1992, reporting on a recent gathering of high-level women formulating a set of proposals on issues of interest to women, to circulate at Clinton's "economic summit." There were recommendations for more flexible work structures, including flex-time arrangements, job-sharing, and compressed work weeks. They also proposed redefining the notion of "infrastructure" to include direct investments in people and communities via housing, child care, health, and recreation.

40. See Debra Renee Kaufman, "Professional Women: How Real Are the Recent Gains;" and Judith Lorber, "Trust, Loyalty, and the Place of Women in the Informal Organization of Work," in Jo Freeman, ed., *Women: A Feminist Perspective*.

41. Joel F. Handler, professor of law at the University of California at Los Angeles, letter to the *New York Times*, July 23, 1991.

42. See David Margolick, "At the Bar," *New York Times*, October 18, 1991. He quotes Nancy Gertner, a civil rights lawyer in Boston, as suggesting after the hearings "that had the Senators asked Judge Thomas for a personal history—when he was divorced, when he remarried, how much he had dated in between—they could have underlined that the accusations against him made chronological sense."

43. See Anita Hill, "Marriage and Patronage in the Empowerment and Disempowerment of African-American Women."

44. Kimberlé Crenshaw, "Whose Story Is It Anyway?" in Toni Morrison, ed. *Racing Justice*, p. 403.

45. Diane McWhorter, "The Real Tragedy of Judge Wachtler," Op-Ed article in *New York Times*, November 13, 1992. See also John Barbanel, "Chief Judge of New York Is Arrested In Extortion Scheme," *New York Times*, November 8, 1992.

46. See Elizabeth Kolbert, "Sexual Harassment at Work is Pervasive, Survey Suggests," *New York Times*, October 11, 1992. "Four of ten women say they have encountered unwanted sexual advances or remarks from men they work for. . . . Five of ten men said that at some point while on the job, they had said or done something that could have been construed as harassment . . . according to the latest *New York Times*/CBS news poll." See Tamar Lewin, "A Case Study of Sexual Harassment," *New York Times*, October 11, 1991. "Lawyers say . . . that with survey after survey showing that 40 percent to 70 percent of working women have experienced some form of sexual harassment, Professor Hill's failure to make a formal complaint or leave the job is also the norm."

47. Cornel West, "Black Leadership and the Pitfalls of Race Reasoning," in Toni Morrison, ed., *Racing Justice*, p. 399.

48. Polls showed, in fact, that a large percentage of professionally employed women were sympathetic to Anita Hill. See "Women See Hearing From a Perspective of Their Own Jobs," *New York Times*, October 18, 1991.

49. See Tamar Lewin, "A Case Study of Sexual Harassment," *New York Times*, October 11, 1991; and Daniel Goleman: "Sexual Harassment: It's About Power, Not Lust," *New York Times*, October 22, 1991.

50. Angela Wright also offered to testify to being harassed by Clarence Thomas, but for various tactical reasons which in hindsight appear foolish, she was not called.

51. See Timothy Egan, "Oregon Now Wonders Who Is Real Packwood," *New York Times*, December 5, 1992.

52. Catharine MacKinnon explains: "Sexual harassment at work connects the jobs most women do—in which a major part of their work is to be there for men—with the structure of sexual relations—in which their role is also to be there for men—with the denigrated economic status women as a gender occupy throughout society." See MacKinnon's *Sexual Harassment of Working Women* (New Haven: Yale University, 1979), p. 220.

53. Deborah L. Rhode quotes a popular Army slogan used to deny or discount charges of sexual coercion: "It never happened, and what's more, [she] deserved it." She goes on to document that according to surveys in the late 1970s and early 1980s "two-thirds of respondents believed that women provoked rape by their appearance and actions, and a majority of respondents agreed that victims in most rapes were promiscuous or had bad reputations." See Deborah Rhode, *Justice and Gender* (Cambridge, Mass.: Harvard University Press, 1989), pp. 245, 248.

54. See Adrienne Rich, "Compulsory Heterosexuality and Lesbian Existence," in *Signs* 5 (Summer 1980); see also Kathleen Barry, *Female Sexual Slavery* (Englewood Cliffs, N.J.: Prentice-Hall, 1979).

55. As Catharine MacKinnon put it, "That consent rather than nonmutuality is the line between rape and intercourse further exposes the inequality in normal social expectations." See "Feminism, Marxism, Method, and the State: An Agenda for Theory," in *Feminist Theory*, ed. Nannerl O. Keohane, Michelle Z. Rosaldo, and Barbara C. Gelpi (Chicago: University of Chicago, 1982), p. 18.

56. See Ruth Colker, "Feminism, Sexuality and Authenticity," in *At the Boundaries of Law*, ed. Martha Albertson Fineman and Nancy Sweet Thomadsen (New York: Routledge, 1991), for an interesting effort to grapple with issues of "compulsory heterosexuality" and women's political responsibilities within intimate heterosexual relationships today.

57. See Susan Brownmiller, *Against Our Will: Men, Women and Rape* (New York: Bantom, 1976); Rosemarie Tong, *Women, Sex, and the Law* (Totowa, N.J.: Rowman and Allanheld, 1984).

58. Deborah Rhode reports that "law review commentators throughout the 1950s and 1960s asserted that it was 'customary' for a woman who desired intercourse to say 'no, no, no' while meaning 'yes, yes, yes.' Since it was 'always difficult in rape cases to determine whether the female really meant "no",' she should be required to convey her resistance by more than 'mere' verbal protest, or 'such infantile behavior as crying.' " See *Justice and Gender*, p. 247.

59. A particularly extreme and poignant example of a sexual abuse of power is demonstrated in a recent case in Glen Ridge, N.J. A 17-year old girl with an IQ of 64 was invited into a basement recreation room one afternoon by a number of the star athletes from the local high school. With the promise of going out on a date with one of them that night, she undressed and performed oral sex on them, and allowed them to stick a baseball bat and a broom up her vagina. None of the boys took her out on a date that night, and four years later four of the former star athletes are on trial for their actions. The trial is to determine whether these were acts of sexual assault or whether the retarded girl consented to the acts. Yet consent can hardly be the point in this case in any literal sense. As *New York Times* columnist Anna Quindlen has said, it is really a situation of child abuse, given the patent and quite pathetic desire of this now 21-year old woman still to do—even on the witness stand—whatever is necessary in order to be liked. Not too long ago, of course, women of normal intelligence were in a not totally different position, due to women's generic lack of social power to refuse consent to the sexual whims and desires of men. See *New York Times* articles on December 11, 12, 13, 16, and 17, 1992.

60. If we consider the Glen Ridge case outlined in note 59 from the perspective of the different dimensions of sexual agency, the moral and legal culpability of the high school stars becomes obvious. Knowing that she was retarded and childlike in her desire to please, it was the boys' responsibility not to take advantage of her simple desire to be liked by them as a means of inducing her to accept their degrading acts upon her body.

61. Notice how cases of self-destructive sexual interaction differ from the cases of self-regarding action John Stuart Mill defended as part of individual liberty. Self-destructive behaviors such as excessive drinking or attempting suicide are responses to the immediate desires of a particular individual, and interventions to prevent these behaviors would constitute excessive paternalism, according to Mill. By contrast, the degrading or self-destructive sexual behaviors of which I am speaking exist as responses to sexual desires of another person, and it is these desires for the humiliation and degradation of another person that are at least highly suspect.

62. Deborah Rhode reports that "between 10 percent and 15 percent of married women experience forcible sex with their husbands, and many suffer severe physical or psychological injuries as a consequence. . . . Indeed, marital rape victims report more long-term injuries than women raped by strangers." See *Justice and Gender*, p. 250.

63. E. R. Shipp, "Tearful Testimony From Accuser's Mother," *New York Times*, February 5, 1992.

64. Kimberlé Crenshaw reports that many black women supported Tyson and were critical of Washington, not because they believed Tyson's story, but because "they believed she should not have been in Tyson's hotel room at 2:00 A.M. A typical response was offered by one young Black woman who stated, 'She asked for it, she got it, it's not fair to cry rape.' " See Crenshaw, "Mapping the Margins," p. 1274, quoting from "20/20" (ABC television broadcast, Feb. 21, 1992). Crenshaw interprets such women as seeking to distance themselves from rape victims as a way of denying their own vulnerability.

65. As bell hooks has explained, this sort of solidarity has not existed, for the most part, between black and white women in the United States. She traces the racial divisions to the time of slavery in this country when a longstanding religious conception of women as the source of bodily sin and sexual lust was transformed through the creation of a racial dichotomy between the sexual images of white and black women. The white male slaveholder could idealize and control white womanhood by denying their sexuality, and could rationalize his sexual exploitation of black female slaves through holding black women to be the embodiment of primitive, wanton female sexuality. hooks convincingly argues that this contrast between the sexually pure white woman and the licentious black woman still prevails today as part of a general cultural devaluation of black women. See her *Ain't I A Woman: black women and feminism* (Boston: South End Press, 1981), pp. 31–34.

66. Crenshaw, "Mapping the Margins," p. 1273.

67. As Deborah Rhode reports, "Courts as late as the 1970s were routinely instructing juries that evidence of 'unchaste character' was relevant in assessing credibility as well as consent. . . . Simulation studies have also found that rape of a divorcee results in shorter sentences than rape of a married women, and interviews with trial judges in the 1970s and 1980s disclosed comparable biases. In their view, victims 'asked for it' if they hitchhiked or dressed 'provocatively' by wearing short skirts, tight jeans, or no bras . . . one judge described rape as a normal response to a permissive society." See Rhode, *Justice and Gender*, p. 249.

68. Michel Foucault notoriously argued that stranger-rape should not be considered a sexual crime, in accordance with his larger argument that sexuality should not be controlled by the state generally. Monique Plaza took him to task for this position, asserting that it showed his insensitivity toward the power differences between men and women in our society, and the need for the law to address these. See Michel Foucault's Introduction to a debate on rape by the Change Collective in *La Folie encerclée* (Paris: October, 1977); and Monique Plaza, "Our Costs and Their Benefits," *m/f* 4 (1980). Stranger-rape is a patriarchal form of criminal assault, and should surely continue to be prosecuted as a sexual form of criminal assault. Yet the whole juridical understanding of rape is so permeated with anachronistic patriarchal assumptions about male and female sexual agency that the crime of stranger-rape probably needs to be redefined. I am not analyzing stranger-rape in this chapter, however.

69. As Catharine MacKinnon explains, "Sexual touching that women do not want has

historically been considered tortious under a variety of doctrines, usually battery, assault, or, if exclusively emotional damage is done, as the intentional infliction of emotional distress. A battery is a harmful or offensive contact which is intentionally caused. While contact must be intentional, hostile intent, or intent to cause all the damages that resulted from the contact, is not necessary. . . . Battery, the actual touching, is often combined with assault, the fear of such a touching. The tort of assault consists in placing a person in fear of an immediate harmful or offensive contact. It is a 'touching of the mind, if not of the body.' " See MacKinnon's *Sexual Harassment of Working Women*, p. 165.

70. Private conversation with Burt Neuborne, January 1991. Deborah Rhode supports Neuborne's statement, maintaining that "for sexual coercion that departs from the traditional paradigm of chaste victim-violent stranger, the burden of proof has been exceptionally high. Lawyers and judges have tended to dismiss acquaintance or date rape as 'personal problem,' rather than a criminal offense—as 'felonious gallantry,' or 'assault with failure to please.' " *Justice and Gender*, p. 248.

71. Eileen F. Wagner, "Campus Victims of Date Rape Should Consider Civil Lawsuits as Alternatives to Criminal Charges or Colleges' Procedures," *The Chronicle of Higher Education*, August 7, 1991. See also Ann Russo, "An Unhealthy Climate for Women," in *Women's Review of Books* (February 1992), for a further discussion of some of the pros and cons of a civil suit.

72. Michael Winerip, "Slain for Race: It's Now Official After 6 Years," *New York Times*, December 20, 1992.

73. Rhode, *Justice and Gender*, p. 245.

74. Susan Estrich's *Real Rape* (Cambridge, Mass.: Harvard University Press, 1987) is a powerful plea for such a broadening of rape laws.

75. Angela P. Harris, "Race and Essentialism in Feminist Theory," in *Feminist Legal Theory*, ed. Katharine T. Bartlett and Rosanne Kennedy (Boulder: Westview Press, 1991), p. 247.

76. Desiree Washington said that she was persuaded to take him to court when her parents asked her whether she could live with herself if Tyson attacked another woman. "I thought about it, and the answer was 'No,'" she said. E. R. Shipp, "Tyson's Accuser Tells Jury of Assault," *New York Times*, January 31, 1992.

77. MacKinnon, *Sexual Harassment of Working Women*, pp. 170–71. MacKinnon has strong arguments for why sexual harassment is a social injury involving workplace power relationships, which should be juridically treated as a form of sexual discrimination rather than as either a crime or a tort. But one of the distinctive features of coercive sexual behavior is precisely its privatized quality, and the lack of any institutional context in which to embed the intimate interaction. MacKinnon is critical of the previous moralistic quality of sexual tort doctrines, and discerningly points out that a corrective "ordinary woman" standard would need to be developed if contemporary women were to resort to sexual tort claims.

78. Martin Heidegger, "The Origin of the Work of Art," in *Poetry, Language, Thought*, trans. Albert Hofstadter (New York: Harper Colophon, 1971), p. 73; "Der Spruche des Anaximander," in *Holzweg* (Frankfurt: V. Klosterman, 1957), pp. 337–38.

79. Jacques Derrida, *Positions*, trans. Alan Bass (Chicago: University of Chicago Press, 1981), p. 34.

80. Jacques Derrida, "Choreographies," an interview with Christie V. McDonald, in *Diacritics* 12 (1982), p. 76. See note 6 in my Epilogue for further analysis of this point.

81. Martin Heidegger, *What Is Called Thinking?* (New York: Harper Torchbooks, 1968), p. 17.

Epilogue: Engaging on a Postfeminist Frontier

1. Jane Tompkins, in *West of Everything* (New York: Oxford University Press, 1992), perceptively points out that the western (as a film genre particularly) is "antilanguage," and that "doing, not talking is what it values." However, she associates the devaluation of lan-

guage with gender and the oppression of women rather too broadly (pp. 50, 52, 66). While women may have experienced themselves as "vanquished by male silence," the chief problem for women on the Western frontier was that their domestic activities represented all the old eastern conventions men were escaping on the frontier. Their activities had little status in relation to those of men who were out forging new worldly relationships, and their articulations of their concerns could thus be dismissed as empty female prattle.

Yet we need to be careful to distinguish the silence of frontiers from the oppression of women on previous frontiers. I think silence may be common to all frontiers, insofar as we experience silence when the actions that are most important are not yet encoded within the available discourses. It so happens that today many of the significant actions that do not yet signify within dominant discourses are those of women. We are culturally silent about new forms of social agency insofar as they do not fit within old narratives. While we may consciously choose to idealize the struggle to speak, and to speak out so as to be heard, it is not appropriate to experience our failure to be heard in terms of gendered structures of oppression like those existing on the Western frontier. Our silence today is a function of the social uniqueness of our agency, still under-articulated and difficult to give adequate voice to.

By contrast, it is frequently men today, still ensconced in their more traditional settings, who seem to prattle on in an annoying way about nothing. Since they usually have a certain amount of social standing, they are rarely required to confront the meaningless of their speech.

2. Women do not have the social power to engage in what Jane Tompkins refers to as "the wholesale and unrelenting" attack on language that occurred on the Western frontier (*West of Everything*, p. 52). Yet the speech of men is frequently annoying to women, whether in its arrogant phallic moments of addressing women on the street, or simply in its capacity for empty pomposity when reiterating the truths of patriarchal discourses. One of the most satisfying aspects of Louise's act of shooting the cowboy is the absoluteness with which she silences his obnoxious voice.

3. See Janet Maslin, *New York Times*, July 1991.

4. See chapters 2 and 4 for my analysis of how masculine notions of social agency and identity have developed upon a foundation of binary patriarchal sexual and social relationships.

5. Both Michel Foucault and Jacques Derrida maintain that the positive aspects of the women's movement lie in its "de-sexualizing component." One assumes they did not imagine desexualization in quite such aggressive and interactive terms. See Michel Foucault, *Power/Knowledge*, ed. Colin Gordon (New York: Pantheon, 1980), pp. 119–20. See Jacques Derrida, "Women in the Beehive," in *Men in Feminism*, ed. Alice Jardine and Paul Smith (New York: Methuen, 1987), pp. 194, 198.

6. It is ironic that in one of his primary discussions of the politics of feminism, Derrida posits "dancing" as a metaphor for "changing places" and enriching gendered relationships while avoiding "reactive" feminist oppositions to men. As Thelma's unfortunate incident with the cowboy illustrates, the problem for the "lone women dancers" Derrida praises is that patriarchal notions of sexual agency rarely allow men to accept women's "desire to escape the combinatory itself, to invent incalculable choreographies" as Derrida recommends. It is men like the cowboy, with their reductively phallic notions of desire, who are positioned reactively today. Women's desires are frequently for incalculable choreographies; it is when they must defend these against male resistance that women become oppositional, as Louise finally did. See Jacques Derrida, "Choreographies," *Diacritics* 12 (1982), pp. 68, 69, 76.

Index

Patricia Mann teaches philosophy at Hofstra University. She serves on the editorial boards of *Social Text* and *Hypatia* and has published many articles on contemporary social and political issues.